PILGRIMAGE

By the same author

Cucumber Sandwiches in the Andes

Prince Henry the Navigator

The Trail of Tamerlane

The Quest for Captain Morgan

Trespassers in the Amazon

The Royal Geographical Society History of World Exploration
(sections on South and Central America)

A Bird on the Wing: Bonnie Prince Charlie's Flight from Culloden retraced

Diplomatic Bag (editor)

The Cossacks

In Search of Nomads

PILGRIMAGE

THE GREAT ADVENTURE OF THE MIDDLE AGES

JOHN URE

CONSTABLE • LONDON

For
HUGO and ARABELLA
travellers as adventurous
as any of the pilgrims
in this book

Constable & Robinson Ltd
3 The Lanchesters
162 Fulham Palace Road
London W6 9ER
www.constablerobinson.com

First published in the UK by Constable,
an imprint of Constable & Robinson Ltd, 2006

A copy of the British Library Cataloguing in Publication
Data is available from the British Library.

ISBN 1-84119-786-6

Printed and bound in the EU

Contents

Illustrations

Line drawings:

A fifteenth-century impression of Satan and his daughter Heresy setting traps for an unwary pilgrim (from *Pilgrimage of the Life of Man* by John Lydgate).

Pilgrims crawling into the tombs of saints, as happened in Canterbury and elsewhere (from *La Estoire de Saint Aedward le Rei*).

An early fourteenth-century depiction of King Henry II quarrelling with Thomas Becket (from *Chronicle of England* by Peter Langtoft).

St Cuthbert, who spent much of his time walking through the Scottish Borders, has his knee healed by an angel, as depicted in the Venerable Bede's account of his life.

Plate section:

Hieronymus Bosch, in his triptych of 1480, gives an impression of the hazards that await a pilgrim on *The Path of Life*.

Erasmus was welcomed as a scholar at Canterbury but wrote very cynically about the display of relics which was shown to pilgrims there (portrait by Quentin Mayes, 1517).

The crusader castle of Krac des Chavaliers was a landmark and haven on the overland route through Syria to the Holy Land (photo by author).

The walled town of Carcassonne was a stronghold of the Cathar heretics who provoked the Albigensian Crusade (photo by Caroline Ure).

The sixteenth-century Hostel San Marco at León is now a parador but still a staging post on the route to Santiago. A bronze statue of a pilgrim sits at the foot of the cross in front of the hostel (both photographs by Caroline Ure).

Montserrat stands among the most spectacular of Spanish sierras. The monastery itself is like a small market town and is a popular destination for *Romerias* (photo by Caroline Ure).

The monastery of San Juan de la Peña nestling under a Pyrenean rock face on the route to Santiago (photo by Caroline Ure).

Romerias, or local pilgrimages, in Spain have always been the occasion for festive equestrian journeys and picnics (both photos by Caroline Ure).

A pilgrim with his 'staff of faith' and 'bottle of salvation' as portrayed in a Pyrenean monastery (photo by Caroline Ure).

Fountain in the cloisters at the thirteenth-century monastery of Poblet, a focus for Spanish Romerias (photo by Caroline Ure).

John of Gaunt is entertained by the King of Portugal on the campaign which included his pilgrimage to Santiago (from a contemporary engraving, *British Library*).

Fifteenth-century pilgrims paying their tolls at the gates of Tyre on their way to the Holy Land (from a contemporary engraving, *British Library*).

Sir John Mandeville taking leave of the King of England before setting out on his travels (*Bibliothèque National 'Livre des Merveilles'*).

Prester John, the fabled Christian monarch of the Orient who features in Mandeville's travels, is depicted honouring the cross.

Acknowledgements

Anyone attempting to write about Christian pilgrimages is aware of a debt of gratitude to all those pilgrims and scholars who have approached the subject over nearly two millenniums, or at least since the time of St Jerome in the fourth century AD. Among recent writings, Jonathan Sumption's book *Pilgrimage* stands out as giving a remarkable overview of the place of pilgrimage in the medieval mind. The fact that my own approach may be a little different from that of others does not diminish my debt.

In particular I am grateful to the Rt Rev. Simon Barrington-Ward for his encouragement at an early stage and for his reading the text at a later stage; to Dr Eamon Duffy of Magdalene College, Cambridge, for pointing me towards some useful sources; to Bamber Gascoigne for introducing me to the work of Brother Felix Fabri; to the Very Rev. Dr Wesley Carr, Dean of Westminster, for information about the Jerusalem Chamber and other matters; and to the late (12th) Earl of Scarbrough for putting me right on a number of points regarding the Pilgrimage of Grace in which his ancestors played a complicated role.

I am also indebted to the Marquis of Tamaron (formerly Spanish Ambassador in London) for arranging for me to visit a number of monasteries and other pilgrim sites in Spain, as the guest of the Carolina Foundation and the Spanish government.

I much appreciate the consent of the travel section of the *Daily Telegraph* and the *Sunday Telegraph* to my quoting (in sections of the epilogue) from my articles about Mount Athos, St Cuthbert and the Cathar castles which first appeared in their columns.

As always, I am most grateful to the country orders desk at the London Library for tracking down relevant books, and also to the archives staff at Canterbury Cathedral for allowing me to use their reading room and enjoy the sensation of working in the scriptorium of a medieval abbey.

My thanks are also due to Sandy and Michaela Reid of Lanton Tower in the Scottish Borders for their hospitality and companionship on my walks from Melrose Abbey to Lindisfarne and across Mull to the island of Iona, as described in the epilogue. Also, though I hope it goes without saying, I thank my wife Caroline who accompanied and encouraged me on these and many other relevant travels.

Looking through these well-deserved acknowledgements, I am struck by the immense authority of many of those with whom I have been in contact regarding this project. The reader should not assume that their aura of gravitas has rubbed off on me: my book is – I hope – an entertainment, not in any sense an attempt to compete with the achievements of those who have been kind enough to help me.

J.U.

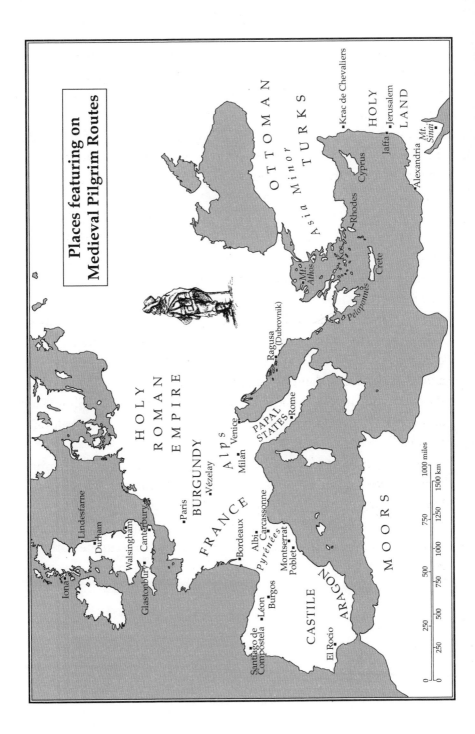

Places featuring on Medieval Pilgrim Routes

OTTOMAN

Asia Minor TURKS

Krac de Chevaliers

HOLY

Jerusalem

LAND

Cyprus

Jaffa

Mt. Sinai

Alexandria

Rhodes

Crete

Mt. Athos

Peloponnese

HOLY

ROMAN

EMPIRE

Ragusa (Dubrovnik)

BURGUNDY

Vézelay

Alps

Venice

Milan

PAPAL

STATES

Rome

Paris

FRANCE

Lindesfarne

Durham

Walsingham

Canterbury

Glastonbury

Iona

Bordeaux

Albi

Carcassonne

Pyrénées

Montserrat

Poblet

Léon

Burgos

Santiago de Compostela

El Rocio

CASTILE

ARAGON

MOORS

0   250   500   750   1000   1250   1500 km

0   250   500   750   1000 miles

1

Prologue: the Adventure of a Lifetime

L IFE IN MEDIEVAL Europe could be nasty, brutish and short; but for some there was a ray of light in their lives. A pilgrimage was both an aspiration and an adventure, an external experience and an internal inspiration. Even kings were not immune to the appeal. Shakespeare memorably portrays Henry IV on his deathbed at Westminster Abbey fantasizing that he is a pilgrim.

> King Henry: Doth any name particular belong
> Unto the lodgings where I first did swoon?
> Warwick: 'Tis call'd Jerusalem, my noble lord.
> King Henry: Laud be to God! – even there my life must end.
> It hath been prophesied to me many years,
> I should not die but in Jerusalem;
> Which vainly I suppos'd the Holy Land:
> But bear me to that chamber; there I'll lie;
> In that Jerusalem shall Harry die.

Before he seized the throne in England, Henry IV had in fact already been on pilgrimage to the Holy Land; he knew better than most of his subjects the hazards of that and similar expeditions. This is a book about those hazards.

Risk and danger were very explicit features of life in the Middle Ages and never more so than when on a pilgrimage. Many pilgrims died on their journeys, and even more were attacked, robbed, cheated, or injured by natural hazards such as falling bridges, Alpine landslides, flooded rivers and desert storms. And yet throughout the Middle Ages Christian pilgrimage was more than a popular pastime: it was the greatest adventure of a lifetime to all sorts and conditions of men.

To go on a pilgrimage was an opportunity for distant – particularly foreign – travel. Lords of the manor might occasionally go to court or join a crusade, but more usually they felt obliged to stay at home managing their estates. And for all others – clerics and lawyers, guildsmen and shopkeepers, craftsmen and apprentices, yeomen and peasants – a pilgrimage was even more surely the only chance of a real adventure, of seeing what was the other side of the hill. The Grand Tour had not yet taken its hold on the aristocracy and, for the rest of society, gap-years, long vacations, Cook's tours and package holidays were centuries away.

In this book I shall concentrate on this travel aspect of pilgrimage. This is not primarily a book about sacred shrines, relics, miracles, the minutiae of the routes or the architectural glories of the great basilicas that were the destination of most pilgrimages. All these have been extensively written about by others better qualified to do so than myself.

Instead I shall try to tell the tale of those who set off – having made their wills and said goodbye to their families – to Jerusalem or Rome, to Compostela or Canterbury, or to any of a host of less celebrated destinations. On these routes the less fortunate faced kidnapping and piracy, broken limbs and undiagnosed fevers, penury and discomfort and even – particularly in the case of those going to Rome during the crisis of the papacy – harassment and imprisonment by fellow Christian activists. Their adventures might or might not lead to the salvation of their souls, but they certainly led to a host of stories on which they doubtless dined out for the rest of their lives.

In the interests of coherence and definition, I have restricted myself to Christian pilgrimages. A different set of conditions applied to those heading for Mecca or the Ganges which puts them outside the scope of this work. I have also concentrated exclusively on the golden age of Christian pilgrimage, that is broadly from around 1066 (before the crusades) until the Reformation and the Dissolution of the Monasteries in England in 1536 – a period of some five hundred years. After that date, the churches, both Roman and Reformed, tended to discount relics and indulgences and adopted a more ambivalent attitude to pilgrimage; the emphasis changed to the allegory of spiritual journeys rather than the actuality of overland travel.

I have also tried to address some of the other phenomena which coloured or affected the adventure of pilgrimage during the Middle Ages. The Black Death was one which upset the pattern. Another was the propensity of medieval man to present other more belligerent activities as pilgrimages: the crusades were the most obvious example of this, but vindictive campaigns such as those against the Cathars in France, or popular uprisings like the so-called Pilgrimage of Grace in Tudor northern England are other examples.

Finally, since some readers may wonder how these sites and routes have survived the intervening centuries, I have devoted a personal epilogue to some vignettes of places I have myself visited over recent (and less recent) years. The road to Santiago de Compostela draws modern pilgrims as surely as it did medieval ones; and I have also managed to visit other key destinations like the fortress of Krac des Chevaliers en route for the Holy Land, Mount Athos in Greece, St Catherine's monastery in Sinai, the Cathar castles of Languedoc, and some of the north British pilgrim sites like

Lindisfarne, Durham and the island of Iona. At all these places the spirit of medieval pilgrimage is not far below the surface of the contemporary scene, and modern encounters can have echoes of those distant days when (according to Chaucer) in all the Christian world 'thanne longen folk to goon on pilgrimages'.

A fifteenth-century impression of Satan and his daughter
Heresy setting traps for an unwary pilgrim

2

The Motivation for Pilgrimage: Saints and Sinners

There's no discouragement
Shall make him once relent
His first avowed intent
To be a pilgrim.

John Bunyan

THE SCOPE FOR entertainment and adventure, even vicarious adventure, was severely limited in the Middle Ages. Public attractions included executions — the more horrible the crime the more grotesque and intriguing the manner of the culprit's death — and popular preachers. The latter attracted phenomenally large crowds: in 1429 one Franciscan friar preached in Paris for six hours on ten consecutive days and if he stopped early his listeners wept from disappointment. Other attractions included formal processions and mystery plays. The processions which enlivened medieval towns on high days and holidays were a visible reminder of the power and glory of the church and state. The plays reminded the populace of biblical stories and were often enlivened with jocular or ribald improvisations. The teaching of the church and the penalties for sin, in this world and the next, were never far from the medieval consciousness. So it followed from this that to go on pilgrimage was a unique way of assuaging the consequences of sin, of visiting spectacular sights, and, above all, of undertaking an adventure. The practice of pilgrimage took man back to his roots.

To go to see for oneself the scene of great events is a deeply ingrained human instinct. The birthplace of famous men, the field on which notable battles have been fought, the site of heroic deeds or great romances, all these have attracted secular visitors over the centuries. So it is little wonder that where people's faith as well as their sentiments or patriotism have been involved, where human events appear to have been touched with the supernatural, the urge to go and see has been even stronger. The concept of going on pilgrimage is not only of distant origin but of deep appeal.

And the appeal of the scene of great, and particularly spiritual, events is much enhanced by vivid evidence of those events. A birthplace is enriched by a cradle, a battlefield by a rusty sword or helmet, a castle by an execution block, or a romantic palace by a lovers' grotto. How much more so therefore is a religious site enhanced by evidence of the divine presence: the bones of a saint, a splinter from the True Cross, or a temple built on the holy place. Those charged with the care and maintenance of such holy sites have always been quick to appreciate this point: they have discovered, acquired or fabricated such attractions. An extreme example of the necessity to provide relics to encourage pilgrims was provided by a group of Umbrian peasants who, in around the year AD 1000, seriously contemplated killing their local saintly hermit, Romuald, so as to secure his bones as a pilgrim attraction. As visitors have increased, so has profit. Mighty abbeys have arisen. Busy markets have sprung up where formerly were sleepy villages or desert sands; and hermit-like custodians of shrines have been translated into bishops, abbots or princes of the church.

An even greater appeal of Holy Places has been the direct evidence of their spirituality demonstrated by miracles and healings. There has also been room for cynicism here: visions have been disputed, cures questioned. But at many pilgrimage destinations the positive evidence has been massive and accumulated over long periods. Faith is a factor in all the world's major religions, and faith-healing a feature of many. From the Middle Ages to the present day there has been a cloud of witnesses to the miraculous, be it from Bethlehem or Canterbury, from Lourdes or Fatima.

If the inspiring power of physical association, relics and miracles have often been inducements to tread the pilgrim road, it is equally true that atonement for sins and punishment for crimes have also been factors in obliging unlikely and often unwilling travellers to set out on far-flung quests. Citizens of all sorts in the Middle Ages went voluntarily on pilgrimages of penance for real or imagined sins. John Moschos, in his book *The Spiritual Meadow* written in the seventh century, relates how a muleteer in Rome had been so stricken with guilt, after his mules inadvertently trampled to death a small child outside his inn, that he voluntarily set off as a penitential pilgrim to the Holy Land. He ventured into the desert in such a state of grief and misery that he attempted to kill himself to expiate the death of the child. But before he had succeeded in doing so, he encountered a lion (not an unusual occurrence at that time in that place). The lion declined to eat him, and the muleteer was so agreeably astonished by this that he saw it as direct evidence of God's forgiveness for the unfortunate accident. Not all self-imposed pilgrimages ended so dramatically or happily.

Another voluntary penitential pilgrim was Charles, Count of Blois, who was captured during the Hundred Years War and spent nine years in captivity in England. To celebrate his release and make amends for allowing himself to be captured he undertook a pilgrim-age – barefoot and through the snow – from the place of his capture to the shrine of St Yves in northern Normandy. The local inhabitants were so impressed that they covered the track he was to take with straw and blankets, but the count disdained this soft option and took to stony side tracks where he lacerated his feet so badly that he was unable to walk for weeks after his ordeal.

Most penitential pilgrimages however were not voluntary at all but imposed by courts, often as an alternative to execution or a long prison sentence. Thus murderers are recorded as sometimes having had to undertake their journeys wearing a belt made from the sword or dagger with which they had committed their crime; knights or noblemen sometimes had to complete their pilgrimages wearing chains forged out of their own armour; heads had to be shaven; shoes or boots eschewed; special penitential shirts were devised for some pilgrims which invited the monks at the hostelries where they stayed to chastise them further.

A particularly harsh case was that of Count Fulk the Black of Anjou. He had been a notorious sinner whose crimes had included allegedly murdering his own wife (an act he excused on the grounds that he had caught her in flagrante delicto with a goatherd) and numerous instances of infidelity, bullying and theft. He was condemned to make three separate pilgrimages to Jerusalem by the overland route – across the snowbound Alps, through the famously lawless Balkans, across Asia Minor and south through the Moslem-dominated Levant. Furthermore, he was to make the journey in shackles. As if this were not enough, he was on occasion dragged through the streets on a hurdle and publicly scourged.

Count Fulk was an exception, not only for the rigour of his sentence but for his aristocratic background. Most penitential pilgrims were poor and uneducated, as well as disreputable. They embarrassed voluntary pilgrims and lowered the prestige of the experience, in the same way as today court-imposed community service can lower the morale and prestige of those undertaking voluntary community service. Dedicated pilgrims were resentful of the company sometimes imposed on them. Jacques de Vitry in the thirteenth century complained that the road to Rome was cluttered with perjurers, whoremongers, jugglers and — worst it seems — actors.

But those working their passage to redemption or pardon were not usually the most dangerous or menacing of the characters to be encountered on the tough roads of medieval Europe or the Levant. There were other predators. Highway robbers frequented the forests (and Europe was much more wooded than now) even on the way to Canterbury. Bogus pilgrims struck up acquaintance with the sole purpose of leading their victims into ambushes. Rapacious innkeepers not only fleeced their high-minded prey, but not infrequently murdered them to cover their traces. (One French hotelier's woodshed revealed eighty-eight corpses after the nearby monastery became suspicious.) Leaky, unseaworthy boats, crewed by unqualified and irresponsible sailors, hazarded the lives of hundreds of pilgrims bound for the Holy Land from European ports, until the Venetians regularized the traffic.

It is difficult now to comprehend the degree of insularity of medieval life. Lords and peasants alike lived in tight communities which had little awareness of what lay over the horizon. Maps were almost non-existent or deeply misleading (being devised from principles of theology rather than geography) and news, including gossip, spread if not slowly then at least arbitrarily. To go on a long journey was taking one's life in one's hands. The clergy were perhaps slightly less at risk than the laity: their better education gave them a wider awareness, and their international status and common language (Latin) gave them membership of a wider fellowship; a Christian priest, monk or friar was never far in Europe from some brother-in-God, some fellow wearer of the cloth.

For those who did undertake long journeys — and these were usually pilgrimages — the problem of finding the way home was not an easy one. Just as simple people tended not to have surnames but to be known as someone's son, or by a trade name (tailor, smith, potter and so on) or by a characteristic which identified them (redhead, long-legs), so hamlets and small villages had only very local names or descriptions in many cases, and these usually related to a natural feature (a hill, brook or ford) which could be replicated many times over even in the same county. To leave home was to enter an alien world full of hidden dangers, some real (like footpads and wolves) and some imagined (like demons and dragons).

Different pilgrimages had somewhat different motives. When Christian pilgrimages first got under way it was naturally to the Holy Land that they went. For several centuries the practice continued with varying degrees of popularity and safety. The Islamic rulers of Palestine and its neighbouring countries, who had dominated the region since the eighth century, did not begin to make life difficult for Christian pilgrims until the eleventh century – and it was this change of attitude that was a major factor in provoking the First Crusade. With the help of Pope Urban II, the concept of a military invasion to recapture the Holy Places for Christendom quickly replaced the earlier notion of visiting these sites in peace and humility. Christian atrocities, notably the slaughter that followed the capture of Jerusalem in 1099, resulted in reprisals and enduring bitterness. The military orders which were set up to succour and protect the civilian pilgrims who were to follow in the crusaders' footsteps also distorted the motivation of pilgrimage. Although the Knights Hospitaller performed invaluable services with their hospitals and hostelries, the Knights Templar (who were the more combatant arm) early earned a reputation for arrogance and intolerance which was inconsistent with the ideals of earlier pilgrims. At the siege of Ascolon, for example, they had breached the walls and then planted sentries to prevent reinforcements joining them to share the glory – a gesture that cost all of them their lives. Not only had the crusaders moved a long way from the original spirit of pilgrimage, but they had incidentally and inadvertently damaged the reputation of holy relics, on which so many pilgrim destinations depended. The suspicious circumstances surrounding the discovery on the First Crusade of the Holy Lance (the Roman lance which had pierced the side of Christ on the cross) did little for the repute of other similar relics.

If the crusaders to the Holy Land did more to muddle than to clarify the motivation of pilgrims, the crusade in Iberia to expel the Moors from Spain and Portugal – the Reconquest – positively encouraged the stream of visitors to one of the other great pilgrimage destinations at Santiago de Compostela, where St James the Apostle was reputedly buried. Knights were excused service in the Holy Land if they volunteered for Spain. The shrine of Santiago and its pulling power helped the kings of Spain in their struggle for independence from Islam. There were other considerations too. The great abbey of Cluny in France took the pilgrims to Santiago under its wing, setting up subsidiary monasteries and giving shelter to travellers. For Cluny, the motivation for encouraging the pilgrimage was largely to extend the influence of the Cluniac order; in this they succeeded greatly, one of their monks even becoming Bishop of Santiago de Compostela at the end of the eleventh century.

Meanwhile, other Christian pilgrimages had grown up in different parts of Europe, each with its own particular lure. Mount Athos in Greece and St Catherine's monastery in Sinai had always attracted a trickle of ardent pilgrims. Local pilgrimages – or *romerias* – had long been a feature of life in Spain, running in complement to the year-long surge to Santiago. In England, the great abbey of Glastonbury in Somerset had remarkable – if tenuous – links with St Joseph of Arimathaea (who had provided the sepulchre for Christ) and with that mythical Christian hero King Arthur; a steady flow of pilgrims to the west country built up through the Middle Ages. The island of Iona, off the west coast of Scotland, had long drawn followers of St Columba; and the island of Lindisfarne, off the Northumbrian coast, and later Durham Cathedral (to which the saint's body had been taken to save it from desecration by the Vikings) had consistently attracted followers of St Cuthbert. At Walsingham, in East Anglia, where the shrine took the form of the Virgin Mary's home in Nazareth, a high church and high-society stream of visitors was established. But at the end of the twelfth century a new and more political destination in England eclipsed all the other national pilgrimages.

The murder of Archbishop Thomas Becket on the steps of the altar in Canterbury Cathedral not only provided a new national saint and martyr but almost overnight a focus for domestic and international pilgrimage. Here lay a hero who had struggled in his lifetime and met a violent death to uphold the rights of the church against those of the state. King Henry II, who was deemed to have incited the murder, tried first to belittle the event, then to profit from it (he levied a charge on the contributions paid by pilgrims at Becket's shrine – surely one of the most audacious of taxes), and finally was forced to go on a barefoot penitential pilgrimage himself to the scene of the murder. The fact that the king's fortune in war changed overnight with his penance (his enemies in Scotland and France suffering instant set-backs) consolidated the aura of effective sanctity that hung over Canterbury. In the following three centuries many of those who took the Pilgrims' Way across the North Downs to Canterbury did so in the awareness that they were honouring a man who had stood out against central secular authority. It was no wonder that, with the Dissolution of the Monasteries and his own assumption of supreme power over church as well as state, Henry VIII closed down the pilgrimage to Canterbury as subversive.

Throughout the Middle Ages – the heyday of European pilgrimages – Rome had always been the most popular continental destination. The motives for going there were not hard to identify, and included the Vatican, its magnificent Basilica of St Peter, its other resplendent churches, the connections with the saints and apostles, and the presence of the church hierarchy. During the period of the

Great Schism (1378–1417) the pilgrimage to Rome was much disrupted, and there was a widespread belief in the closing years of the fourteenth century that the end of the world was nigh and that since the start of the Schism no one had been admitted to the kingdom of heaven. With the end of the Schism, confidence and pilgrimage to Rome briefly recovered. But with the coming of the Reformation, Rome ceased to be a destination for Protestants, and indeed with the Counter-Reformation some aspects of the apparatus of Roman pilgrimage – relics and indulgences in particular – were also discredited within sections of the reformed Catholic church. The practice of pilgrimage was not over, but its motivation and conventions were changed, and its impetus much reduced.

One of the ways in which the change had been becoming apparent for some time, with the growth of nation states and the decline of a universal (or at least western European) Christian church, was the proliferation of national regulations affecting pilgrims. For a long time, rulers had had mixed feelings about large numbers of randomly assorted visitors walking or riding across their domains. Even if they had not been vagabonds and beggars themselves (and many were) they had attracted criminal elements. In both France and Spain unlicensed pilgrims were treated as undesirable aliens. In England (as a foretaste of things to come) currency restrictions and other hurdles were put in the path of would-be pilgrims. No longer, as in medieval times, could educated pilgrims be sure that their knowledge of Latin would provide a lingua franca which reached across frontiers. And increasingly pilgrims were returning from overseas with a marked distaste for foreign manners and practices. The Basques, across whose territory most pilgrims to Santiago de Compostela had to pass, were especially singled out as 'bestial' and predatory. The motive for pilgrimage, which in medieval times had been at least in part the consolidation of Christendom and the spread of mutual understanding, was markedly less so after the Reformation.

But one element in pilgrimages which remained a motive for many throughout the Middle Ages and right up to the present time was the element of tourism. It had never been an approved motive. As early as the sixth century, St Augustin had denounced curiosity for its own sake as 'worthless stock . . . an interruption and distraction from our prayers'. Similarly, Thomas à Kempis in the fifteenth century deplored curiosity and sightseeing in pilgrims because 'one seldom hears that any amendment of life results . . . their conversation is trivial and lacks contrition'. But tourist curiosity survived such denigration and remained a major motive for both rich and poor. There had always been a privileged minority of luxury pilgrims: princes and prelates, noblemen and knights, wealthy merchants and rich widows . . . all these had featured from the earliest times. Pilgrims such as John of Gaunt or William of Aquitaine had travelled with liveried retainers, silken tents and silver plate. For them, curiosity about foreign parts had often played as large a role as piety, indeed almost as large a role as it was to do on the secular Grand Tour which took over from upper-class pilgrimage in the eighteenth century. Even Chaucer's Canterbury pilgrims, though they were not leaving the shores of their own country, intended to enjoy themselves: they assembled at an inn, they all had mounts, and they entertained each other with storytelling of a highly secular – and on occasion ribald – nature. Further down the social scale, for peasant pilgrims the allure of travel was not so much tourism as escaping from the narrow confines of a feudal state to the wider horizons of a world beyond their own village.

The single event which gave most encouragement to the touristic content of pilgrimages was the publication in the fourteenth century of *The Voiage of Sir John Maudevile*, which is the subject of a later chapter. This purported to be an account of a journey to the Holy Land but was in fact a cocktail of invention and plagiarism written under the pseudonym of the non-existent Sir John Mandeville (as he has become known). It was promptly translated from the original French into English, Latin, German and other languages, as it was an entertaining work combining elements of geography, natural history and wild imagination: fountains of eternal youth, and anthills of gold dust enliven a trip which goes beyond even its proclaimed destination of the Holy Land. It was an open invitation to the curious and adventurous to avail themselves of the possibilities and advantages of taking to the pilgrim road because, as the author said, 'Many men have great liking to hear speak of diverse countries.'

Apart from the moral and other-worldly attractions of dubbing a journey a pilgrimage, there were practical advantages too. Though far from safe, it was still somewhat safer than other ways of travelling. Papal interdictions and national laws prescribed specially severe penalties for those who robbed or molested pilgrims. On sections of some routes there was an element of policing, notably by the Templars and Hospitallers on the routes to Palestine; and monasteries sent out search parties for lost pilgrims in the Pyrenees. There was cheap accommodation and often meals in monasteries and hospices, and companionship on the journey was easy to find. In most countries in medieval Europe, pilgrims also had certain legal privileges: they could make legally binding provision for their families and could stave off creditors until their return.

Sir John Mandeville's book had not only encouraged people to go on pilgrimages, it had also encouraged them to write about it. Chaucer's *Canterbury Tales* was not so much a book about pilgrimage, as using a pilgrimage as a literary vehicle for telling a series of good stories. But others made their travels the subject of books, and even guidebooks appeared, notably on the hazards – fast-flowing rivers, treacherous swamps, avaricious landowners who extracted tolls with threats and so on – on the various routes to Santiago de Compostela. The tradition persisted: in the early years of the twentieth century Hilaire Belloc was writing *The Path to Rome* about the spiritual and physical vicissitudes of walking through France and over the Alps to meet a religious goal, clearly with one eye on future travellers.

The best known of all books about pilgrimages is of course a purely allegorical one. John Bunyan would have been unlikely to set out on foot (and even more unlikely on horseback) to one of the classic European destinations such as Rome, Santiago or Canterbury because – even if he had not been in Bedford jail at the time – as a Puritan he would have disapproved of such traditionally papist activities. He followed very closely in *The Pilgrim's Progress* the actual risks and dangers that beset real-life pilgrims: not only those hazards mentioned in the paragraph above but also the risks of predatory and corrupt traders in market towns, fickle or boring companions, and a host of other difficulties and temptations. Bunyan's hero, Christian, is unlike most real-life pilgrims in that his motives are entirely pure: not for him the lure of conquest, or tourism or of literary aspirations. It was said of many of the simpler peasant recruits for Peter the Hermit's 'People's Crusade' that they thought they were being led not to Jerusalem in Palestine but to the New Jerusalem in heaven. Bunyan's allegorical hero really was travelling to the New Jerusalem.

Returning from the literary and imaginary to the real and historical, some things are clear. Just as the motivation for the pilgrimages with which this book is concerned have been mixed and at times muddled, so the nature of the pilgrims themselves has varied from the saintly to the scurrilous, from the virtuous to the vicious. The pilgrimages have taken place in different countries, in different centuries and by different forms of locomotion. The tapestry is broad. One idea remains constant: a 'first avowed intent to be a pilgrim'.

3

Jerusalem: the Archetypal Pilgrimage

B<small>Y THE MIDDLE AGES</small>, pilgrimage had become such an established feature of the Christian church that many imagined it had always been so. But the earliest Christians – unlike the earliest followers of Mahomet – did not immediately think in terms of revisiting the scenes of their founder's life; they concentrated on the universal application of his teaching rather than on its local aspects; St Paul and the Apostles took the Christian teaching out into the world of Asia Minor, Greece and Rome, rather than attempting to bring followers back to Palestine. The Emperor Hadrian – no lover of things Jewish – went so far as to build a temple dedicated to Venus on the scene of Calvary, to make Christians feel less at home there. In general, the Roman emperors for the first three centuries AD discouraged travel to Palestine, a region associated with disaffection and turbulence.

All this changed with the conversion of the Emperor Constantine to the Christian faith in 312. It was his mother, the Empress Helena, who set the new trend. As well as being an ardent Christian, she was an early amateur archaeologist; she combined her two enthusiasms

17

by visiting Palestine and digging up parts of Calvary in search of relics; she also encouraged her son to build the Church of the Holy Sepulchre there – a lasting magnet for pilgrims. From then on, a steady trickle of devout Christians made the journey from the West. And soon there was to be an additional draw: St Jerome settled himself in a cell in Bethlehem and, while intent on translating the scriptures into Latin, drew to his new home a stream of fashionable followers from Italy. By the year 400, there were already some two hundred monasteries which took in pilgrims visiting Jerusalem, and later in the same century the ranks of the visitors were swelled by large numbers of Byzantine grandees from Constantinople.

Inspired by Helena, the fashion of collecting relics from the Holy Land spread throughout the western church. Sir Steven Runciman, in his celebrated *History of the Crusades*, quotes the example of a western lady who brought back from her pilgrimage the thumb of St John the Baptist, and whose friends' enthusiasm was so awakened by this modest relic that they set off themselves to see the saint's body in Samaria and his head in Damascus. One visit bred other visits.

Throughout the first several centuries after Christ, the standard of life in the East – whether in Byzantium or the Arab lands – was noticeably higher than in the West: luxuries moved from the Orient to Europe. The traders who conducted this commerce often took pilgrims as passengers and even more often brought back news and travel information which encouraged the flow.

There were of course occasional set-backs: in the middle of the fifth century the Vandals, who had made incursions into the Roman empire, also dominated the sea-lanes to the East and piracy became a temporary hazard. A further problem was the Arab conquest of Jerusalem in 638. Although this was conducted in a relatively gentlemanly manner (the Caliph Omar paid his respects at the Holy Sepulchre) it also temporarily reduced the number of pilgrims from the West; women stopped coming altogether and only the robust felt able to cope with Arab administration.

But in the following century the pilgrim traffic picked up again. The Emperor Charlemagne was a patron and supporter of pilgrims. The first detailed records of pilgrim journeys began to surface, and by the tenth century numerous routes had opened up and the Arab rulers of Jerusalem appeared to welcome the trade that accompanied the western visitors. Aristocratic pilgrims brought lesser personages in their train. Some became serial pilgrims: the Bishop of Parma – later to be canonized – made no less than six separate journeys to Jerusalem. It was beginning to be taken for granted throughout the West that there was a right of way to the Holy Land, and the great age of pilgrimage, that coincided with the later Middle Ages, was gaining pace.

Whereas the earliest pilgrimages had almost always been private initiatives, from the tenth century onwards there was an element of institutionalizing the practice. The Cluniac order of monks not only positively encouraged the great and good to go to the Holy Land, but they helped with the organization of travel arrangements. The Dukes of Normandy and the Counts of Anjou – from Cluniac strongholds – were persuaded to go; and where they beat a path, other rulers followed from regions as distant as Sweden, Denmark, Iceland and Norway – the last being represented (in legend if not in certifiable fact) by no lesser a pilgrim than Olaf Tryggvason, their first Christian king. Some of these Nordic leaders were violent men with lists of crimes to their name which gave added purpose to a pilgrimage of atonement: Swein Godwinsson was sent barefoot in 1051 to expiate a murder and died of exposure in the mountains of Anatolia on the way.

When, at the end of the tenth century, the rulers of Hungary were converted to Christianity, overland travel to the Holy Land via

Constantinople – that great metropolis with its unrivalled store of Christian relics – became a better proposition than going by the expensive sea route. There were good and relatively safe roads across Asia Minor to Antioch and thence down the Syrian coast to Palestine. It was possible to congregate in fairly large groups for the journey, which further added to the feeling of security; but it was not unknown for parties of two or three to undertake the walk or ride without escort. So long as Byzantium was friendly, so long as the Arabs could maintain law and order within their own domains, and so long as the pilgrims themselves behaved quietly and unprovocatively, there was no reason to think that the Holy Land would not remain an accessible destination for westerners of all classes who could spare the months or years that such a journey took. The sacred road had become part of the rich pattern of medieval Christendom.

But the decades of peaceful pilgrimage were numbered. Before the end of the eleventh century, two developments had occurred that completely undermined the status quo. The Byzantine empire had been invaded by the Seljuk Turks and Asia Minor was largely overrun, with the predictable consequence that the overland pilgrim route was effectively closed. And secondly, in 1071 the Turks had also taken Jerusalem itself and the new regime there was less hospitable towards Christians and in particular towards western visitors. The most valued Christian pilgrimage in the world had ceased to be viable.

The process by which the crusades were launched to try and rectify this state of affairs is recounted in Chapter 13. For the purposes of this chapter, the story is best resumed when the turmoil of the crusades is over. By the fifteenth century the preferred route for most pilgrims was by sea, and sea travel effectively had to be by courtesy of the predominant maritime power in the eastern Mediterranean – the Venetian Republic.

The decision as to whether or not to embark on the voyage was never an easy one. When Eberhard, Count of Wurtemburg, returned from Jerusalem in 1480 and was asked about the advisability of following his path to the Holy Land, he replied: 'There are three things that can neither be recommended nor discouraged – marriage, war and a voyage to the Holy Sepulchre. . . . they may begin well and end very badly.'

To reduce the chances of them ending badly, detailed instructions were prepared for pilgrims in 1481 by the Cavalier Santo Brasca who had been to the Holy Land from Milan the previous year. The first injunction was probably the hardest and the least observed: it was that the voyage should be undertaken with the sole purpose of 'contemplating and adoring the Holy Mysteries . . . and not with the intention of seeing the world and being able to boast "I have been there".' The spiritual and material requirements for pilgrimage meet in one of his next injunctions: that the voyager should take with him two bags – one full of patience (to sustain him in the fatigues and boredoms of the journey) and another bag containing 200 Venetian ducats (to sustain the way of life of one who is accustomed 'to live delicately at home'). Other hints and instructions are mostly of a practical nature: he should take an overcoat reaching down to the ground to wear when sleeping in the open air, two barrels (one for water and one for wine) and a 'night-stool or covered pail' (for self-evident reasons). Recommended provisions included 'a great deal of fruit syrup, because that is what keeps a man alive in the great heat, and also syrup of ginger to settle his stomach'.

When it came to landing in Palestine, Brasca insisted that the pilgrim should be 'humble in his behaviour and in dress' and avoid arguing about the faith with Saracens 'because it is a waste of time and productive of trouble'. Despite the humble and modest posture recommended however, pilgrims should be generous with largesse, and Brasca lists an alarming number of crew members on any

Venetian galley – ranging from trumpeters to crossbow men – who require tipping on disembarkation. Although he claims not to want to discourage poor men from venturing on the voyage, one is left with the impression that the project is not to be undertaken cheaply – let alone lightly or wantonly.

Not only because of Venice's control of the seas, but because of her chain of ports and extensive fleet of mercantile galleys, Venice was well placed to mastermind the pilgrim traffic from western Europe to the Holy Land. Indeed, under tight governmental control, Venice organized a virtual Cook's travel agency service. It was a profitable business. The captains of the Venetian galleys were usually the owners or at least part-owners of the vessels, so the temptation to maximize profit was considerable and, in the interests of preserving their long-term prospects, they had to be constrained by a whole raft of regulations. Captains were required to employ scribes to note down all the passengers' particulars; luggage was restricted to one chest (pilgrims' servants had no luggage allowance); excess baggage became the property of the captain; overloading was expressly forbidden; the crew had to be provided with weapons, including a sword and three lances for each mariner; even if some passengers failed to complete the voyage by jumping ship at ports on the way because of fatigue, fear or shortage of cash, the captain was obliged to take the remaining pilgrims on to their destination; there was a special rule forbidding the misclassification of pilgrims as crew members.

As well as all these constraints on the captains, there were similar rules governing the conduct of the crew, chief among which were that they had to take an oath before embarkation 'not to steal more than the value of five small *soldi*', and not to desert in the event of shipwreck but to stay around and help recover cargo etc. for fourteen days. One feels that the Venetian authorities knew the limits – both in terms of honesty and of loyalty – that could be expected of their sailors. There was even a well-developed system by which complaints by pilgrims could be registered with the authorities on return to Venice.

With all these regulations affecting both captains and crew, designed to protect the rights and interests of pilgrim passengers, the Venetian authorities realized that they risked damaging the attractions of the traffic for their own seafarers; so they reluctantly allowed the captains and crew to carry a certain amount of private goods on the voyages to be sold or bartered en route. Doubtless the fact that the galleys were therefore, at least in part, on trading missions, increased their acceptability at their Arab ports of call. The Venetian government, for its part, secured a measure of profit by selling licences to ship-owners to participate in pilgrim transportation. The idea was that everyone should be happy with the arrangements. But despite all the red tape, occasional scandals occurred, as when some Flemish and German pilgrims in 1465 complained that their captain had tried to extort an extra payment from them in mid-voyage as a condition of their safe return.

Among those who sailed from Italy to the Holy Land were a number of pilgrims of great distinction. Probably the most celebrated was St Francis of Assisi who, with a band of missionaries, landed at Acre in 1219, visited the Holy Places, and on his return journey entered a Saracen camp and, possibly because no one understood what he was saying, managed to preach a sermon criticizing the Koran without apparently giving any offence. In 1392, Henry Bolingbroke (the future King Henry IV of England) was provided with a galley at the expense of the Venetian Republic to sail to the Holy Land. When he succeeded to the throne after the deposition of Richard II, one of his first acts was to write an appreciative letter to the Doge of Venice promising to treat Venetian visitors to England with the same favour as his own subjects. In 1446, a noble party of pilgrims sponsored by the Duke of Burgundy were given similar preferential treatment. Some of the more eminent pilgrims were distinguished more for their martial valour than their piety: in 1458 the *condottiere* Roberto da Sanseverino, a notable soldier of fortune, made the voyage.

However distinguished the passengers on some specially sponsored trips, the voyage still had its share of discomforts for most pilgrims. Hans Von Mergenthal, who accompanied Duke Albert of Saxony in 1476, reported that 'the sleeping space allotted to each pilgrim was so narrow, that the passengers almost lay one on the other, tormented by the great heat, by swarms of insects, and even by great rats that raced over their bodies in the dark'. (This despite the fact that Venetian regulations laid down that every passenger should have a berth a foot and a half wide.) In the daytime the passengers were shunted round the decks to make way for the seamen to handle the sails. Many succumbed to seasickness and some, who fell more seriously ill, died on the voyage. As for the provisions, the meat was rotten, the bread was full of worms and the wine was 'hot and tasteless'. The hardships persisted even after the pilgrims had landed, and the overland journey often involved sleeping rough. One of the embarrassments about these harsh conditions was that a number of supposedly simple pilgrims were in fact grandees travelling incognito; they not only noticed the hardships more than others, but they reported on them to a wider circle on return.

Hardships were one thing: dangers were another. And the main danger was always from Turkish privateers and pirates; however much Venice might dominate the sea-lanes to Syria and Palestine, there were frequent attacks on their galleys, resulting not only in the sequestration of ships and cargoes but, all too often, in the death or sale into slavery of passengers and crew. When the *Quirina* was attacked in the Gulf of Satalia by a Turkish ship in 1408, there were many deaths and the ship would almost certainly have been lost altogether had it not been for the courageous fight put up by the non-Italian civilian pilgrims on board. At times when Venice was specifically at war with the Ottoman empire, the Venetian senate ordered extra precautions to be taken: the *Contarina* in 1472 was equipped with two rowers to each bench and twenty crossbow men including – presumably to maintain morale and discipline – 'two patricians'.

With so many hardships and dangers, what, one wonders, was it really like to go on such a pilgrimage from Venice to the Holy Land?

4

Canon Casola: the Privileged Pilgrim

THE BEST ACCOUNT we have of a fifteenth-century pilgrim to the Holy Land taking the Venetian galley route is by a Milanese priest called Canon Pietro Casola, who was well connected to aristocratic circles, had been for many years attached to the Milanese embassy in Rome and who knew that city well. Casola made his journey in 1494 at the age of sixty-seven – a very advanced age for such an adventure – and wrote a full report entitled *Voyage to Jerusalem*. His previous publications had been strictly theological, but his account of his pilgrimage is full of practical and illuminating detail; he proved himself to be a keen observer, a cultivated man of the world and not without a certain dry humour. Casola is the first to recognize that possibly because of his age, status and connections, he was given a degree of privileged treatment by the captain of his galley. If he was to survive, he probably needed it.

Casola had always wanted to go to the Holy Land, but in his youth there had been too many other distractions. By the time he reached sixty-five, he realized it was now or never, and took a solemn vow to go to Jerusalem at all costs. He set his affairs in order (there was a serious risk he might not return) and set about collecting some congenial companions for the voyage – mostly monks. But as the departure date grew nearer, the prospective companions fell away with one excuse or another. So he lobbied among his congregation but none came forward to accompany him, and Casola was left to go alone. The only support he could get was from his bishop, who blessed the emblems of his pilgrimage: his cross, his pilgrim's staff and – most important – his wallet.

Casola then rode across the plain of Lombardy, and through Brescia, Verona, Vicenza and Padua to Venice, which greatly impressed him with its size, wealth and beauty, and also with the fact that it was cheaper to hire a boat here than to hire a horse elsewhere. He toured the surrounding monasteries, the Arsenal and the glass factories of Murano. He noted how proud the Venetians were on account of their great dominions: 'When a son is born to a Venetian gentleman they say to themselves – "A Lord is born into the world".' He admired the richness of the men's clothing, but was more critical of the women's high heels ('they are not safe from falling as they walk'), false hair-pieces and décolleté dresses. ('The pretty ones show their chests, I mean the breasts . . . so much so that I marvelled that their clothes did not fall off.') He appeared to disapprove of the Venetian women's habit of hiring jewellery which they could not afford to buy, and of painting their faces 'and also the other parts they show'. Casola is at pains to justify his observation of all these things; he explains that he had no wish to enquire into the private lives of these women, but he had 'thought it my duty' to have a good look around on the way to the monasteries and churches. Quite so. Reading between the lines, he seems to have thoroughly enjoyed his venture into these lush and unfamiliar pastures.

All too soon he had to turn his attention to more serious matters like securing his berth. Up to the last moment he hoped that 'some Lombard would arrive with whom I could join for the living on the galley', but none showed up. He paid the captain of the galley 30 gold ducats in advance, and for this the captain undertook 'to keep me by sea and by land as far as the River Jordan . . . and give me a place at his own table'. Another 30 ducats were to be paid later. He bought a chest and a mattress and sent them aboard the galley. All was set for departure on 4 June 1494.

Casola had a good look round the galley the moment he went on board. He noted the ballast in the hold – sand and gravel, and wedged in among it 'many barrels and casks of wine for the majority of the pilgrims'. He also noted many weapons, including crossbows and swords, slung from the overhead decks. He explains that above the poop was 'a place called the Castle' where the captain and 'any great persons that happened to be aboard' lived; here there was a curtain of red cloth embroidered with the arms of the Holy Sepulchre and of the Contarini family. The latter coat of arms reflected the fact that the passenger list included 'the Magnificent Don Agostino Contarini, a Venetian patrician, who had four young men to serve him'. There were three trumpets, each with a good trumpeter. All in all, there was a good deal of protocol to be observed, and Casola clearly felt reassured by this and by the fact of himself being on the captain's table.

At a more practical level, Casola was impressed by the size and weight of the rudder, which took more than two men to operate in heavy seas. He noted that there were cages for live animals, which could be killed for food if this was not obtainable in port; and – as a good Catholic – he was relieved to find that there were fish-sausages (a Milanese speciality) for Fridays. The galleys were propelled by sail as well as by oars, and Casola was overawed by the circumference of the main mast 'which in its lower part could only be embraced by three men'; and he describes in detail the mechanism for hoisting the sails. With his usual eye for money matters, he records that the ship's cables alone cost over a thousand ducats. There were thirty-six pieces of artillery, and plenty of powder and shot – something he would be glad of later on. He even reports that the ship's lavatories (or, as he more euphemistically calls them, 'places necessary for purging the body') projected outside the galley and overhung the sea, and is reassured by the fact that the seat is 'on timbers well tarred and joined together'. One feels that not much was missed by the hawk-eyed cleric.

The total crew and armed guard amounted to 140 men, and Casola noted that every one of them had brought some kind of merchandise aboard, to augment his pay by a bit of private trading on the side: 'there were more than three thousand pieces of cloth alone . . . no man could believe the galley was capable of carrying so much cargo in addition to the passengers and crew'. Despite being so weighed down, there was still room for 170 pilgrims, most of whom – including Casola – were promptly seasick on setting sail. Casola prudently went below decks immediately to take possession of his sleeping space before others laid claim to it. Had there been sun-loungers, one feels he would have grabbed one early on.

From the first day at sea, Casola reveals that, however much he was intent on 'contemplating the Holy Mysteries', he was not averse to 'seeing the world' – in fact, in indulging in any tourism that was on offer. When the captain of the galley said that the pilgrims could not go ashore at Parenzo (on the far side of the Gulf of Trieste), he joined forces with another reverend father and they hired a boat for an hour's trip round the harbour and a run ashore. He makes it clear in his journal that he intended to do this whenever possible. The two fathers did a little wine-tasting and declared the local reds to be very drinkable. At the next port of call, Zara, Casola complained that the city was paved with hard pebbles that made it difficult for a gouty Milanese like himself to walk at all comfortably on them, and also, he noted wryly, 'I did not see a single fine palace'. He did however admire 'fourteen very large figures all covered with gold' in the cathedral, and was much impressed with the principal relic of the place – the body of St Simeon (he of the *Nunc Dimittis*) which he described as perfectly preserved, even noting that the saint's mouth was open, revealing the old man to be as toothless as might have been expected. But he was not able to hover too long in the cathedral because one of the ship's trumpeters was sent to go round the town sounding a warning blast that everyone should embark quickly to catch the favourable wind.

The captain had been over-optimistic about the wind: soon they were battling against such an adverse gale that he contemplated returning to Zara. Worse was soon to happen. While the pilgrims were below decks having dinner, the pilot ran the ship on to a sandbank. There was general alarm, as most of the pilgrims thought they had hit a rock, holed the hull and were about to sink. Casola admits he was among those panic-struck. However, 'God had mercy on the many souls aboard . . . and especially as so many of them were religious [i.e. priests] of all kinds'. He concluded that, although they had been in great peril, no lasting harm was done. Adventure was being added to tourism.

Casola's curiosity about all matters took a new turn at Ragusa: he made a detailed survey of the city walls. Noting that these were higher on the landward than the seaward side, he measured them and found them over twenty feet thick. But the defences of the city also come in for criticism from Casola: a castle outside the walls was thought by the priest to be too isolated to receive supplies in the event of an assault, and the local commander's protestation that it could be supplied from a tower 'by means of a cord' was dismissed as 'an absurd answer'. But he noted that they were constructing a wider moat around the city and a larger harbour. While the city did not appear under an immediate threat, he learnt that they were paying a hefty tribute to the Ottoman Sultan and also made an annual gift to the King of Hungary. The Balkans were not a secure environment even in the fifteenth century.

Be that as it may, Casola found much to enjoy: commented favourably on the local malmsey and other wines at Ragusa, but he deplored a local law that prohibited citizens from keeping wine in their own houses and required them to send out to a tavern every

31

time they wanted a drink – though he added that there would be fewer citizens with gout in Milan if the same rule applied there. And, as usual, he was impressed by signs of ecclesiastical wealth, commenting that in the main church 'everything is of silver'; but he speculates that some of the jewels may be fakes or they would be better guarded. In the city council chamber, the critical connoisseur notes with disapproval that the chairs are not gilded, as had been the case in Venice. He found the women of Ragusa to be good-looking, well dressed and adorned, but considerably more modest than their Venetian counterparts. All in all, Herr Baedeker himself could hardly have given a closer commentary on most aspects of the city which is now Dubrovnik.

Ever since the adventures of St Paul during his missionary expeditions in the eastern Mediterranean, Christian scholars had been aware of the storms and high seas that occur there. It cannot therefore have been a total surprise to Casola when his ship ran into yet another storm after leaving Ragusa. This time it was worse than before, and the captain of the galley declared that in forty-two years at sea he had never had such a long and fierce battering. The pilgrim passengers panicked as usual: as water cascaded below decks into their sleeping quarters there was shrieking and a surfeit of last-minute confessions. Casola says that although he did not join in the screaming, he did contemplate the fact that (as he had often said in jest before) it seemed likely he would have 'a fish as his sepulchre'. Happily, once again the prayers of the pilgrims or the vagaries of the weather saved the day, and they sailed on to Corfu.

Here Casola fell on his feet. He had been given a letter of introduction to a leading local churchman from an Italian bishop and, while his fellow pilgrims were complaining about the quality of the wine in the local taverns, he was wined and dined as if he had been the bishop himself. But he did not greatly take to the town of Corfu, finding the inhabitants 'for the most part of a low class', the archbishop's palace 'not worthy of such dignity', and the streets 'very narrow and dark' and rather frightening to explore on his own, particularly as he saw 'a great many ugly faces'. Casola's local host did him proud however, accompanying him back to the ship and giving him a leaving present of fruit and geese and – following a heavy hint from Casola – also giving the captain a very generous present which enhanced Casola's prestige on board.

Casola's social antennae were also quick to pick up indications that a 'very young and magnificent' new pilgrim who embarked at Corfu was a nephew of the King of Spain. This rich and rare young man included among his accoutrements for the journey some horses and sporting falcons given to him by the King of Naples. In fact, so large was his baggage train that he had to have his own special *greppo* (a one-masted trading vessel) sailing alongside the galley to carry his kit and possessions. Another lord (the ruler of the Greek island of Kos) also embarked and Casola remarks, 'I made myself known to him and he showed me many attentions.' The pilgrimage was fast becoming a gratifyingly social experience.

From time to time however there were events which reminded all aboard that this was essentially a pilgrimage. For instance, over the feast day of St John the Baptist – while the ship was becalmed – the passengers were subjected to several hours of sermon on two successive days from one of the other priests on board, and then in the evening the sailors put lamps up the rigging and 'sounded the trumpets, let off many fireworks, fired off mortars and made great illuminations'. Whatever else might be overlooked, the Christian calendar was always in mind.

The next port of call was Modone in the Greek Peloponnese, which Casola found scruffy and not at all to his taste. He was introduced to *retsina*: 'a wine made strong by the addition of resin . . . which leaves a very strange odour which does not please me'. But the thing that really upset him was the Jewish colony, who were engaged in the silk industry. Casola displays the anti-Semitic sentiments that were so rife in medieval and Renaissance Europe, describing the Jews as 'very dirty people in every way and full of very bad smells . . . their society did not please me'. There seemed to be increasingly many features of the journey which displeased this fastidious pilgrim.

In one respect at least Casola was becoming more cheerful: he was less seasick now, even when further storms buffeted the galley on the crossing to Crete. But, like most of the pilgrims, he was annoyed that the captain and crew insisted on putting in at Candia (Iraklion) – when they could have pressed on, taking advantage of a favourable wind – so that they could set up their customary market and sell the trade goods they had brought with them from Venice. It was ironic that, having survived so many storms at sea, no sooner had they landed at Candia than a violent earthquake shook the town. Casola, who was visiting a friary on shore, was 'almost thrown from the seat on which I was sitting' and feared the whole place was going to collapse around him, as the beams of the roof came out of their sockets and clouds of dust engulfed everything. The pilgrims thought they had escaped the sea only to perish on land.

In the event, they spent several days at Candia and, as usual, Casola found a good deal of which to disapprove. Although he admired the tall hats of the Greek priests, he found most of those wearing the hats 'very ignorant'. But what he really took exception to were the sanitary arrangements. There were no proper lavatories and people used chamber pots during the day and then in the evening, at the sound of a bell from the tower of St Mark's church, 'they all empty the vessels from the windows without taking any precautions . . . though the contents should fall on a person's head, no penalty is incurred . . . and there is a great stink.' He says they seem to think the scents of the cypress trees 'confound these stinks' – but he maintains they don't.

Throughout the voyage and overland journey there was a fairly steady stream of fatalities, which illustrated the need – that had been impressed on all of them before departure – for pilgrims to make their wills. On leaving Candia, Casola's neighbour on the dormitory deck died of no specific ailment, except that he had been ill when he came on board. More deaths were to follow.

Sailing from Crete (which was firmly under Venetian rule) to Rhodes, the pilgrims became aware that they were getting to the very fringes of Christendom. From here on, Venetian outposts were always at risk from the Turkish Sultan's forces and the seas were more heavily infested with pirates and other hostile shipping. Constantinople had fallen to the Turks only forty years before, and the battle of Lepanto – at which the Ottoman naval advance was to be decisively halted – was not to take place for nearly another eighty years. These were difficult times: at best, a period of stand-off in hostilities.

As if to illustrate these dangers, the moment they reached the island of Rhodes the pilgrims heard that two Venetian merchants vessels (with 60,000 ducats' worth of goods on board) sailing from Cyprus to Rhodes had just been seized by Turkish pirates. This predictably threw the pilgrims into 'a great alarm'. Their confidence was not much restored by a tour of the citadel of Rhodes which revealed traces in every quarter of the damage done during the siege by the Turks a few years earlier. Everywhere there were stones and cannon balls – some said five thousand of them – lying around where they had landed. Casola was convinced the survival of the town had been 'more a miracle than due to the power of man'. He found everything on the island was highly cosmopolitan: carpets came from Turkey, cloth from Italy, and the inhabitants mostly 'foreign knights or merchants from every nation under the sun'.

However, Casola's spirits improved when he was invited to a dinner at one of the palaces and found 'such a display of silver, such diversity of viands, and everything so well decorated and served that it would have sufficed for any great lord'. He also called on the Grand Master of the Order of the Knights of Jerusalem who paid him 'many attentions'. While he was with the Grand Master, news was received that the ships which had been taken by the Turkish pirates had been recovered. The knights had only managed to take one prisoner, a boy who had been 'cut in pieces' in the customary manner. (This was a war in which no quarter was given by either side: a few years earlier when some 250 Turkish seamen had been captured by the knights, they had all been impaled – a form of execution also favoured by the Turks themselves.) The morale on the pilgrim galley was much restored by this news and, while they had been apprehensive about continuing towards Cyprus, now they pressed on – merely cursing the lack of wind in a way not altogether appropriate for such dedicated pilgrims.

But when they reached Limassol in Cyprus, they found a town which, unlike Rhodes, had never recovered from the Turkish incursions. It struck Casola as a bleak place: no proper harbour, ruined city walls, a tumbledown cathedral, and bales of cotton in place of beds for those foolish enough to stay ashore.

The locals blamed some of their woes on the havoc wreaked by King Richard Coeur de Lion of England when he had stopped there in the course of the Third Crusade, but since that had been some three centuries before Casola's visit the accusation seemed a little unfair. The hard fact was that the pilgrims were now entering lands where Ottoman destruction was a regular feature of life. Indeed, while they were in Cyprus there were further rumours of Turkish pirates lying in wait for the galley, and the captain requested escort vessels from the local governor. In the event, escorts were not available and the passage to Jaffa (now Tel Aviv), the nearest port of Jerusalem, was said to be clear. And this proved to be the case.

While they were moored off Jaffa, waiting in baking heat for permission to land, one of the Franciscan friars on board preached a sermon to the pilgrims exhorting them to prepare themselves spiritually for the Holy Land. The indulgences associated with the pilgrimage would only be forthcoming if they renounced their sins: the journey – however hazardous – was not sufficient in itself to win salvation. The following day, amid the mounting impatience of the pilgrims with the Islamic formalities that had to be complied with before they could disembark, the same friar preached another sermon: this time it was on the theme of 'make to yourselves friends of the mammon of unrighteousness' – a clear reference to the need to keep in with the tiresome Turkish authorities until the red tape had been complied with. And to add to the gloom, while they were waiting to go ashore, another pilgrim died. This time it was a young Dane who had scarcely enough money with him (when they went through his baggage) to pay for his burial, so they put his body, rather unceremoniously, in a cave by the beach. Casola reckoned the lad had died as a result of eating too many unripe grapes in Crete.

Casola's patience was clearly wearing very thin. He complained that 'the Moorish dogs would not let us go on our way . . . they made difficulties, now about one thing, now about another'. Even their presents to the captain of the galley (surely a token of goodwill?) were shrugged off by Casola without much grace: the ox that was sent was too thin, and the fruit overripe. In any case, Casola noted, the Moorish officials were all placemen who had bought their jobs from the sultan. There was not much effort to make friends with the mammon of unrighteousness – at least from that quarter.

It was at moments like these that Casola recalled Brasca's advice about every pilgrim needing two bags or sacks – one of patience and the other of money. He comments wistfully that 'it was necessary to tie everything up in the sack of patience, as we did not want to loosen the sack of money'. To pass the time, the captain suggested that they indulged in some fishing from the ship, making his suggestion sound more appropriate by claiming that these were the waters where St Peter used to fish. In the event they caught a shark, and the sailors frightened the pilgrims with tales of its man-eating habits. They also saw turtles. One way or another, the captain tried to keep them amused until he could get permission for them to land.

But it was a losing battle. Casola reports that 'the pilgrims began to murmur still more against the captain, as did the Children of Israel against Moses'. Some of them – especially the French – said insulting things to the captain's face, but he retorted that the delay cost him more than it did them as he had to feed them while they remained on board.

After eight long days of sitting aboard in growing frustration, a message was finally sent to the effect that the pilgrims could land but could not set off towards Jerusalem until the Moorish governor of Gaza had arrived to escort them. The captain advised them they would be safer and more comfortable on the ship until such time as they could start their overland journey. But some refused to listen and went ashore regardless and were obliged to lodge in a cave. Some of these subsequently died, at least in part because there was no medical help and no comforts ashore, so when they got ill it could be fatal.

Meanwhile tension was rising on the galley. A party of Moors were invited on board to placate them and the ship was decorated to celebrate the event. But it was not a success. The chief Moor lay down, together with his slaves, on one the carpets which had been laid out on the poop and took a two-hour siesta. Some of the pilgrims suggested to the captain that the time for patience was over and the time for money – extensive bribes – had arrived. But the captain was reluctant to pay out, claiming that it would set a bad precedent and that all future pilgrims would suffer. He had good reason to mistrust the Moors who had forced him to part with a hundred ducats as the price of being allowed to return to his own ship.

When eventually the governor of Gaza arrived, a very ugly incident occurred. The captain was offering some gifts to the governor in his tent, when the latter produced ten Christian prisoners in chains who had apparently been shipwrecked on the coast and captured by the Moors who accused them of theft. The governor told the captain and the Prior of Mount Zion (the local Christian resident representative) that the pilgrims must pay a ransom for the prisoners or 'he would flay them alive before their eyes'. In the ensuing altercation, the governor had one of the prisoners stripped and stretched out by the executioner as if to be flayed. The governor demanded a 1,000 ducats. Bargaining followed and the final price for their release was 150 ducats. A collection was made among the pilgrims (Casola contributed one ducat) and 'the prisoners were redeemed and taken naked and famished on board the galley'. Realizing he was on to a good thing, the governor next produced a Jew and a Frenchman and threatened to flay them alive if a ransom were not paid. The captain told him this time he could do as pleased, providing the pilgrims were allowed to go on their way to Jerusalem. The Jew was then badly beaten, but the Frenchman was so frightened that he instantly converted to Islam – or (as Casola rather uncharitably put it) 'that coward of a Frenchman denied Christ'.

Finally, after two full weeks of promises, privations, threats and extortions, the surviving pilgrims were allowed to proceed on their way. Mounts of one sort or another had been found for them: some rode horses, some mules, some asses. As well as what the captain had paid for these animals, the individual owners required a separate tip or else 'they make a rider tumble off his animal and then extort more before they will help him up'. Casola was allocated a mule and struck a hard bargain with the muleteer. The pilgrims were accompanied by an escort of Mamelukes, armed with bows and arrows, who travelled on foot. They departed on 1 August – the hottest time of the year – on a dusty, shadeless road. The Mamelukes, when not regaling the pilgrims with tales of all the robberies they might expect (the road from Jerusalem to Jericho was nothing to this, and there were no Good Samaritans around), diverted themselves by hunting hares. Whenever they passed a place of Islamic significance, they infuriated the pilgrims by making them all dismount.

The first night of the overland journey was spent at a monastery outside Rama, a bleak building set aside for the use of pilgrims and run by an order called the Christians of the Girdle. Casola was none too happy with it. He had to sleep on a plank, wrapped in his mantle and using his purse as a pillow. The next day they were diverted from the path to see a tiny church where St George had reputedly been beheaded; it was said to be much venerated by the Moors, but Casola reckoned the only veneration they practised was charging Christians an entry fee.

There is nothing ecumenical about Casola's approach to Islam: he seldom misses a chance to deride its practices. For instance there are frequent references to imams 'yelping like dogs' and calling on the male population to 'multiply upon the earth' – a task which Casola says is all the easier as they have so many wives. He says it is madness to talk to the Moors about their faith 'because they have no rational sentiment in them' and they are easily excited to anger. Even the Mameluke escort are accused of staging false alarms of non-existent attacks as a means of demanding extra money from their charges.

So far Casola had survived better than most of the pilgrim group, but now an accident – which lost nothing in the telling – befell him. His muleteer, no doubt anxious to get the most for his none-too-generous tip, had packed fodder and merchandise on to Casola's mule, as well as a young boy who was apparently his son; the animal was seriously overloaded, and when the boy fell off he brought Casola down with him. Stopping only to grab his wallet, Casola set off on foot to catch up with the rest of the cavalcade, by which time his arm had swollen up so much that he had to unsew the whole of the sleeve of his doublet. Casola was so badly hurt that he maintained that even after he had returned to Milan 'his wounds were still not healed'. It must have been an unpleasant experience for a man in his late sixties.

But Casola's morale improved, as so frequently before, when he received some special attention and privileges. On arrival at Jerusalem – surely the climax of his trip? – his first comments are all about his own accommodation which was with the captain in a comfortable house (quite different, he assures us, from the poorer pilgrims) and where he was given extra carpets and cushions to lie on. 'We lived like lords,' he declares with palpable satisfaction.

Having survived all the hazards and discomforts of the journey, it is not surprising that Casola and his fellow pilgrims were determined to make a very thorough tour of the Holy Places. This included the Mount of Olives, Mount Zion, the Holy Sepulchre and Bethlehem among other sites. Casola, who had already referred frequently to his bag of patience and his bag of money, now added a third necessity – a bag of Faith. This was particularly required he explains because 'those Moorish dogs' had not marked the sites with the care and precision they deserved, so they had to be taken largely on trust. He also blames the resident Christian friars for not conducting proper prayers and ceremonies at the sites as he expected them to do. He was also shocked that at the Pool of Bathsheba, where Christ had performed a miracle, the Moors now washed their hides; he adds with obvious disdain that 'many of the pilgrims drank the water . . . when I saw that filth I left it alone'. In fact, rather surprisingly, he shows more interest in the local markets and the magnificent mosque than he does in most of the sacred sites that he has come all this way to see: there is no denying (despite Brasca's injunctions) that even here in the Holy Land seeing non-Christian curiosities is a fairly high priority.

The one site which totally absorbed Casola's interest and was the exception to the carping above was, predictably, the Holy Sepulchre itself. The pilgrims were kept hanging about until after dark when eventually the Moorish custodians finally condescended to open the door of the church. They all lit candles and processed around the main points of sacred significance: the place where Christ first appeared to Mary Magdalene after the Resurrection, the place where his garments were divided, the place where he was held a prisoner while the cross was erected, the scene of the deposition from the cross, and numerous other relevant locations. At several of these there were most important relics: a large piece of the True Cross, a part of the marble column at which Christ was scourged, and so on. On this occasion the friars performed to Casola's satisfaction, singing and chanting and preaching. Casola concluded that even 'the Moorish dogs' would have been moved had they been present and able to understand.

The next major destination was Bethlehem. Although Casola enjoyed the scenery on the ride from Jerusalem, and admired the church there – 'the most beautiful since Venice' – he reverted to his criticism of most other things: the Armenian Christians who inhabited the church 'lived there on the ground, like pigs'; regrettably a toll was payable to the Moors on entry; and 'to our great shame' cattle were allowed to graze right up to the door of the holy manger. (The fact that this might have been the case at the time of the holy birth does not seem to have occurred to Casola.)

On the night after their return from Bethlehem a formal ceremony took place: ten of the most distinguished pilgrims were dubbed as Knights of the Holy Sepulchre. Casola acted as secretary and wrote the documentation for the Superior of the Order to seal. This was one of the rituals that encouraged grand and aristocratic figures to embark on pilgrimages to the Holy Land, and Casola was obviously pleased to be associated with the ceremony.

Everything was slightly an anticlimax after the Sepulchre. An optional journey to the River Jordan was proposed. Casola rather smugly decided not to go, because 'it appeared to me that the expedition was prompted rather by curiosity to see the country than by any sentiment of devotion' – not an argument that usually deterred him. However at the last moment he joined the Jordan expedition after all. There was the usual hang-about for the

Mameluke escort. When eventually they got going it meant riding through the night; everyone was very tired; Casola's mule wandered off the road into thorn bushes that tore his mantle and doublet; Jericho, which they passed by, 'was nothing but ruin'; the escort chivvied them at every turn – to dismount, remount and hurry up; the daytime heat was intense; one of the elderly fathers collapsed; the Jordan turned out to be 'like a mud bath' and Casola thought those who drank from it were very unwise; to cap it all, when they got back to Jerusalem the guards at the gate had to be bribed to let them in. All in all, it had not been a joyous or uplifting excursion.

But worse had happened to those who had stayed behind in Jerusalem. A Jewish doctor (there is never any shortage of fuel for anti-Semitism in Casola's story) had denounced the stay-behinds to the Moorish authorities as spies, claiming 'they have refrained from going to the River Jordan in order to spy out and explore Jerusalem, and he had heard certain of the pilgrims say that within two years the Christians would be masters of Jerusalem'. The Moors had been all too ready to believe – or pretend to believe – that the pilgrims were the vanguard of another crusade; they arrested them and took them off to prison in chains. Casola was glad after all that he had been to the Jordan as 'if I had been in the house I should have been led in chains like the others'. After much negotiation, the local governor agreed to release the pilgrims on payment of a fine or bribe – reduced from 1,000 to 25 ducats. 'The malice and iniquity of that Jew' had resulted, as usual, in an excuse for the Moors to milk the pilgrims of their funds.

Casola did some final sightseeing in and around Jerusalem before departure. He was astonished by the number of different Christian sects which were represented at the Holy Places: these included Georgians, Armenians, Abyssinians (shades of Prester John?), Syrians, Maronites, Copts and 'Jacobites'. These last evoked Casola's particular disdain: 'they have a very strange way of chanting

43

the offices . . . which rather provoked the company to laughter'. Once again, ecumenism was not on Casola's agenda.

The overland journey back to the port of Jaffa was just as fraught with problems as the journey out. The Moorish governor of Gaza 'invented another bewildering fraud': he demanded the return of those Christian captives whose freedom had been purchased by the pilgrims when they arrived. The pilgrims paid up – a further 128 ducats – so as to be free to go on their way. But this was not the end of the matter: later the governor demanded that 'the slaves' be returned to him anyway, and the unhappy captain felt he had to order that they be handed over. The ransom money was returned to the captain but, Casola records with annoyance, his own single-ducat contribution was not refunded to him. It had been a sorry tale of threats, dishonesty and cruelty by the Moors, and of capitulation and self-interest by the pilgrims.

No one wanted further delays and casualties. Some pilgrims had already died in Jerusalem; some had been left behind as too sick to travel; and some of those who were travelling were in very bad shape. The Prior of Mount Zion delivered a farewell sermon in which he begged the pilgrims to dissuade others from following in their footsteps for at least another two years to avoid 'the great vexation inflicted by the Moors'.

At one point on the route, the town of Rama, they were warned that they would be attacked and robbed at night. An alarm was sounded in the middle of the night and Casola was so agitated that he fell off the plank on which he was sleeping – the only casualty of the incident. The pilgrims then realized that, as they had no weapons of any kind, they might as well go back to sleep and hope for the best.

The next day they pressed on towards Jaffa, their embarkation and their escape from the tribulations of the Holy Land. A final set-back remained in store for them: on return to the galley one of the grand and affluent German pilgrims who had been created a Knight of the Holy Sepulchre died, and the grasping Moors would not let him be buried ashore without further payments and risk of detention. No one was sorry to put out to sea.

But their relief at escape did not last long. The winds were either adverse or non-existent. When they eventually put in at Cyprus, they found that there was an outbreak of the plague and 'certain impatient Germans' disregarded the captain's warnings to give the place a wide berth and went ashore to explore the island and rejoin the galley at Limassol. When a few days later the friar who was the favourite preacher on board was found to be gravely ill with swellings on his throat, there were fears that the plague might have broken out. The captain's reaction was superstitious rather than medical: he ordered all Jordan water (which, however efficacious for baptisms and drinking on the spot, was curiously considered an unlucky souvenir) to be thrown overboard, and the ship to be searched for items which might have been stolen from churches in the Holy Land as illicit relics, and thus bring bad luck or divine retribution. The friar died but the plague scare abated.

Now the main worry was being becalmed while fresh water and provisions ran out. The doomed friar had earlier preached about the need to focus on spiritual rather than material sustenance when rations were low. Now they were in more dire straits than ever, and the friar was no longer there to give them comfort. Other passengers died and Casola wrote: 'I never thought to see land again after so many days without seeing any.' (One wonders how he would have survived had he been on Columbus's first Atlantic crossing just two years earlier.) Eventually, in mid-September, they sighted Rhodes.

The news of the plague at Cyprus had gone before them, and no one was allowed to land from the galley at Rhodes, particularly after the port authorities heard of the suspicious death of the friar. However, 'through the efforts of the Lord of Longo', the Grand Master was persuaded to let the pilgrims go ashore: social clout had triumphed over medical precautions. Casola was swept up in a round of 'very sumptuous banquets every day' paid for by the Lord of Longo (who was that same ruler of Kos with whom Casola had earlier taken care to make his number): he was in his element again. Other pilgrims and crew were busy trading: 'more than four thousand carpets were carried aboard'. This was a pilgrimage on which everyone seemed to have their own set of priorities.

The next halt on the return voyage was the island of Kos. Here the Knights of St John paid flattering attention to Casola because they understood he was a person of importance in Milan. The Lord of Longo had a castle on the island which was protected from marauding Turks by a pack of dogs which ranged the countryside for several miles around the castle and, if they encountered Turks who could not escape, they 'worried them to death'. If, on the other hand, the dogs encountered lost Christians they 'recognised them at once and led them to the castle'. These remarkable animals also apparently looked after each other, and if one did not show up at mealtimes one of the older dogs would go and look for it. Casola – with his firm grasp on finances – declared they were 'worth their keep'.

Between Rhodes and Crete rations again ran short and everything to eat on the galley became very expensive. But an unplanned stop at the island of Nio (Ios) enabled them to take on fresh water and provisions. Here there was a castle on a great rock which Casola compared unfavourably with its Italian counterparts: 'in Lombardy it would be an important fortress, but here it appears to be a pigsty.' Casola says he would not dare to spend so much as a single night there in case it fell down. One senses the feeling of superiority of a citizen of one of those Italian city states which were about to burgeon into full Renaissance.

Having put in at Nio, now they found themselves becalmed there, and the non-Italian pilgrims formed up to the captain to complain, once again behaving like the feckless Children of Israel with Moses. The captain explained he was the victim of the weather and, when 'very injurious words had been said on both sides', Casola acted as a diplomatic intermediary. The discontents among the foreign pilgrims always seem to have suspected that the captain was pleading inclement weather when really he was prolonging his stay in port to give himself and his crew more time to trade with the locals. When eventually they were able to sail again, stiff winds gave the French pilgrims (another group not in favour with Casola) an excuse to remain below decks and miss out on attendance at choral Mass.

Casola himself is at great pains to reassure his readers that he takes no part in all the commercial activity. When describing how he witnessed the making and storing of cheeses in Crete, he justifies spending a whole day there by saying he was 'looking at those things in order to be able to tell about them, not with the idea of trading'. Curiosity about the world around him and the strange ways of foreigners may not be a proper reason for going on pilgrimage, but at least it is better than conducting business, it seems. Similarly, on the rare occasions Casola confesses to spending money not on essential food, it is usually 'on articles of devotion'.

Just when they thought they were about to reach Corfu, the worst storm of the whole voyage struck them. Casola blames this on his fellow pilgrims' ingratitude to the Almighty and disregard of the Commandments: 'good works were limited to a very few persons' (among whom, one gathers, Casola himself was numbered). The sirocco lashed the galley so that everyone fled below decks and 'it was no use to say "this is my place" because in that hour all things were common . . . death was chasing us'. Even the least pious among the crew called on Jesus to help them 'like souls tormented in hell'. It is interesting to note that the reaction of many of the pilgrims was to make solemn vows to go on further pilgrimages if they survived this one; separate undertakings were given to visit Our Lady of Loreto and St Anthony of Padua; money was collected towards the cost of these trips, and lists of volunteers were drawn up. The promises appear to have been successful because once more, despite conflicting sailing directions from the captain, the governor of Crete (the most influential passenger, who was hitching a lift back to Venice) and the chief officer, the winds abated and the vessel sailed on into calmer waters.

When they reached the Dalmatian island of Curzola (Korcula), Casola had so fully recovered from his fright and good resolutions that he allowed himself to start noticing again the charms and manners of the ladies, who 'arrange themselves so that their breasts hold up their clothes and prevent them from falling down on their feet'. Apart from the ladies, the other good feature of the island was declared to be the wine. Life was returning to normal.

Slowly but surely the galley completed its northerly passage up the Adriatic to Venice. When Casola arrived there it was to a gratifyingly warm – if not exactly heroic – welcome. The Milanese ambassador to Venice kept Casola, telling him of his adventures until late into the evening. But not everyone was as impressed by the achievement: the Venetian authorities, in a thoroughly tiresome way, detained the pilgrims' luggage in customs for several days, and were only prevailed on to release it after application of Casola's 'second sack' – money. Clearly to Venetian officials, pilgrims to the Holy Land were a useful source of revenue rather than a category of visitor to be treated with any special consideration. Casola was none-the-less impressed by other aspects of the Venetian establishment: he witnessed the Doge's procession to Mass and greatly admired the sumptuous costumes and good order of the whole performance. And he was taken on a tour by the Milanese ambassador of various opulent palaces where the good cleric displayed his usual quick eye for material values: 'the bedstead alone was valued at 500 ducats', and he speculates that some of the Venetian damsels were wearing jewellery worth 100,000 ducats. But despite all these worldly distractions, Casola did remember to say a special Mass in gratitude for his survival of the worst storm at sea.

Leaving Venice, Casola returned on horseback to his home city of Milan by the same route which he had come. He avoided towns where 'the place was full of soldiery' and one is reminded that this was the age of the *condottiere* and of the continual fighting between the city states of northern Italy: a pilgrim like Casola was never really safe until he was back within his own city walls. When at long last Casola reached Milan he paused for a night outside the city, because he wanted to avoid making his arrival at a time when he would have been overshadowed by the grand entry of Ludovico Sforza, the Duke of Milan. Instead, Casola entered the gates of the city the following day 'in pilgrim's dress and alone' and was received 'most graciously' by the archbishop.

Casola had risked his life and abandoned his comforts to go on an unquestionably dangerous pilgrimage at an age when most men – and certainly most clerics – would have chosen to stay safely and comfortably at home. By writing such a full and frank account of his travels and adventures he has revealed himself – and his motives – to us as thoroughly as Chaucer revealed the personality of any of his Canterbury pilgrims a century earlier. One suspects he was not untypical of pilgrims to the Holy Land in the fifteenth century, setting out as he did with a thoroughly mixed set of motives: he sought and expected spiritual advancement; he wanted to see how other people lived in other lands; he hoped to have a tale to tell on his return which would captivate the attention and admiration of his friends; he did not want to spend more money on the expedition than he needed to; and he aspired to enhance his social credentials by mixing with grander and more influential travelling companions. But above all he wanted to have the greatest adventure of his life, and – like most medieval pilgrims – he did.

5

Rome: the Eternal City Pilgrimage

WHILE THE HOLY LAND was the most obvious and natural destination for Christian pilgrimage, there were long periods when it was either impossible or very difficult to reach. The second most popular destination had the advantage of being on continental Europe and never in the hands of non-Christian enemies. Rome also had many positive attractions of its own.

Although there was no direct connection with Jesus, Rome was believed to be the site of the martyrdom and burial of two of the most significant figures in the Christian story: St Peter and St Paul. Both saints were commemorated from an early date by suitably grand basilicas. A third and almost equally impressive basilica was the Lateran Palace – home to many of the popes. By the late Middle Ages there were to be no less than seven essential sites for every pilgrim to visit.

Another reason for the pulling power of Rome was, of course, its role as the seat of the papacy and the launching pad for the Christianization of western and northern Europe. Successive popes over the centuries capitalized on this factor by granting indulgences and spiritual favours to those who made the journey to their capital:

St Peter was, after all, not only the rock on which the church was founded, but the keeper of the gates of heaven, so a pilgrimage to his city and his shrine could convincingly be portrayed as a positive factor for those seeking admission to paradise or at least the avoidance of an after-life in hell or an indefinite period in purgatory.

To augment these natural advantages, successive popes maximized the collection and deployment of Christian relics as additional lures to pilgrimage. By the eighth century AD, Pope Paul I had begun the process of redistributing the bodies and bones of the early Christian martyrs from the catacombs below Rome to the ever-burgeoning number of churches around the city. After the sack of Constantinople by the western crusaders during the Fourth Crusade in 1204, there was a huge influx of looted relics from the eastern Christian (Orthodox) church. In 1208, the Pope started exhibiting publicly the *sudarium* of Veronica (the napkin with which it was believed Jesus had wiped his face on the hot and hard climb with the cross to Calvary): this was a star among relics. Other particularly popular treasures of Rome included such colourful – and occasionally improbable – items as the tablets of Moses, the rod of Aaron, the hair-shirt of John the Baptist and the five loaves and two fishes with which Jesus had fed the five thousand. Indeed when former popes had parted with some of the relics of saints who were part of the heritage of Rome – notably the body of St Sebastian – the action had provoked riots in the streets from the citizens who relied on such objects for the protection of their home city; later Roman citizens were to prize their relics not only for their spiritual insurance value but also for their drawing power for pilgrim visitors.

Rome has always attracted visitors for secular reasons. However decayed and neglected the architectural ruins of the ancient world of the mighty Roman empire might be, there were always those who were moved by the monuments of antiquity. Throughout the medieval period, the neglect of such a heritage was a recurring theme of visitors, until the Renaissance awakened both a constructive reverence for antiquity and a surge of neo-classical construction of a quantity and value rivalling the original. Although few admitted it openly or in their written accounts, the antiquarian appeal of Rome to scholars, students and sightseers was an undoubted factor in the city's appeal to pilgrims even in the Middle Ages.

But the appeal of Rome, though strong, was not consistent: there were periods when the Eternal City was slighted or ignored. King Henry II of England forbade his subjects to go to Rome during the time of his quarrel with Thomas Becket: he saw allegiance to the papacy as a dangerous rival sentiment to loyalty to the crown of England. Richard I – that arch-crusader and Christian warrior – passed within a few miles of Rome on his way to the Holy Land in 1190, but saw no reason to make even a marginal detour. Edward I actually passed through Rome on his way to talks with the Pope but did not consider it worth giving up the time to visit any of the Christian shrines there. In the early Middle Ages it had been normal – however arduous the journey – for Archbishops of Canterbury and other primates and prelates to visit Rome on the first possible occasion, to obtain papal blessing on their appointments. But by 1300 this process was already falling into decline: not only did fewer monarchs make the journey to pay their respects to the successor of St Peter, but fewer archbishops and bishops found it necessary or convenient to do so. By 1400 even newly appointed cardinals did not always go to Rome. This was partly because the religious orders, which had originally always congregated in Rome for their assemblies and conventions, were finding other more local, accessible and attractive venues. The papal evacuation to Avignon in the fourteenth century contributed to the fall-off of Rome as a natural magnet.

With this reduction in pilgrimage and attention to Rome, it would be natural to speculate that the declaration of a Jubilee Year in

1300 by Pope Boniface VIII was an overt attempt to attract visitors. The reality was more complicated. The idea of more generous indulgences had been steadily gaining ground: the participants in the Albigensian Crusade were encouraged to view it as a form of pilgrimage by the award of special 'jubilee' indulgences. When New Year's Day in 1300 was approaching it seemed to the citizens of Rome that some extraordinary recognition of this Christian centenary was called for, and a jubilee plenary indulgence – a remission of sins – was the obvious way to achieve this recognition. Huge crowds gathered in and around St Peter's in the last hours of the old century.

The Pope consulted his college of cardinals and decided to take advantage of public expectation. The greatest treasures and the most popular relics were unexpectedly put on public display. By February 1300, the Pope issued a bull confirming what was so widely hoped for: all those who visited the appropriate basilicas during the centenary year and were genuinely penitent would indeed receive the much-desired plenary indulgence. The fact that forgiveness of sins was dependent on a confession by the sinner and absolution by his priest was often forgotten or overlooked by the thousands flocking to Rome in the expectation that the visit in itself wiped out the consequences of their sins.

Other factors helped swell the numbers. The weather shone fine over the Eternal City, and the approach roads to Rome were less hazardous than in most of the immediately preceding years as the recurring wars between Italian city states were mostly in temporary abeyance. The French flocked in and a more than usual number of Englishmen: Edward I sent a personal representative.

All this was welcome to Pope Boniface and the church establishment in Rome. But it put a considerable strain on the municipal arrangements – rather as in more recent times the Olympic Games might do. Accommodation was overstretched and numbers of Roman citizens opened their houses to visitors – at a fee. Food too would have been a problem had it not been – appropriately and providentially – an exceptionally good harvest in that part of Italy. Some people went so far as to say that feeding the pilgrims was another miracle of the loaves and fishes. At focal points crowd control got out of hand. The chronicler William Venturer saw women as well as male pilgrims being trodden underfoot in the press of people. And the poet Dante, who was himself in Rome for part of that year, describes in his *Inferno* the crowds on the bridges. The historian Jonathan Sumption, in his scholarly study *Pilgrimage*, gives a vivid account of all these factors.

Like all popular events, the Jubilee Year was the subject of many post-mortem assessments: some saw it as a greedy attempt to wring more money out of pilgrims – there were reports of priests literally raking in money with forks at St Peter's as if it were a casino – while others saw it as a gross extravagance. Nor could contemporaries agree on the numbers who had come, and estimates ranged from two hundred thousand to two million.

Be that as it may, before 1350 there was a move afoot to have a repeat jubilee. In the intervening years the papacy had evacuated Rome for Avignon, but it was to Rome that pilgrims were once more invited in large numbers in 1350 by Pope Clement VI. But this time conditions were not so auspicious: the truce in European wars was well and truly over, the roads were dangerous and governments reluctant to see their citizens embarking on foreign travel and expenditure. The plague, or Black Death, was scarcely under control. To cap it all, an earthquake damaged many of the principal Christian sites in Rome. But despite all these set-backs, once again huge numbers of pilgrims flocked to Rome – probably at least some fifty thousand extra people being in the city at any one time.

An increasingly familiar development in and after 1350 – though not an entirely new one – was the proliferation of forged papal bulls and fraudulent promises of indulgence. All sorts of special indulgences were offered by particular churches or the owners of particular relics to increase attendance and donations. For instance, each of the altars in St Peter's offered separate and competing dispensations to sinners; for every hour that a pilgrim spent contemplating the sudarium of Veronica, a foreigner would, it was claimed, reduce his time in purgatory by twelve thousand years. As Sumption comments, it was remarkable that these practices were not challenged earlier than the Reformation in the sixteenth century.

After 1350 also, the whole 'industry' of Roman pilgrimage accelerated. Guidebooks proliferated, and often were written to suit the expectation or hopes of those in whose language they were written. Thus an English guidebook quietly converted references to St Thomas – the doubting apostle – to Thomas Becket. With Avignon as a rival attraction for much of the fourteenth century, Rome was not only asserting its attraction within Europe, but was trying to outbid the Holy Land at a time when the pilgrimage to Jerusalem was again firmly re-establishing itself. The vernicle (a badge depicting St Veronica's relic) was introduced for Roman pilgrims to rival the palmer's badge of Jerusalem and the cockle-shells of Santiago de Compostela. National hostelries enjoyed a revival and, as well as the celebrated English hospice, there were other houses set aside for the shelter and accommodation of Portuguese and Swedes, Castilians and Sicilians and even Hungarians and Irish.

As the decades passed after the original Roman jubilee of 1300, other complications arose. Crowd management had not improved: in December 1450 there was an incident on the Ponte Molle when nearly two hundred pilgrims were crushed to death and a further score of bodies pulled out of the Tiber. These were disasters almost on the scale of more recent catastrophes among Moslem pilgrims to Mecca. But by then the Great Schism had ended: Rome was once more predominant and the requirement for jubilees was over. By 1500, the year of the last jubilee, the fluctuation in the number of pilgrims to Rome was no longer the Pope's main concern: the corruption associated with indulgences was stoking a far greater threat – the Reformation.

With so many reasons to come to Rome throughout the Middle Ages, and with such a numerous, if erratic, flow of pilgrims, one wonders how they made the journey from all over western and northern Europe. Englishmen naturally tended to come through France, with the complications that ensued in times of war between the two countries. Scandinavians tended to come via the German states. Some came from even farther afield: Nicholas of Munkathvera had to sail from Iceland to Norway before he could even begin the overland journey. But all of their routes converged on the great obstacle of the Alps. Ice, snow, avalanches and vertiginous passes were a feature of most crossings. The Great St Bernard Pass, 8,000 feet above sea level and covered in snow for three-quarters of the year, was the most popular crossing point, partly on account of its famous hospice, founded by St Bernard himself in 962. But others chose to cross by the Simplon or Mount Cenis Passes.

Travellers' tales of the hazards are all too numerous. James Harpur has recounted a number of the more spectacular mishaps in his *Sacred Tracks*. Aelfsige, Archbishop of Canterbury, froze to death while attempting the Alpine crossing in 959. John of Canterbury, less seriously, found his ink bottle frozen solid on the St Bernard Pass in 1188, and his beard 'congealed in a long icicle'. Adam of Usk, when banished to Rome in 1402, had himself blindfolded when he was carried over the passes in an ox-wagon, so that he would be spared the horrid vision of the perilous falls below. It was not until the romantic movement of the nineteenth century that such Alpine phenomena were to be considered stimulating rather than merely frightening.

To help with finding the best route and keeping to it, a number of maps and guides were produced at different periods. One of the most memorable of these was either devised or copied by the chronicler Matthew Paris from St Albans in 1253. His map consists of a long series of strips, indicating places and features on the road, not only to Rome but to the Holy Land as well: rivers, mountains and lakes are shown to warn the intending pilgrim of hazards or obstacles. His map was to be the forerunner of many such road charts in subsequent centuries, for use not only of pilgrims but of all travellers.

As well as all the natural hazards which beset pilgrims and travellers to Rome, there were man-made dangers which were often even worse. During the period in the twelfth century, when there was a rival – an anti-pope – to Alexander III (elected by a minority of the cardinals and supported by the Holy Roman Emperor), those making the journey to Rome had to traverse lands dominated by the Emperor Frederick Barbarossa.

One such was an Englishman called Brother Samson (who was later to become Abbot of Bury) who wrote a graphic account of his journey to Rome in 1161. He was not only making the pilgrimage for the good of his own soul, but on his return he was also carrying a letter back from Pope Alexander III to his flock in England. He knew – and recounts in his journal – that all clerics who carried Alexander's letters were seized by order of Barbarossa and 'some were imprisoned, some hanged, some had their lips and noses cut off and were then sent thus [back] to the Pope to his disgrace and shame'.

Samson decided that the best protection against being thought of as a papal messenger was to pretend to be a Scot – a dialogue between Rome and Scotland at that moment apparently being considered improbable. He therefore 'put on the Scottish costume and Scottish manner'; the latter appears to have involved shaking a stick at people and uttering uncouth threats. In this way he managed to get through to Rome, but on his return path he passed by a castle whose officers captured him and declared 'this vagabond, who pretends to be a Scot, is either a spy or a messenger of the false pope Alexander'. They then body-searched him, examining 'my rags and my hose and even the old shoes which I carried on my shoulders in the Scottish manner'. Samson had his wits about him: he stuffed his incriminating correspondence into a drinking goblet and held this above his head while they strip-searched him without realizing there was anything in the cup. His interrogators contented themselves with taking all his money off him and leaving him to beg his way back to England.

Another pilgrim traveller – Peter of Blois – who was making the journey from Bologna to Rome at the same period was intercepted by agents of the Emperor (whom he describes as 'executioners') and, although his companions were 'cast into chains', managed to escape – probably by judicious bribery – 'through the wall in a basket'. He records with chagrin that, although grateful for divine protection, he regretted having to abandon his clothes and other possessions in making his dramatic exit.

Samson and Peter of Blois came into danger because of backing the wrong pope. Others were endangered purely because of their importance and wealth. Prominent among these was Archbishop Anselm of Canterbury at the end of the eleventh century. One of his retinue – a certain Brother Eadmer – told the story of his master's adventures.

Eadmer explains that the archbishop's progress towards Rome was attended by much – often unwelcome – publicity. His itinerary reached the ears of those determined 'to take him and spoil him of his possessions' which were rumoured to include 'a great weight of gold and silver'. The Duke of Burgundy in particular had his eye on the archbishop's saddlebags, and personally led a party of armed soldiers who waylaid the rich primate.

Eadmer tells how the duke rode up and demanded 'with a roar' to know which was the archbishop, and how the latter 'sat his horse looking very stern'. Suddenly the duke realized the enormity of what he had intended to do; he blushed and fell silent. Meanwhile the archbishop, who must have been a man of nerve and considerable presence, said: 'My lord duke, I wish to embrace you and save you, and I sincerely rejoice in the Lord at your arrival.' Thereupon the archbishop gave him a kiss of peace and told the duke he was delighted to see him and had always wanted to make his acquaintance. The whole encounter ended up with the duke offering in all sincerity to provide the archbishop with a suitably aristocratic escort for the rest of his journey. Eadmer understandably comments: 'For our part, we thanked God!'

Anselm continued on his way to Rome, being received with appropriate honours at Cluny and at Lyon. But his perils were not passed: 'some persons moved by evil greed laid snare to catch him'. Wilbert, Archbishop of Ravenna, had been expelled from his post and was bent on taking revenge from passing church leaders. He had already 'captured certain bishops, monks and priests in his fierce persecution, had robbed them and loaded them with abuse and killed them'. He saw Anselm as his next victim. Knowing this, the archbishop delayed for some while at Lyon, making the excuse of ill-health, but the Pope urged him to press on, and so he did. But prudently he presented himself anonymously with Eadmer and another priest at the next monastery on the route, only to be told by the local monks that it was folly to press on to Rome as 'no one in clerical garb can go that way without being seized and greatly harmed'. The monks went on to reinforce their argument for caution by saying that even the Archbishop of Canterbury had sensibly gone no further than Lyon. Undaunted, Anselm continued his pilgrimage in the guise of a simple monk and safely reached Rome, to be received in state by the pontiff and accommodated in the Lateran Palace.

Another pilgrim with a special agenda was Archdeacon Gerald of Barri who, in 1199, set out to Rome to seek the Pope's blessing on his election to a Welsh bishopric and to make the case for independence of the Welsh church from Canterbury. Gerald wrote his own account – one of the earliest of travel writers. On the way out, the forest of Ardennes had proved to be 'full of thieves and robbers' and, having survived them, he fancifully declared himself Bishop of the Ardennes as well as of Wales. But it was on his third journey to Rome, in 1203, that his most traumatic adventures began. By then the see of Canterbury had realized that he was on a mission of which they disapproved and the English church were determined to thwart him.

Gerald eluded the authorities at Canterbury by stowing away in the hold of a ship sailing from Dover to Gravelines. In France things proved tougher than in Kent. On the third day he was spotted by an agent of 'the evil warden of Artois who robbed all Englishmen and spared none' and was obliged to pay a heavy ransom before he was allowed to go on his way. Having negotiated the dangers of Burgundy and the Alps – frightening equally because of their snow and their much-feared robbers – he was nearly betrayed to his enemies (presumably representatives of Canterbury and the English church) by two canons of Llandaff whom he had assumed to be Welsh supporters but who had 'treacherously sided with his enemies'. Making a wide detour to avoid the notoriously dangerous Tuscany, he eventually reached Rome safely once more. After all his efforts, the Pope rejected his case.

His return journey was to be bedevilled by money troubles. The problem was that when he ran out of money, which he quickly did, he borrowed from the locals who detained him, running up interest and further living costs, until fresh financial support arrived. The spectre of 'captivity for the rest of his life' in a debtors' prison was a real and constant worry. His immediate troubles in Italy were relieved when his principal creditor in Bologna allowed him to proceed with his journey into France, where he had arranged to collect fresh funds at the Troyes fair (on the Seine, south-east of Paris) provided that he did not seek to escape from the escort which the creditors provided. In fact, he was to travel as a debtor let out on licence until he could repay obligations which were mounting alarmingly as time and travel went on.

This plan was going remarkably well until he was overtaken by an apparent stroke of bad luck at Châtillon-sur-Seine near Troyes. Gerald and his escort had joined up with a larger band of French pilgrims, but he was spotted as a foreigner and when questioned confessed to coming from Wales 'which belonged to the King of England who was then at war with the King of France'. So Gerald and all the pilgrims travelling with him were arrested. Gerald was very upset, not only for himself but because he had brought this misfortune on his travelling companions who, as pilgrims, should also have been immune from such arrest. When it transpired that these companions, who claimed to be from Rouen (within the King of France's domain) were really from Gisors (within the King of England's domain) matters looked even worse for them, until a genuinely French priest, who was returning from Jerusalem, told their captors a 'virtuous lie' confirming their provenance from Rouen and so secured their release. But this did not help Gerald who was indisputably Welsh and therefore in his captors' eyes an Englishman. Indeed the officious officers from nearby Châtillon nearly detained some of the other pilgrims on suspicion of being in Gerald's retinue as 'a man of such importance to be elected head of a metropolitan church' must, they thought, have a sizeable band of retainers with him. Once more the virtuous liar – this time telling the truth – explained that Gerald was travelling with one foot-boy only and thus secured the release of these remaining pilgrims.

But then it transpired that Gerald's identification as a foreigner and 'Englishman' had not been as random as supposed. In conversation with his captors, Gerald explained that the Archbishop of Canterbury had sent agents to work against his case (for an independent Welsh bishopric) in Rome. His captors enquired who such agents were and, on being told that one of them was called John of Tynemouth, they declared 'you must thank him for your detention'. It then became apparent that this John of Tynemouth, not satisfied with having successfully undermined Gerald's case in Rome, had then passed his description to the French authorities at various points along his return route. In particular, he had described Gerald's 'bushy eyebrows' which had led the young officer who had spotted him to suspect he was neither French nor a simple pilgrim. Gerald, who emerges from his tale as a spirited figure, amused his captors by saying that 'if he had known his bushy eyebrows would lead to harm, he would have cut down their wooded growth by fire or sword!'

Gerald now made a plan to escape. His warders allowed him to go to vespers in the local church, and he resolved to 'seek sanctuary by clinging to the altar and its relics'. But at the last minute, he was told there was a good chance that the seneschal (the responsible officer) would release him after all. This turned out to be the case, but Gerald increased the chances of his own release by telling the seneschal that John of Tynemouth – who was also under the seneschal's jurisdiction – was a wealthy priest with rich livings at his disposal, and that, as a favoured emissary of the immensely rich Archbishop of Canterbury, he would be worth a far larger ransom than Gerald himself. This argument appealed greatly to the greedy seneschal who was quick to add that since the archbishop was councillor to the King of England, and Tynemouth his agent, this made Tynemouth a specific enemy of the King of France. Gerald, under extreme provocation and with an obvious relish, had completely turned the tables on his betrayer.

From then on, fortune smiled on Gerald. He was allowed to go free on his way, while John of Tynemouth languished in the prison he had vacated. He reached Troyes fair and found his bankers who paid his debts to the Bologna creditors (what had happened to the creditors' escort/custodians is not clear). Continuing to Paris, he was well received by the visiting Archbishop of Dublin who helped him to cross over into English-held territory in Normandy. His tricky and dangerous mission to Rome was ended – albeit unsuccessfully. Undeterred, he returned to Rome yet another time in 1204–5 'solely by way of pilgrimage and devotion' with no complicating and embarrassing special mission. Altogether he had earned ninety-two years of indulgences and, by enrolling himself in the English hostelry in Rome, got further credit to set against his sins. He dropped his case for independence from Canterbury 'and so made his peace with the church'. All had ended for the best.

Gerald's tale does however present a sobering picture of pilgrim dangers unrelated to the natural hazards of continental travel or even to the accustomed hazards of brigandage and robbery. The malice of churchmen against other churchmen extended even to those who were engaged in following the sacred tracks to Rome.

6

Margery Kempe: the Unpopular Pilgrim

IF ANYONE DOUBTS the social and convivial aspects of medieval pilgrimages, they only have to look at the treatment accorded by fellow travellers to one pilgrim who was considered by her associates to lack the spirit of companionship-of-the-road which formed an essential element in all such journeys.

Margery Kempe was a fifteenth-century English pilgrim whose devotion and dedication went far beyond the normal bounds of accepted pilgrim practice. To some she was a pious and saintly figure, to others a fanatic, and to many of the more conventional lay and ecclesiastical people she encountered she appeared marginally mad and dangerously close to heresy. In 1411 she was convinced she received a divine call to go on pilgrimage to Jerusalem, Rome and elsewhere and, having made the necessary deployments, set off on a whole series of sacred journeys that were to occupy most of her energies from then onwards. To understand the extent of her commitment it is necessary to be aware of her background and life prior to 'the call'.

Margery Kempe came from a reputable background. Her father was mayor of Lynne (now King's Lynn) in Norfolk and she and her husband lived a comfortable life with children, plenty of servants and plenty of money for fashionable clothes. She had her own independent brewing and later milling businesses (medieval ladies not being as housebound as is sometimes imagined) which she pursued despite a history of some mental instability. However the businesses did not prosper. She felt conscience-stricken and began to see herself as a Mary Magdalene figure, with a sinful past but a peculiarly close relationship with Christ.

In this state of mind she first became a vegetarian and then, more radically, set about persuading her husband that all sexual relations between them should cease. She told him she would rather he was dead than that they should 'turn again to our uncleanness', and (in her own words in *The Book of Margery Kempe*) she 'asked her husband what was the cause that he had not meddled with her for eight weeks, since she lay with him every night in bed'. He said he was so frightened of her that he dared not touch her. She was clearly a strange and scary lady, even before she set off on her travels.

In 1413, convinced that she was following divine guidance, she set out – without her husband – for the Holy Land and Rome, having first settled all her debts at home in the manner recommended for pilgrims. From Yarmouth she sailed to Holland as the first stage of what was then to be an overland journey to Venice. And from the outset Margery Kempe upset her fellow pilgrims: 'they were much displeased because she wept so much and spoke always of the love and and goodness of Our Lord, as much at table as other places.' One can visualize the exasperation of her companions at their jovial mealtimes being interrupted by her excessively pious behaviour, which clearly struck them as exhibitionism of the worst sort. Her companions warned her explicitly that 'they would not put up with her as her husband did when she was at home'. As they travelled across Europe, even the more sympathetic of her companions had had enough and told her 'she could no longer go in their fellowship' and they 'forsook her that night'.

This was an impossible situation for a lady: travelling in a group was arduous and dangerous enough, but travelling alone and unprotected was just not possible. So Margery was persuaded to approach the group again and 'meeken herself', begging that they allowed her to stay with them at least as far as Lake Constance (after which the Alps had to be crossed and a new stage of the journey begun). The party reluctantly readmitted her, but with no very good grace and even less charity: 'they cut her gown so short that it came but little below her knee', so that she should look foolish and immodest, and they made her wear a canvas apron, presumably to make her look like a servant. They even insisted on her sitting at the end of the table 'below all the others' where she was excluded from the conversation and where, if she started her sobbing and praying, she would not disturb the secular cheerfulness of the other pilgrims.

But Margery was not easily phased by such childish and malicious behaviour. She notes in her book (in which she refers to herself – like royalty – in the third person) that – despite their snubs – she was treated with more deference than the others, and that the landlord, 'though she sat lowest at the table's end', always served her first. This probably did little to endear her to her companions. She also told them that she had had a message from the Almighty to the effect that while she was with them no harm would come to them. They felt now that she was being patronizing as well as embarrassing.

When they reached Lake Constance they met up with an English friar who was a Master of Divinity and the Pope's representative there. He promptly took Margery's side against her bullying fellow travellers. The latter had told the friar that he should tell her to eat meat and stop weeping and preaching to them all the time. But the friar supported her, and said that if one of them had made a vow to go to Rome barefoot (a far cry from what they intended no doubt) he would not have absolved them of their vow while they were able to do it, so he did not see why he should persuade Margery Kempe to eat meat while she was still able to keep her promise not to do so, and 'as for her weeping, it is not in my power to restrain it'.

This was too much for the other pilgrims. They told the friar that if this was the sort of person he wanted to be with, he could keep her: 'they would no more associate with her.' The friar then took Margery under his wing but this did not help her progress because of course she needed someone to chaperone her on the next stage of the journey. At this point an old bearded man from Devonshire miraculously appeared on the scene and offered to be her guide. She set off with him with some misgivings, since 'she knew not the language, or the man who would lead her'; but it all seemed to work out better than could have been expected because the next we hear of her she had reached Bologna safe and sound and in quicker time than the disagreeable pilgrims who had expelled her from their party. In fact, her original pilgrim group now offered to readmit her if she agreed 'not to speak of the Gospel where we are, but to sit still and merry, as we do, both at meat and at supper'. Rather surprisingly, Margery – who had probably received quite a fright at her former abandonment – agreed, and she travelled on to Venice with them and stayed there thirteen weeks awaiting a ship bound for the Holy Land.

Margery soon found she could not, or would not, keep to the new agreement. Before long she was at her old practices of spouting Gospel texts over dinner. They banished her to her room in Venice for the remaining six weeks of their stay, and her own maid, who had not stuck with her before, boycotted her again and did the laundry for everyone else except her eccentric employer. The other pilgrims chartered a ship and obtained wine and bedding for themselves for the voyage, but not for Margery. Undaunted she bought her own bedding and even found her own galley to take her to Palestine.

By now her fellow pilgrims seemed to begin to think that Margery led such a charmed life that perhaps – after all – it would be tempting fate to go in a separate ship from her. She had told them often enough that the divine protection that apparently followed her would be extended to them so long as they remained with her. So they rapidly unchartered their ship and joined her galley. But, glad as they were to cash in on her divine protection, they could not forgo their old vicious habits: they hid her clothes and stole her bedding. Margery sums it up philosophically enough: 'And so she had ever much tribulation till she came to Jerusalem.'

Predictably, the Holy Places set Margery off on her weeping fits and self-dramatization again. On Calvary she 'fell down . . . and rolled and wrestled with her body, spreading her arms abroad, and cried with a loud voice'. She records proudly that some people were astonished by the volume of her crying 'unless they had heard it before'; some assumed she was drunk and others 'wished she was in the harbour, or wished she was on the sea in a bottomless boat'. She must have been an embarrassing companion on the regular tour of the Holy Places which lasted some three weeks because 'wherever the friars led them . . . she always wept and sobbed wonderfully'. Afterwards Margery rode an ass into Bethlehem 'with much weeping and sobbing, so that her fellows would not let her eat in their company, and therefore she ate by herself alone'. Ironically, the Saracens seemed to be impressed with her 'boisterous sobbing' and made much of her; indeed she records that 'she found all people good to her and gentle, save only her own countrymen'. One feels that it was her own countrymen who had heard it all too often to be impressed.

While in Jerusalem she received divine guidance that she should proceed to Rome, rather than return directly to England. The first stage to Rome was of course to return to Venice by sea, and many of her companions were 'right sick' on the voyage. But they appear to have derived some comfort from Margery's assurances – however smug they may have thought them — that no one would die on the ship in which she was sailing. But, as before, they no sooner touched land and safety than they dumped her saying 'they would not go with her for a hundred pounds'. Possibly one reason was that Margery at this point had a new injunction from the Almighty, her intended compliance with which her companions doubtless found exhibitionist: she was to wear white from head to foot, making her more conspicuous than ever 'so that all the world should wonder at me'.

As at Lake Constance, so now again a guide materialized at the crucial moment. This time it was an Irishman 'with a great lump on his back' called Richard, who was hesitant about attempting to lead her across Italy to Rome because he had no weapon 'save a cloak full of clouts [patches]' and was convinced they would be robbed and Margery raped. But Margery reassured him and they set out, accompanied by two Grey Friars. It must have been a curious cavalcade: every day Richard went begging and Margery did her public weeping performance; the former secured money for their food, and the latter secured 'a good soft bed' from sympathetic 'good women' along the route. But some of the good women were not as innocent as they appeared. In one lodging she found that her gold ring, which she somewhat ambitiously described as 'a wedding gift to Jesus Christ' and which she had rather carelessly left hanging in her bedroom, had disappeared. The wife of the house joined in the search for the ring and with the aid of a candle purported to find it under the bed, but then as good as admitted she had stolen it herself in the first place.

The route to Rome lay through Assisi where Margery met another English friar (further evidence of how widely they were spread throughout Christendom) who told her that he had not met anyone except her who was 'so homely with God'. Margery responded with a spectacular cataract of tears. She was still worried about her safety on the last leg of the journey to Rome, and the admirable hunchbacked Richard interceded for her with a very superior lady pilgrim – Dame Margaret Florentyne who travelled with a retinue of Knights of Rhodes – requesting her to admit Margery to her entourage. In this rather grand company Margery reached Rome safely and once more astonished her former travelling companions by having done so. To celebrate the accomplishment Margery now decked herself out in the all-white outfit which she had earlier resolved to wear.

It was not long before she was making enemies again. This time it was a priest at the Hospital of St Thomas of Canterbury (the normal place for English pilgrims to stay in Rome), a fellow Englishman who 'slandered her name in the Hospital' and ensured that she was expelled. Again the loyal Richard came to her rescue and persuaded a local priest to take her in. Unfortunately the Italian priest in question could understand no English, so Margery had some difficulty in making her routine confessions until, she announced, Our Lord sent St John the Evangelist personally to hear her confession. Like other pilgrims she spent much time in the church of St John Lateran in Rome, and here she met a sympathetic Dutch priest with whom she managed to converse, despite a lack of any common language. These special revelations and communications, coupled with her customary crying so loudly that 'people were often times afraid and greatly astonished', ensured that the general community of English pilgrims in Rome continued to find this noisy, white-clad figure, with her special relationships with God and his saints, both bizarre and unacceptable. More and more people began to feel she was not only mad but bad.

Margery's response to these accusations was, as always, dramatic: she adopted an impoverished old lady and gave her her own mantle, fetched firewood and water for her, begged meat and wine for her, and generally 'served her as she would have done Our Lady'. As so often, she rather overdid it, not only giving the old lady all her own money but also all of the unfortunate Richard's money. The latter, not surprisingly, was 'greatly moved and evil pleased', but had to be content with an assurance that Margery would refund him in England.

But as usual when Margery was down on her luck someone turned up to help her. This time it was the same affluent Dame Margaret Florentyne who had protected her on the road from Assisi to Rome, who now gave her money and food and 'sat her at her own table above herself'. Slowly she became something of an institution in Rome and had quite a following among the local people there. Even the master of the Hospital of St Thomas of Canterbury, which had expelled her earlier, now asked her to return and said he was 'right sorry that they had put her away from them'. Margery now spent time studying the works of St Bridget of Sweden, clearly seeing this aristocrat and saint as a role model for herself. She was much gratified when, at a time of unusual lightning and storms, citizens came to her to ask for her intercession for their safety. Visiting priests from England sought her out and were left in wonder at her boisterous sobbing. When she visited the church in Rome where St Jerome was buried – the Basilica of St Maria Maggiore – the saint herself consoled Margery with 'a manner of dalliance'. As always, Margery's humility was of a distinctively high-profile variety.

By Easter 1415 Margery decided she should head for home, once again comforted by a divine assurance that everyone travelling with her would be as safe as if they had remained in St Peter's church. She made an uneventful journey to Middelburg in Holland where she planned to embark by sea for England. The only ship available was 'but a little smack' and she embarked on this 'amid great tempests and dark waters' but the tempests ceased in answer to her prayers and they arrived in Norfolk in time for evensong and in very 'merry' form.

But it was not long before such a controversial and unclubbable pilgrim was arousing criticism at home too. The first accusation to be made against her was that she had been away such a long time because she had been giving birth to an illegitimate child: what had she done with the baby, she was promptly asked.

Nothing daunted, Margery set off on yet another pilgrimage, this time to Santiago de Compostela. She sailed from Bristol – her fellow pilgrims threatening to throw her overboard . . . nothing had changed – and spent a fortnight in Santiago, returning again by sea to Bristol. She had now completed the trilogy of great pilgrimages; Jerusalem, Rome and Santiago. But her troubles were only beginning.

Margery's eccentric behaviour on pilgrimage had been widely reported, and she continued to draw attention to herself at home. This was a period when individual interpretation of the Gospels and direct communication – as opposed to through the church – with the Almighty was highly suspect: it reminded men of that peculiarly English heresy, Lollardry. The case of Mr Badby, a tailor who had blasphemed against the Holy Sacrament saying 'a spider or a toad were superior to the consecrated Host' and who had been burnt for heresy in 1410, was fresh in memory at Canterbury and elsewhere. Sir John Oldcastle, a prominent Lollard, was brought to trial and execution in the very year (1417) that Margery was undergoing interrogation. She was frequently heckled and called a Lollard and eventually arrested by the mayor of Leicester and accused not only of Lollardry but also of immorality: her white clothes – worn by somebody who was clearly not a virgin – were for some strange reason considered a temptation to the good wives of Leicester to indulge in loose living. Later she was also to appear on similar charges in front of the Bishop of Lincoln, the Archbishop of York and the Duke of Bedford – the henchmen of the duke claiming that she was in some way connected with Sir John Oldcastle. In all these ordeals, Margery, for all her customary extravagant behaviour, remained calm and collected, and defended herself with considerable skill. In particular, she declared in her evidence that she believed that the fact a priest might be corrupt did not invalidate the power of his ministry and the sacraments he administered. By making this point she came out in support of the church and in flat contradiction of the doctrine of the Lollards. It was her saving. She survived, and even went on further pilgrimages in the 1430s.

It is difficult to know what to make of Margery Kempe. She dictated her own account of her travels and travails; in fact, *The Book of Margery Kempe* is arguably the first autobiography in the English language. A mystic she certainly was; also a publicity-seeker whose visions and divine inspirations often coincided with her own convenience and plans, and who in consequence attracted charges of hypocrisy and charlatanism in her own lifetime. She stands out among medieval pilgrims as one whose obsessive behaviour exasperated and even enraged her travelling companions; for those who sought a foreign experience, a modest adventure and some quiet spiritual credit, she was an uncomfortable companion. But so perhaps would St Paul have been.

7

Santiago de Compostela: the Romantic Pilgrimage

IN THE MIDDLE AGES, only the pilgrimages to the Holy Land and to Rome took precedence before that to the shrine of the Apostle St James the Greater in Galicia in Spain. This fact owed much to the significance of St James himself. The son of Zebedee and the brother of St John the Evangelist, he was one of the earliest to be recruited by Jesus, from his fishing boat on the Sea of Galilee. James was also with Jesus at many of the most significant moments of his ministry: at his agony in the Garden of Gethsemane, and at his transfiguration on the Mount. He himself was a martyr, put to death by Herod Agrippa in AD 44. Together with St John and St Peter he was one of the pre-eminent Apostles.

His connection with Spain is more controversial. There is a strong tradition that after the Resurrection James preached first in Judaea and Samaria and then went on a mission to Spain, at that date a thriving part of the Roman empire. Accounts vary as to the duration and success of his mission in Spain. Some of the most staunchly held convictions include his presence in Galicia, and his summons by the Virgin Mary to build a temple in her honour around a jasper column which to this day forms the spiritual basis of the long-standing Basilica of Our Lady of the Pillar in Zaragoza.

It was therefore not altogether surprising that after his death in Palestine, there should have built up a strong body of belief that St James's body was returned to Spain. The nature of the saint's return was reported to be a miraculous journey in a ship without sail or rudder which crossed the Mediterranean and the Atlantic coast of Spain to Galicia. More miracles followed, the most famed of which was the conversion of the local Queen, Lupa, after the saint's body had been drawn into her palace on a cart pulled by wild bulls, which she had earlier described as oxen to the saint's followers, in the hope that the followers would be killed when trying to harness them.

Be that as it may, there was then a total silence on the subject of St James and Spain for nearly seven hundred years. During this period the Moorish invasion of Iberia from north Africa took place, and Islam surplanted Christianity as the dominant religion of the peninsula. The great mosque of Cordoba replaced the earlier Visigothic church.

It was to fall to St Beatus in the eighth century to resurrect the legend and effectively consolidate St James as the patron saint of Spain. Beatus was not only a holy and learned figure, but an influential one. His reputation extended to the court of Charlemagne. And, most importantly, he was one of those who led the resistance to the Moorish occupation of the Iberian peninsula at a time when others were inclined to reach an accommodation with the Moors. Don Claudio Sanchez-Albornoz, the eminent Spanish historian, has argued that Beatus not only provided his country with a patron saint, but he also created an expectancy that St James's grave would be found in Spain. And less than twenty years after Beautus's death, the grave was indeed found in dramatic circumstances. During the reign of Alfonso II at the beginning of the ninth century, a hermit called Pelayo saw a bright star burning over fields and a wooded hill in Galicia. He also heard choirs of angels singing. Investigation revealed a small shrine in the undergrowth and within the shrine a sarcophagus. With little hesitation, the local bishop pronounced the body in the sarcophagus to be that of the long-awaited St James. The place where the star had been seen over the fields was henceforth to be known as the starry field – or Compostela. The king accepted the finding and promptly informed both the Holy Roman Emperor Charlemagne and Pope Leo III in Rome of this exciting discovery. (The fact there was already reputed to be a body of St James preserved in Toulouse does not seem to have given anyone undue concern.)

This was just the boost to Christian morale in Spain which had for so long been required. Once again battle was joined with the Moors and in 845, at Clavijo, St James appeared to the Spanish king on the eve of the engagement and promised him victory; the saint was as good as his word and was reported to have descended from the sky on a white charger during the battle and personally to have slain large numbers of the infidels. St James was periodically to make similarly spectacular interventions on the battlefield in the following centuries, notably at Simancas in the tenth century, at Coimbra in the eleventh century, and at the decisive battle of Las Navas de Tolosa in the thirteenth century. During this time there had of course been set-backs to the Spaniards. In 997 for instance, Compostela had had to be evacuated and the Moorish commander had removed the bells from the church, forcing his Christian captives to carry them on their shoulders all the way to Cordoba, where the bells were hung upside down in the great mosque and used as lamps; when the Spanish eventually recaptured Cordoba they sent the bells back to Compostela on the shoulders of Moorish captives. But whether appearing as a vision on the battlefield or providing less immediate intervention, St James was a most effective patron saint and it was little wonder that he became known as Santiago Matamoros – St James the Moor-slayer. (He was reputed to have one other less than charitable characteristic: tired pilgrims who showed disrespect by falling asleep at his shrine were as likely to wake up blind as cured.)

77

From the earliest days of the Reconquest of Spain from the Moors there had been a trickle of pilgrims to the saint's tomb at Compostela. But to start with it was only a trickle. A small church had been built on the site soon after its discovery, and a larger church – the one with the much-travelled bells – had replaced it less than a century later. The bishops and archbishops who presided over the 'apostolic see' at Compostela became ever grander, as did their cathedrals. It was Archbishop Diego Gelmirez, in the early twelfth century, who constructed the present cathedral; he had seven of his canons made into cardinals, and between them they owned vast estates and had a standing army to help the King of Spain in furthering his campaigns against the Moors. But all this expenditure was not supported by the donations of pilgrims; it was financed by a special decree that obliged farmers throughout 'free' Spain to make an annual donation of corn and wine to the canons of the cathedral at Compostela. In time, this arbitrary tax (which lasted until 1812) was to become resented, but throughout the Reconquest it seemed a reasonable enough tribute to Santiago Matamoros.

From the beginning, some of the pilgrims came from far afield. The bishop of Puy in France came with a large retinue in 950; some English coins from the reign of Ethelred II (979–1016) have been found on the pilgrim route; Duke William X of Aquitaine went there in 1137 to atone for his war crimes in an earlier campaign in Normandy; foreign reinforcements – often from Germany or England – coming to help with the later stages of the Reconquest tended to break their sea-journey at Compostela to seek the saint's blessing. Later, even more distinguished visitors arrived: St Francis of Assisi in 1212; St Bridget of Sweden came to celebrate her silver wedding in 1341; and John of Gaunt, Duke of Lancaster, came in 1386 en route for a campaign to assist the new King of Portugal. Perhaps the most dramatic visit in the fourteenth century was that of Sir James Douglas who brought the heart of the Scottish King Robert the Bruce on his way to make the longer pilgrimage to the

Holy Land; however, Douglas and his precious cargo did not get any further because – like the good Christian knight he was – he passed the time while in Spain by fighting the Moors and was killed in the process (Bruce's heart eventually being returned to Melrose Abbey in his home country). Many other prominent rulers and churchmen were credited with having made early pilgrimages to Compostela; but in some cases it seems that there was little evidence beyond the conviction of their hagiographers this was a necessary entry on their subject's curriculum vitae.

The relationship of the pilgrimage to Compostela and of the Reconquest to the concurrent crusades to the Holy Land is a complex one. Spanish knights were excused from participating in the crusades because they had their own holy war closer at hand. Foreign knights were encouraged to think of service in Spain as an alternative to, or postscript to, some of the later crusades: Chaucer's Knight in *Canterbury Tales* had been present at the siege of Algeciras. There was even a special order of chivalry – the Knights of St James – set up to act as knights-errant to protect weary and defenceless pilgrims to Compostela, in the same way as the Knights Templar and the Knights Hospitaller did in respect of travellers to the Holy Land: they were to be 'lions in battle and lambs in the convent'. The Knights of St James also fulfilled a practical diplomatic function: they acted as negotiators with the Moors for the return or ransom of prisoners. All in all, the pilgrimage basked in the reflected glory of the Reconquest: for much of the Middle Ages, when normal pilgrimage to the Holy Land was virtually impossible, to have been on foot to Compostela was the next best thing to having fought in a crusade.

The motives for a pilgrimage to Compostela were by no means always as noble as those of the early saints and crusaders. For many the journey was not only a penance, it was quite specifically a punishment. Occasionally the pilgrimage would be imposed as a collective penalty: Charles IV ('le Bel') of France made it a condition of his peace treaty at Arques in 1326 that a hundred citizens of Courtrai should take the road to Compostela.

Though not strictly a penalty, the pilgrimage would also be often imposed as the condition of an inheritance or other provision of a will. In such cases the pilgrim would be required to offer prayers for the soul of his benefactor at the shrine of St James and other chapels along the way. Frequently too the pilgrimage would be undertaken following a vow made by an invalid or one of his relatives as a thanksgiving for recovery.

With so many reluctant pilgrims on the route or facing the prospect of it, there was a constant temptation for richer potential pilgrims to hire or bribe others to make the journey on their behalf, in the spirit in which (in certain countries at certain times) it has been possible to pay poorer citizens to do military service in the place of their richer contemporaries. This practice, not surprisingly, was frowned upon by the church authorities, and it was always a moot point whether such substitutes really counted in terms of legal obligations or spiritual credit. Indeed, some priests and bishops maintained that shirking a pilgrimage in this manner was in itself a sin carrying dire penalties.

The pilgrims on the road to Compostela constituted a microcosm of medieval life. There were plenty of princes, bishops and knights to be encountered. There were also genuine pilgrims from all classes of society and from a wide variety of nations: merchants and labourers, scholars and priests. There were additionally those who lived off the other pilgrims: minstrels, jugglers, beggars (who feigned wounds and disabilities) and vagabonds. Not infrequently there were more serious criminals, including murderers on the run from the authorities in their own countries.

Quite apart from the more disreputable pilgrims, there were others who lived along the route and made a living more by exploiting the passers-by than by providing for their needs. Bandits preyed on them in wooded country; crooked ferrymen demanded extortionate charges; dishonest innkeepers fleeced them and sometimes even murdered them in their beds for the sake of their possessions. Bogus guides would lead unsuspecting pilgrims into unnecessarily expensive lodgings or even into ambushes. Among these villains were an appreciable number of Englishmen who often disguised themselves as pilgrims. One such, known as John of London, is reputed to have robbed pilgrims as they slept in a hostelry near Estrella fairly regularly in 1318; and in 1319 a whole band of bandits – all of them Englishmen – were captured by the authorities near Pamplona.

All this vulnerability prompted protective measures from other quarters apart from the Knights of St James. The Emperor Charlemagne made provision for cheap lodgings and food along the parts of the route for which he was responsible. The Lateran Council of 1123 made the crime of robbing pilgrims punishable by excommunication. Some of the Spanish kingdoms granted immunity from road tolls to pilgrims, and in Castille pilgrim roads were patrolled by archers of Santa Hermandad. Religious orders such as the monks of Cluny (who codified the miracles that took place at Compostela) and Augustinian canons set up hostelries along the route. Benevolent landowners sometimes repaired the pilgrim paths or even built bridges over dangerous rivers. In the fastnesses of the Pyrenees, some monasteries tolled their bells throughout the night to guide lost or mist-bound pilgrims to their sheltering gates. The bigger hospices along the way – usually financed by the church or by princely landowners – often provided such additional amenities as hospital beds, barbers, emergency tailoring for those whose clothes had fallen to pieces, and overnight cobblers to fix up the shoes or boots of those whose footwear had been broken up by the stony paths. Even makeshift Christian burial could be arranged for those whose condition was terminal.

The vast majority of those who walked to Compostela during the Middle Ages came by one of the four main routes across France.

There was a complex network of well-established and interlocking paths. Often pilgrims collected in Paris, where the Guild of St James had premises in the Rue St Denis. Vézelay, with its great Benedictine abbey, was another favourite collection point. The routes converged on passes over the Pyrenees, or took the easier road hugging the coast round the Gulf of Capbreton. There were chapels dedicated to subsidiary saints – such as St Gilles near Arles or St Leonard near Limoges – at some points even before the route entered Spain, and these maintained the morale of pilgrims on the earlier stages of the journey. Once in Spain, the route was well punctuated by chapels and shrines as it wended its way through Burgos and across the hot plains of Old Castille and León.

Others came by sea. Pilgrim ships came from as far away as Scandinavia and north Germany to disembark their passengers at Bordeaux or Corunna. The maritime traffic from Britain was particularly heavy at some periods: in the first half of the fifteenth century it has been calculated that well over a hundred English ships made the direct voyage entirely for the benefit of pilgrims.

With such an uncontrolled flow of pilgrims, the wanton and rowdy behaviour of a few gave a bad reputation to the many. Monarchs and governments started imposing regulations. By the time that Philip II was on the throne of Spain at the end of the sixteenth century, he forbade his own subjects to adopt pilgrim attire – the staff, scrip, broad-brimmed hat and cockle-shell badge – and insisted that foreigners had a licence from their own government or their local bishop to qualify them as genuine pilgrims. Louis XIV of France was to become even more demanding about those going through his territory in the seventeenth century: unlicensed so-called pilgrims risked being picked up and shipped off for service in the galleys. As in later centuries, currency restrictions were also imposed: English pilgrims were not allowed to take out of the realm more silver and gold coin than it was deemed they strictly needed for the trip. They further had to swear not to give away state secrets while they were abroad, although it is hard to imagine that any except the most distinguished pilgrims had any state secrets to give away – except perhaps some vague observations of coastal defences.

Throughout the Middle Ages an important aspect of the pilgrimage to Compostela – as of many pilgrimages – was souvenir-hunting. The ultimate trophy for the wealthy and devout was some saintly relic. Matilda, the daughter of King Henry I of England, brought back a part (undefined) of the hand of St James, although how she acquired it remains a mystery; her father was so elated by this important acquisition for his realm that he established an abbey at Reading to celebrate the event. (Matilda's grandfather, William the Conqueror, had had to be satisfied with a Spanish horse which had been brought back from Compostela by one of his knights, and which had proved its special value by carrying him to victory on the field of Hastings.) For those who could not afford relics or handsome horses, there were lesser souvenirs. The connection of the scallop shell with the Compostela pilgrimage goes back to a legend involving a runaway horse and a rider who emerged from the sea covered in shells to be baptized. Certainly from the early days of the pilgrimage travellers returned with scallop-shells as evidence (surely rather flimsy?) of their having completed the journey, and as mementos. Shells or replicas of shells were worn on cloaks and hats to indicate the status of a pilgrim. El Cid wore one on his charger's bridle to indicate the holy nature of his campaign against the Moors. Also at the cheaper end of the souvenir hunt were the carved models of St James which were (and are) sold in the square at the north end of the great cathedral at Compostela.

Another permanent reminder and benefit for the returning medieval pilgrim was the membership of guilds or fraternities of St James. These sprang up in London and all over the continent, as clubs for those who had made the pilgrimage; they conferred status and prestige on the members, and they helped to advise and even finance future pilgrims. They had their own songs, traditions and superstitions: those who ate oysters (a relation of the scallop-shell) on St James's feast day – 25 July, when there is no R in the month – would never feel poverty.

But the benefits of the pilgrimage to Compostela went far beyond those to the individual pilgrim. Chaucer's Knight was not alone in having had an introduction to the Iberian struggle against Islam. English pilgrims usually returned with some knowledge of France as well as Spain, and French pilgrims with a knowledge of Spanish secular as well as religious ways and customs. For most medieval pilgrims to Compostela, the trip would have been their first exposure to foreigners of any sort. Not only was there shared devotion and fatigue, but shared conviviality and commerce. Pilgrims were not self-sufficient (like twentieth-century caravan-travelling German tourists) but depended on hospitality and purchases to survive the long ordeal. Some returned with a heightened awareness of art and architecture. To all, it had broadened horizons in an era when horizons were normally very restricted.

As with so many Christian pilgrimages, the high period of the trek to Compostela was the Middle Ages. The Renaissance brought both scepticism towards the concept, and military conflicts which disrupted the practicalities. Prominent among the sceptics was Erasmus who inclined to mock the pilgrimage in his *Colloquia* at the beginning of the sixteenth century; he points out that pilgrims were frequently neglecting their real responsibilities at home, and comes near to accusing them of indulgence in what (had the term existed) he would have called tourism. Luther was, as so often, much blunter: 'justification was by faith and not by pilgrimage', he wrote; he rejected St James at Compostela 'as an idol': he was in favour of banning pilgrimages and destroying the shrines along their routes. In England, Henry VIII turned against pilgrimages, including to Compostela, in 1538 and required their supporters publicly to retract. Protestant thinkers and travellers like Sir Walter Raleigh were inclined to look on pilgrimages as 'an interior journey'.

The Counter-Reformation put more pilgrims on the road, but the wars of religion that raged through much of central Europe and the Low Countries made the longer journeys even more hazardous than before. With the Age of Enlightenment in the eighteenth century, more sceptics emerged: Rousseau, Voltaire and the Encylopaedists in France poured scorn on the legends, relics and other motivations for the pilgrimage. Alexander Pope was writing dismissively in England of

> . . . happy convents, bossomed deep in vines,
> Where slumber abbots, purple as their wines.

The Grand Tour was taking over as the acceptable motive for travelling across Europe for the upper classes: the ruins of antiquity, the salons of the elegant and rich, and the studios of the fashionable artists . . . these were to replace shrines and monasteries as the draw for the new generation of travellers. Despite his love of most things Spanish, Richard Ford in his *Handbook for Travellers in Spain* of 1845 described some of the much-admired shrines along the route as 'fricassees of gingerbread'. Even the status of St James received a set-back in his adopted country when, in 1814, St Teresa (whose Spanish credentials were somewhat more historically based than his own) was formally declared to be the patron saint of Spain in the light of her exemplary convent life in sixteenth-century Avila.

But through all these vicissitudes, a trickle of pilgrims continued to take up their staff and scrip and head for Santiago de Compostela, returning with their prized scallop-shells. The shrine had received a latter-day boost when in 1879 St James's bones were refound behind the altar at Compostela, and five years later Pope Leo XIII confirmed by papal bull that they were genuine. For Roman Catholics at least, the question of authenticity was definitively resolved. The twentieth century, like the sixteenth, saw wars and rumours of wars shaking the tranquility of Europe; the Spanish Civil War disrupting religious life in Spain to an unprecedented degree. But as prosperity returned after the two world wars, so did the incidence of travel. Books about the road to Compostela proliferated. Photographs of the beauties of the cathedral and its mighty *botafumeiro* (the gigantic silver incense censer), which was alleged to have been introduced to drown the odour of the sweaty pilgrims, illustrate the guidebooks and further entice the visitors. The pursuit of scholarship, love of beauty, desire for exercise, and the hope of salvation, together make an enduring appeal. And when all is said and done, as in the time of King Ethelred, what better reason for a continental journey than a pilgrimage to the holiest shrine in northern Europe?

Pilgrims at Canterbury and elsewhere not infrequently crawled into the tombs of saints, sometimes getting stuck in the process

8

John of Gaunt: the Overmighty Pilgrim; and Andrew Boorde: the Merry Pilgrim

AS HAS BEEN seen, pilgrims of all nationalities, social classes and temperaments set out for Santiago de Compostela during the Middle Ages. But one man and his entourage epitomized the grand and powerful pilgrim: this was John of Gaunt, son of King Edward III of England and father of King Henry IV of England, Duke of Lancaster, Earl of Derby, Lincoln and Leicester, Seneschal of England and Constable of Chester. Few people in the realm had so many titles, so much land, such a splendid court, so many retainers and such a dominant influence on national life. It was not for nothing that Shakespeare to put into the mouth of 'Old John of Gaunt, time-honoured Lancaster' some of the most evocative lines in the English language about 'this scepter'd isle'; John of Gaunt was the standard-bearer for the principles and practices not only of the House of Plantagenet but of the ruling class throughout Europe. He was the grand seigneur par excellence: the Lord Mountbatten of his time. Not for such a man as this a humble foot-pilgrimage to Compostela, nor even a journey on horseback with a suitable band of followers. When John of Gaunt set out for Compostela it was to take over the church, the monastery, the shrine and everything to do with place;

he came not as a supplicant but as a conqueror; not as a penitent but as a reformer and an enforcer.

In fact, John of Gaunt's expedition to Iberia in 1386, although presented as a pilgrimage, was not in reality any such thing; it was a military campaign to consolidate his claim to be King of Castile and León, a title which he claimed through his wife who was the daughter and heir of the murdered King of Castile. Although not lacking in regal and aristocratic connections and titles, John of Gaunt was anxious to acquire a kingdom of his own. And this ambition in turn was part of a wider design which he shared with his nephew King Richard II. The Hundred Years War between England and France had already been raging for some fifty years and still had another fifty years to go. England was anxious to build up an alliance against France to further the English claims on the French throne. If Castile could be prised away from France and to the English side, a major asset would have been gained. John of Gaunt's marriage to the Princess Constanza of Castile was an important step in that direction. An alliance with Portugal – which was to become the longest-lasting alliance between any European powers – was another such important step. When John of Gaunt set out on his Iberian adventure, it pleased him to make Compostela one of his first destinations; but he had an agenda of his own that went far beyond the remit of any pilgrim. To the archbishop and monks of the sacred shrine of St James, the impending visitor must have been a terrifying prospect.

Gaunt's arrival had been long expected and long delayed. He would liked to have come to Spain to make his pilgrimage and claim his kingdom much earlier. But events had intervened. He had been deeply involved with the Peasants' Revolt in England in 1381. Because he had been such an overmighty subject, many of the failings of Richard II's government had been laid at his door, particularly the hated Poll Tax. In fact when the rebels had marched on London, it was Gaunt's palace of the Savoy that had been the first target of their destructive venom. The incident had added its own legacy of bitterness, because thirty-two of the rebels had been trapped in the wine cellar by falling masonry and had been left to die of starvation there. Fortunately for him, Gaunt was away at the time in Scotland. His support for the king was immediate and all the more effective for the fact that he declined to lead a Scottish army south into England. Meanwhile relations had been further complicated between Castile and Portugal: first there had been a truce, then the decisive battle of Aljubarrota in 1383 had established João, the Master of the Order of Aviz, as an independent sovereign in Portugal. But João's appeals for help from England were now – in 1386 – at last being answered.

Even after setting sail for Corunna, in north-western Spain, Gaunt allowed himself to be deflected; an English garrison at Brest was being besieged and needed rescuing by the gallant expeditionary force. Eventually he landed at Corunna on 25 July 1386 – appropriately St James's Day. To indicate his intention of staying until his business was completed, Gaunt sent his transport ships and their crews back to England: it was the equivalent of burning his boats. His first and immediate destination was Santiago de Compostela. His arrival there was more like that of a conqueror than of a pilgrim. Froissart records the scene in some detail:

> About two kilometres from the town, the clergy carrying their special relics, the Cross, with men, women and children, the municipal councillors with the keys of the gates of the city, the nobles and gentlemen, one and all with the semblance of good will, came towards the Duke and Duchess, knelt down to welcome the seigneur and his wife.

The procession then entered by the city gate and proceeded straight to the cathedral to pay their respects to the tomb of St James. For all that he had other reasons for coming to Spain, Gaunt was part of a strong family tradition of going on pilgrimage: most of the Plantagenets had visited several of the great shrines of Europe and Gaunt's son – the future King Henry IV – was to be an inveterate pilgrim.

His arrival at Compostela must, none-the-less, have caused considerable disarray to the religious community. His attendant army was much too numerous to find billets within the city itself, and camped outside the walls in bivouacs constructed from branches off the trees in the surrounding woodland. Froissart records something of the flavour of the occasion:

> They were all at ease and had food and strong wine in plenty; the archers regularly drank so much that they went to bed each night quite drunk. It was the season of the grape harvest and the wine flowed freely. On the following days, the archers had drunk so much that they were incapable of action.

In fact, it was the normal behaviour of a medieval army on campaign.

Although the rough soldiery were accommodated outside the city, Gaunt and his wife, together with his two daughters and the senior members of their household, were lodged at the abbey itself. Very quickly Gaunt showed who was in control. It was not the abbot or even the archbishop, but the visiting pilgrim, the all-conquering claimant to the throne of Castile. Gaunt was a supporter of Pope Urban VI who resided in Rome and claimed to be the only true recipient of the mantle of St Peter. In fact, Gaunt had been specifically granted the title by Pope Urban of 'Standard Bearer of the Cross for the Pope and the Roman Church'. Such a title in itself made him a very special sort of pilgrim, . . . more, it could be argued, a personal representative of the Pope than a humble penitent. This was certainly how Gaunt himself saw the situation.

The Archbishop of Sandiago de Compostela on the other hand was a supporter of the rival pope – Clement VII who resided in Avignon. This was an affront to Gaunt. But worse was the fact that the archbishop was chancellor to Don Juan, the de facto King of Castile and, as such, the rival of Gaunt. The archbishop's position until this moment had been supreme in Galicia and all this part of Spain; he was in every sense a prince of the church; his post normally carried a cardinal's hat as part of the dignity of the job; sometimes even his canons were cardinals too; his writ ran through the secular as well as the spiritual life of all this corner of the Iberian peninsula. Faced with this formidably installed prelate, Gaunt did not hesitate; he immediately relieved him of his office, and appointed his own man (naturally a supporter of Pope Urban) in his place.

Having sorted out the abbey at Compostela to his satisfaction, Gaunt pressed on with his wider objectives. He embarked on a full-scale military campaign in support of King João of Portugal against King Juan of Castile. As an earnest of his good intentions, Gaunt proposed a marriage between his daughter Philippa and King João. This idea was readily accepted and the wedding took place at Oporto Cathedral on 2 February 1387. The Archbishop of Braga scarcely had time to preside over the torch-lit wedding ceremony that followed before marching orders for the forthcoming campaign arrived at the scene. The following month the young King of Portugal and his elderly father-in-law launched a joint invasion of Castile. Gaunt was used to being the dominant partner in any undertaking, and he resented the inevitable fact that João's forces were superior in number to his own. The campaign was fraught with misunderstandings from the outset. 'There was a certain knight-errantry in his [John of Gaunt's] adventures that touches them with romances,' wrote his biographer Sidney Armitage-Smith. This was never more in evidence than during the Castilian campaign.

Although committed to England's cause in the Hundred Years War, Gaunt was on friendly terms with many of the French knights and aristocracy; they were imbued with the same spirit of knight-errantry and were from the same social strata as himself which the newly arrived King João and his distinctively provincial Portuguese followers were not. As one town after another was besieged by the invaders, Gaunt would send heralds forward to enquire whether any knights of renown were to be found among the enemy ranks. If the answer were positive, hostilities would be suspended until a jousting competition or some other chivalric festivity could be organized. King João was at the same time bemused, impressed and exasperated by this display of amateur-gentlemanly behaviour. Matters reached a climax at Salamanca, where Gaunt was so delighted to find some former sparring partners among the enemy garrison that he joined them for a feast of French wines and venison (supplied by his opponents) while his Portuguese allies went hungry. As the campaign slowly lost its initial impetus, Gaunt gave further evidence of his priorities to the Portuguese king: he began arranging for his other daughter to marry the heir to King Juan, his opponent and rival as the reigning King of Castile. Gaunt no longer had to win a military campaign to ensure that his family — even if not himself — would secure the Castilian throne. By the time he had finally embarked for England, few would have foretold that the newly formed Anglo-Portuguese alliance would endure for more than six centuries.

John of Gaunt had made his pilgrimage and fought his war. Both events had been bizarre. The war had been more like a protracted tournament than a serious military campaign. The pilgrimage had been more of a tour of inspection and a display of authority than an act of devotion. But both events had been what John of Gaunt had above all intended and what — in one way or another — so many of his contemporaries expected from a pilgrim journey: it had been incontrovertibly an adventure.

At the other end of the social spectrum from John of Gaunt was a much more light-hearted and down-to-earth pilgrim called Dr Andrew Boorde – or 'Merry Andrew' as he was known to his travelling companions.

Boorde was born around 1490 (150 years after John of Gaunt) and started life as a Carthusian monk; he spent twenty years in that austere order, subjecting himself to all the rigours of its discipline and the mortifications of the flesh. He had then, at his own request, been released from the order to study medicine at Montpellier, and immediately threw off his former ways and became a hard-drinking, convivial and somewhat wayward medical student. He went on to practise in Glasgow and wrote various books, not only on diet and health, but also on such random subjects as beards ('some weer berdes bycause theyr faces be pocky or maungy') and a compendium of jests and jokes. His best-remembered book however is a prolonged travelogue in which he gives vignettes of the character – and drinking habits – of other European nationalities. This work was published under the misleading title *The First Book of the Introduction of Knowledge* and has some claim to be the first continental guidebook (as opposed to travel book) in the English language. It is partly in verse and partly in prose.

As well as having much to say about pilgrimages, Boorde's book is also a drinking man's guide to the continent. On national drinks, for instance, he says 'ale is the natural drink for an Englishman, even as beer is the natural drink for a Dutchman'. He also strongly recommends all pilgrims to have a good draught of wine at the end of the day's walk, since 'wine doth quicken a man's wit, comfort his heart and scour his liver'. He devotes a whole chapter of his book to

93

the relative merits of drinking white or red wines, ale, beer, cider, mead and a variety of fairly disgusting-sounding drinks such as whey ('which doth come of butter), metheglyn ('honey and water and herbes, boyled and soden together') and posset ('hot mylke and colde ale'). Although he goes through the motions of cautioning against excess, one feels that Merry Andrew was not one to turn down a chance of doing justice to the local brew wherever he found himself.

And he found himself almost everywhere, as he was a vociferous traveller. He gives advice to those going on pilgrimage to the Holy Land ('You must bye a bygge cheste with a locke & kaye to kepe-in wyne . . . and other necessary things') but he devotes a longer section of his book to describing how he took under his wing a group of nine English and Scottish pilgrims, whom he met up with at the university of Orleans, who wished to go to Santiago de Compostela. He warned them in advance of the rigours of the journey, saying he would rather go five times to Rome than once overland from Orleans to Santiago. He went so far as to say that had he been on the King of England's Council, he would have put anyone in the stocks who set off for Santiago without a proper licence, as they would be all too likely to die by the way. When his companions refused to be put off by his warnings, Boorde 'having pity they should be caste away' wound up his business at the university and escorted them across France to 'the barren country of Castile' after which they arrived very hungry at Santiago de Compostela. Things got worse on the return journey through Spain. Despite his cautions against drinking the local water, all nine of the English and Scottish pilgrims persisted in this and 'for all the crafte and physycke that I could do, they dyed, all of eatynge of frutes and drynkynge of water, from the which I did ever refrayne my self'.

The Compostela pilgrimage had been a disappointment to Boorde in other ways also. He was disillusioned about the *raison d'être* of the pilgrimage – the body of St James – and said: 'I assure you there is not one hair or bone of St James in Compostela . . . but only the sickle and hooke whych [they said] dyd saw and cutte off the head of St James.' Boorde made his confession in church to a doctor of divinity who admitted that there were no true relics of St James in Compostela because Charlemagne had taken them all to Toulouse. It seems likely that Boorde's scepticism owed something to the period of his visit. We do not know the exact date, but it was certainly after the Reformation was getting under way – in the 1530s – and in England Henry VIII (to whom, incidentally, Boorde was later to give medical advice) had already begun the process of debunking shrines and relics. Boorde's cynicism was politically correct for his decade.

Despite his reservations about the relics of St James, Boorde seems to accept unquestioningly a much more improbable tale which has long attached to the church of Santo Domingo de la Calzada on the pilgrimage route. Here a white cock and hen were kept in a cage and their feathers given to pilgrims to commemorate an ancient story of an earlier pilgrim's plight. This was the tale – as retold by Merry Andrew – of a father and son who were on the pilgrimage to Compostela when the son was approached by 'a whenche whych wolde have him to medyll with her carnally'; the young lad declined her advances and 'the whenche repleyted with malice for the said cause' planted a silver cup in the bottom of the young man's scrip and then claimed it was stolen and sent the town officers to pursue the pilgrims. (The tale was a variant of the classic biblical story of Joseph planting the silver in Benjamin's sack of grain in Egypt.) The lad was apprehended, judged and hanged, with a stipulation that his corpse was not to be cut down but left suspended from the gibbet as a warning to other thieves. The bereaved father went on his way to Compostela and on return several weeks later went to mourn at his son's gibbet – only to find that the boy was still surviving, having been preserved alive on the gallows by the active intervention of St James. The boy asked his father to go to the judge and ask that he should 'come hyther and let me down' which the father promptly did. When he arrived at the judge's house he found him having supper, 'having in his dyshe two greate chykens, the one a hen chyck and the other a cock chyck'. The judge responded to the father's request by saying that it was about as likely that the boy was alive as that his two cooked chickens should stand up and start crowing. At which point that was exactly what the chickens did. So the judge set off in full procession to the gallows and 'did fetche in alive that sayd young man'. And ever after they have kept a white cock and hen in a cage in the church to commemorate the remarkable miracle. Merry Andrew, who had a keen ear for a good story, clearly enjoyed this one.

In general, Boorde found Spain very poor, particularly inland. There were no convenient markets and he complains that when you go to supper you must fetch your bread in one place, your wine in another, and your meat in yet another. Pigs were roaming every-where and 'in many places shal be under your feete at the table, and lice in your bed'. The best fare was to be had in the priests' homes 'for they do keepe typlynge [tippling] houses'. Moving from Castile to Navarre, things became even worse: 'the people be rude and poore, and many theves . . . the country is barren for it is full of mountain.' Altogether, Boorde was highly relieved when he got back to France and 'did kiss the ground for joy'.

In fact, although Boorde travelled very widely and noted in his book useful details of the countries he visited (and some he didn't) – their currency, their words for basic numbers and other vital information – he is a good example of that growing impatience with foreigners and foreign practices which became a by-product of the development of nation states as the Middle Ages drew to a close. By this period, no longer was pilgrimage an exercise in consolidating the bonds of Christendom: it had become an experience that showed up the cracks in the fabric of that edifice, and accentuated differences with other races and faiths. Merry as Andrew Boorde may be, he finds as he wanders on his pilgrimages that whatever is strange is usually unappealing: the Hungarians are stay-at-homes; the Poles are crafty merchants; the Bohemians are opinionated and 'standing much in their own conceits'; the Barbary Moors have thick lips and 'there is nothing white but their teeth and the whites of their eyes'; the Egyptians are light-fingered and have bad manners; the Turks have been seduced by Mahomet, 'a false fellow'; the Jews fail to keep even the laws of Moses, and so on.

In short, writing at the conclusion of the great age of pilgrimage, Andrew Boorde suggests that the risks and discomforts of the pilgrim life outweigh the pleasures and rewards.

Putting his monk's hair-shirt behind him, and resigning himself to the fact that most foreigners are a bad lot, Merry Andrew finds consolation in the conclusion that at least continental wines are better than English ones.

An early fourteenth-century depiction of
King Henry II quarrelling with Thomas Becket

9

Canterbury: the Political Pilgrimage

JUST AS CHRISTIAN shrines were built at Glastonbury and elsewhere on earlier pagan holy sites, so at Canterbury the sixth-century basilica of St Augustine was built on the site of an earlier Roman temple. Some of the early Christian bishops – notably Dunstan and Anselm – had been canonized and, in consequence, a modest flow of pilgrimages to Canterbury was already taking place before the twelfth century.

After the murder of Archbishop Thomas Becket on 29 December 1170 this modest flow became a torrent. Almost overnight, Canterbury was to become one of the great focal points for European pilgrimage, rivalling Santiago de Compostela and even Rome itself. There were several reasons for this. The obvious sanctity of the victim was one. The dramatic nature of his death was another. A sudden eruption of miracles was a third.

On the night of the murder itself, the first miracle – the restoration of sight to a blind man – was reported at Canterbury. Others followed thick and fast: two days later a prayer invoking the martyred Becket resulted in a miracle in Sussex; two days after that a girl in Gloucestershire recorded a healing in similar circumstances, and another reputed miracle occurred in Berkshire the next day. A monk was quickly appointed to collect and sift the evidence of these incidents, and cross-examined the beneficiaries and witnesses. He did not accept as genuine all the scores of almost immediate 'miracles' but the body of evidence convinced him and his superiors (despite some reluctance from the clergy who had been critical or jealous of the archbishop) that Becket was a potential saint as well as a martyr.

Biographies (or hagiographies) began to appear in the years immediately following his death. And the pilgrim traffic that resulted from this eruption of miracles and adoration had a new ingredient which distinguished it from other English or continental pilgrimages: this was a political factor. Becket was perceived not only as a saint, but as a champion of the church against the state, of the underprivileged against the establishment. To understand how this came about it is necessary to recapitulate, at least in outline, the remarkable story of Becket's life and career.

Like many great men, Becket was to accumulate myths around the story of his life. One of the most dramatic concerned his parentage. A story started circulating soon after his death that his Norman father, Gilbert Becket, had been captured on a crusade to the Holy Land and that the daughter of an Arab sheikh had fallen in love with him and, following his escape, had pursued him to London and married him, later giving birth to the infant Thomas. Be that as it may (and the historical evidence belies the legend), Becket grew up with characteristics which were unusual in a member of the Norman ruling caste: he was aloof, single-minded and intellectual – a romantic and faintly mysterious figure in the coarse and brutal world of feudal England.

Young Thomas was educated by the church and his father secured him a position in the ecclesiastical household of Theobald, Archbishop of Canterbury. He distinguished himself from the start, and was employed on delicate diplomatic missions, one of which helped to determine the succession of Henry II to the English throne. By the time Becket had reached the age of thirty-six, Henry was so impressed with the qualities of the young cleric (not yet a priest) who had become his friend that he appointed him chancellor – effectively his chief minister. The partnership between the young King Henry and the still youthful (but fifteen years older) chancellor flourished. They hunted deer together, and they discussed affairs of state together. The king confided absolutely in his protégé.

Becket even proved a faithful servant of the king in affairs where church and state appeared to clash; in 1157 when the Bishop of Chichester, with the support of the Pope, attempted to establish his authority over the Abbot of Battle Abbey by claiming a limitation of the royal powers in favour of papal authority, Becket came down on the side of the crown, and the bishop was frightened out of further resistance. This was a man Henry felt he could trust absolutely to help him to restore the law and order of the Norman kings. When Theobald, the Archbishop of Canterbury, was dying in 1162 it seemed natural to him and to the king that Becket should succeed him; indeed, Henry's first thought was that Becket could take on the church post while retaining the chancellorship. Becket on the other hand saw the acceptance of Canterbury as necessitating a complete change of loyalties: so far he had been the king's man, now (hurriedly being ordained a priest and consecrated a bishop on successive days) he was to be the church's servant.

The basic bone of contention between church and state was the question of ecclesiastical courts. The church maintained that priests should enjoy 'benefit of clergy' and not be subject to the arbitrary judgements and harsh penalties of civil courts, while the king maintained that all Englishmen should be subject to one Common Law under the Crown. When Henry codified the state's position in his Constitutions of Clarendon, Becket found himself unable or unwilling to implement them. A rift had arisen.

101

Soon matters went from bad to worse. Both the king and the archbishop entrenched themselves in their positions, carrying their arguments to extremes and imputing wrongful motives to their opponents. Henry summoned Becket to a council at Northampton where the archbishop was accused of a variety of crimes and reviled by the barons, who behaved like the gross bullies they were – shouting abuse, hurling dung at him, and threatening physical violence. Meanwhile the populace outside the castle cheered and endeavoured to protect him. Becket realized that he could not long survive in this clime of royal hostility, and fled to France, invoking the support of the Pope. Henry reacted viciously, rounding up and deporting Becket's family and the families of his supporters.

For six years there was a stand-off. Becket retired to a Cistercian monastery in France and wrote conciliatory letters to Henry, but without giving ground on matters of substance. In due course, the king visited him in France and a reconciliation of a sort was patched up. Becket – now over fifty years old – was emboldened to return to England; crowds met him rapturously at Sandwich in Kent and accompanied him to Canterbury where he resumed his duties as archbishop. But Becket had not forgiven those clergy – including the Archbishop of York – who had turned against him; and many of the barons and knights, who saw their future depending on the king's favour, found ways to persecute Becket (they molested his servants and cut off his supplies from France) and to misrepresent his activities to the king. In particular Becket's enemies suggested to the king that the archbishop's fury at the enthronement of Henry's son as heir to the throne – a task which Becket saw as the Archbishop of Canterbury's own prerogative – was an attempt to unsettle the succession to the throne. It was such slanders that provoked Henry's desperate cry of 'Who will rid me of this turbulent priest?' which was to trigger off the four knightly assassins.

Becket had from the moment of his return foreseen the prospect of death. In a Christmas sermon in Canterbury Cathedral he declared 'I am come to die among you . . . in the church there are martyrs and God will soon increase their number.' When he had visited the capital a few weeks earlier, an anonymous voice from the crowd at London Bridge had called out: 'Archbishop, beware the knife!' For Becket, as surely as with Julius Caesar at the Ides of March, assassination was looming inexorably. But Becket seemed not to shrink from death; indeed there was undoubtedly an element of welcoming the prospect of martyrdom. Even when he heard that the knights who had arrived from France were gathered at nearby Saltwood Castle, a property which was owned by the archbishop but which was currently in the hands of his enemy, De Broc, he took no precautions. On the contrary, he knowingly provoked his enemies by including in the Christmas service a solemn denunciation of those who had wronged the church and himself during the time he had been abroad: while each of their names – including De Broc – were read out, he extinguished a candle and threw it to the ground. This was the language of confrontation and not of reconciliation.

Four days later, on 29 December, the four knights – having hardened their resolve at Saltwood Castle – rode over to Canterbury and burst in on the archbishop's palace while Becket was in discussion with his clergy. At first he ignored them, but when he finally turned to them they interrupted the peace of the meeting with demands that Becket should accompany them back to France to apologize for his conduct to the king in person. (Henry II, as so often, was still in France.) Becket, who may have regretted his long period in exile, said he would never again put the sea between himself and his flock at Canterbury. The knights withdrew, but only to collect their swords. Becket's supporters pressed him also to withdraw – from the palace to the cathedral itself, since they felt that the greater sanctity of the holy precincts might make murder less likely. Becket consented only with great reluctance, and when he got there refused to hide in the darkened corridors or the crypt.

He also refused to allow the doors to be barred behind him: the house of God was not to become a fortress.

When eventually the four knights burst in Becket faced them in the transept – the spot which has ever since borne the title of 'The Martyrdom'. Even to a pack of loutish and enraged Norman knights, the archbishop must have been a daunting figure, standing mitred and enrobed in the solemn hush of the mighty cathedral. They hesitated for a moment, plucking up their bravado by calling him a traitor, before they struck him down with their swords, slicing off the top of his head. One monk (a Cambridge scholar called Grim) attempted to deflect the first blow and suffered a nearly severed arm. The knights then ransacked the palace, looting and stealing horses, while a fearful thunderstorm and sheet lightning lit up the cathedral close. Seldom in the annals of Christian history, at least since the first century AD, can there have been such a dramatic martyrdom: no wonder Canterbury was to loom large on the pilgrim scene.*

The miracles and the pilgrims began almost immediately. For three and a half centuries (until deterred by Henry VIII) pilgrims continued to ride or walk to pay their respects at Canterbury. Many came from the north of England, via London; others used the well-trodden 'Pilgrims' Way' from Winchester across the Downs; a surprising number came from France. Their motivation was as mixed as their adventures: for some it was a penance, for some a holiday, for some a political act of protest against central authority. For all it was a memorable landmark in their lives.

We know a good deal about the numbers and origins of the pilgrims in the early years after Becket's death. Jonathan Sumption

---

* In more recent times there has however been one similarly dramatic martyrdom. Archbishop Oscar Romero, the champion of the poor in El Salvador, was gunned down and killed by assassins on the steps of the Chapel of Divine Providence Hospital in San Salvador as he concluded the celebration of the Mass on 24 March 1980. The author had met him shortly before this event.

has identified, from the records of miracles performed between 1171 and 1177, some 665 pilgrims of whom a third were either from the nobility or orders of knighthood; he rightly points out that the great and good were more likely to have their pilgrimages recorded than the mass of yeoman or peasant visitors, but, even making allowance for that, it still suggests that Canterbury (like Walsingham) was a fashionable pilgrimage.

This aroused some jealousy among the custodians of other relics and centres of pilgrimage. The guardians of the shrines at Durham, Glastonbury, Reading (associated with St James of Compostela) and others denigrated the Canterbury miracles, suggesting that they were unfounded or exaggerated. They were helped in this task of debunking by the highly dubious nature of some of the claimed Canterbury events. There had, for instance, been so many reported healings that it was feared that rivals might try to remove Becket's remains, or pilferers might chip bits off his tomb. In consequence, the monks at Canterbury constructed a wall around the shrine with holes in it just large enough to allow devotees to put their heads through and kiss the stone tomb. One of the more improbable stories was that of a corpulent pilgrim who managed to contract his body sufficiently to squeeze through one of the holes and then uncurled himself to his full stature like a genie released from a bottle.

Other miracles seemed hardly more convincing as evidence of divine intervention. When the king's favourite falcon was run through the eye by the bill of a crane on which it had swooped, a vow to St Thomas was alleged to have restored the predator's sight; similarly a kite dropped dead when the starling it was attacking warbled the tune of an incantation to St Thomas. Such tales did nothing to add to the credibility of Becket's reputation for sainthood, and rival institutions fastened on them as evidence of frivolity or chicanery.

105

The monks of Canterbury responded by sending summaries of the more convincing miracles performed in St Thomas's name to bishops and religious houses as far afield as Vézelay and other pilgrim-orientated centres in France and elsewhere on the continent. Donations poured in, although not all of them were equally desirable: one man – instead of sending the expected monetary contribution – donated to adorn the cathedral the tapeworm which had been removed from his intestines after St Thomas's intervention.

But despite the dodgy nature of some of the evidence, and the unsavoury nature of some of the donations, by and large the shrine of St Thomas grew in reputation with remarkable speed. And many of the pilgrims, whether grand or simple, demonstrated unequivocal devotion. Considerable numbers came not only on foot but barefoot. Matilda of Thornbury walked to Canterbury on her crutches at the end of the twelfth century, and the Countess of Clare threw away her shoes on setting out on the journey – in the same spirit as some crusaders would throw away the scabbards of their swords on setting out to Jerusalem.

One enduring tribute to Becket was that the number of children who were christened Thomas rose dramatically, and indeed it has remained one of the most popular English names. Almost as enduring was the fashion for naming church bells after the new saint: in steeples up and down the country Great Toms far outnumbered Big Bens.

From the outset, the journey to Canterbury was not without its hazards. Although it was the west-to-east route – from Winchester to Canterbury – which was to become known as the Pilgrims' Way, in reality far more pilgrims approached from the north: not only did Londoners come this way, but all those from starting points north of the capital. Most of the latter group chose to go through London where London Bridge provided the cheapest and easiest way of crossing the river. (Ferrymen were well known for fleecing their non-regular customers.) And it was south-east of London that the hazards intensified for the travellers. Shooters Hill at Blackheath was to become notorious for its highwaymen only in the eighteenth century, but already in the Middle Ages it was a vulnerable stretch of the road, as was Gad's Hill near Rochester. Although by Shakespeare's time the pilgrimage to Canterbury was in sharp decline, he wrote in *Henry IV* Part I of one such imagined raid taking place at Gad's Hill on 'pilgrims going to Canterbury with rich offerings and traders riding to London with fat purses' as it would have been two centuries before his own time and two centuries after Becket's death. Further along the route, between Charing and Chilham on the North Downs in Kent, there remain chapels built as assembly points for pilgrims who dared not undertake the more heavily forested parts of the route until they could do so in strength of numbers. The road to Canterbury may not have been as dangerous as that to Jerusalem, or even to Rome or to Compostela, but it was not without its own risks.

But nor was the Canterbury route without its pleasures. The archetypal pilgrims' jaunt will always be that described in Chaucer's *Canterbury Tales* at the end of the fourteenth century. In fact, Chaucer says very little about the pilgrimage itself and stops short of describing the entry into Canterbury, possibly because he felt that the raunchy nature of some of his tales would sit uncomfortably alongside an account of the shrine of 'the holy blessed martyr'. Chaucer's period was the heyday of the Canterbury pilgrimage: it was well established and renowned throughout Europe and the cynicism and hostility of the sixteenth century was still far off.

Chaucer's disparate group of pilgrims assembled at the Tabard Inn at Southwark and took the route that most travellers from London and all points north would have chosen. Although he adds nothing to our knowledge of the route, Chaucer does add greatly to our comprehension of the spirit of a certain type of pilgrimage – what might be called the tourism of the Middle Ages. Like a randomly selected group on a package holiday, Chaucer's pilgrims mostly had little in common with each other, which is what has always made them such a fascinating social study for students of history as well as literature. The group doubtless felt safer and more secure because of its numbers and the inclusion of some senior and formidable figures – most notably the Knight who was familiar with campaigning in such distant and dangerous regions as Russia, Prussia, Spain and north Africa. Other old troupers – like the formidable Wife of Bath – had already been on far more adventurous pilgrimages to the 'big three' destinations of Jerusalem, Rome and Compostela, as well as less familiar ones such as Cologne: she was obviously an addict who found the companionship and adventure of pilgrimage was the key to an enjoyable and rewarding middle age. All of them were bent on enjoying their springtime excursion, and the landlord of the Tabard Inn captured the spirit of the occasion with his suggestion that they should all tell each other stories to pass the time as they rode. It was of course significant that they did ride and were not making the journey on foot, as the poorer and more devout pilgrims did from necessity or choice. The hire of their horses or mules would have cost as much as their accommodation.

Another aspect of medieval pilgrimage which is encapsulated in Chaucer's tale is the social one. In a society as strictly in strata as that of medieval Europe there were few occasions when members of different classes could or would meet in a social context: even on the hunting field or the battlefield each knew his place and there was little opportunity for exchanging reminiscences or telling favourite stories that crossed the class barrier. Henry V's intimate talk with his soldiery on the eve of Agincourt (even had it been real and not fictional) would have been a quite unique experience and only made possible by the anonymous appearance of the king. Yet on a pilgrimage such as that described by Chaucer there was an opportunity for fraternizing, if not on equal terms at least on much more familiar terms than was probably possible in almost any other circumstances. The humbler members of the party might be gratified by the attention of a knight and a prioress with exquisite manners; the grander members of the entourage might be amused and curious to hear the outpourings of such earthy figures as the Miller and the west country Shipman. The landlord of the Tabard recognized this and – like an assiduously flattering modern cruise director – complimented his customers (in the words of Nevill Coghill's spritely translation) on being an unusually interesting and lively group:

> You're very welcome and I can't think when
> – Upon my word I'm telling you no lie –
> I've seen a gathering here that looked so spry.

The conclusion is inescapable: although some of the more serious-minded pilgrims – like the Poor Parson – might be wholly bent on a religious experience, most of the jolly band of pilgrims that set out that April morning in the late fourteenth century from Southwark were anticipating a pleasurable expedition spiced with adventure and social opportunity.

But popular as the Canterbury pilgrimage was, there had never been a time when there were not some critics of that institution. John Wycliffe at the end of the fourteenth century (in the same decade as Chaucer was writing his *Canterbury Tales*) had attacked in his sermons the cult of Becket and the vast accretion of wealth which it brought to the monks and chapter of Canterbury. Wycliffe memorably remarked in this connection that 'God gave his sheep to be pastured, not to be shaven and shorn'. In fact, when Wycliffe suffered a fatal stroke in December 1384, it was widely maintained at Canterbury that this was an act of God to prevent him preaching against the commemoration of Becket's martyrdom on its anniversary on 29 December that year. Elements among the Lollards had always inveighed against Becket. Nor had they been the only detractors: as late as 1530 one William Umpton had been clapped in irons in the Tower for having posed the question why St

Thomas should be a saint rather than Robin Hood? And three years later James Bainham had been burnt at the stake for calling Becket a traitor rather than a saint.

So Henry VIII, having embarked on his Dissolution of the Monasteries and his despoiling of the pilgrimage shrines, was not blazing an altogether new trail when he turned his destructive attentions to Canterbury. It was however a reversal of policy to the extent that both Umpton and Bainham had been condemned by Henry's own regime for their derogatory remarks about Becket. But, as his reign progressed, special reasons emerged for Henry's determination to focus his wrath on Becket's shrine and the Canterbury pilgrimage: first was of course the fact that Becket had always been a symbol of the church's resistance to the monarchy of Henry II (in the same way as Sir Thomas More was becoming a symbol of the church's resistance to Henry VIII); and second was the well-known and inordinate wealth of the shrine (as observed by Erasmus and others) which provoked the cupidity of the king. The fact he took so long to tackle the Becket shrine probably reflected the hesitation of even such a formidable monarch as Henry VIII to challenge head-on the legend of England's most revered martyr and saint.

But when he did turn to Canterbury there were no half measures. The opening gambit in the campaign against Becket was the trial of Friar Forest in 1538 who had – among other 'treasons and heresies' – affirmed that St Thomas of Canterbury had died for the rights of the church. A well-known and discredited wooden image was broken up and used as fuel on the bonfire on which Forest was burnt alive.

Next came the assertion by Archbishop Cranmer that 'I have in great suspect that St Thomas of Canterbury his blood, in Christ's church in Canterbury, is but a feigned thing and made of red ochre or some such like matter'. Cranmer set in train a formal examination or trial of the tincture that was sold to pilgrims. It may have been this 'trial' that formed the basis of the long-believed reports (emanating predictably from Rome) that Henry had staged a full-scale public treason trial of Becket *in absentia* (hardly surprisingly since he had been dead for over three centuries) with prosecuting and defending counsel; predictably, Becket was found guilty and – according to the papal reports – his bones were burnt. In reality, they were removed from the shrine and reburied amid same confusion and obfuscation.

A further temptation – if any were needed – for Henry VIII to seize jewels and valuables donated to Becket's shrine was provided unwittingly by a distinguished and aristocratic French visitor, Mme de Montreuil. After being shown round the treasure house in 1538, rather as Erasmus and Colet had been a few years earlier, she had a meeting with the king at Dover. At this she is believed to have regaled the king with descriptions of the dazzling opulence of all she had been shown, and in doing so further incited his greed to get his hands on it. He would also have been aware that the monetary offerings from simple pilgrims at Becket's shrine were far greater than at other altars at Canterbury: a typical year in Tudor times produced £3 2s 6d at Christ's altar, £63 5s 6d at the Virgin's altar, and £832 12s 3d at Becket's shrine.

By September 1538 the king was ready to move. He was himself making a royal progress through Kent, so his presence – and that of his large armed escort – gave a royal imprimatur to the sacking of the shrine by the king's commissioners. While the bones of the saint were whisked away and the other relics dispersed or destroyed, all the treasure donated by pilgrims over the centuries and otherwise accrued by the monks, was loaded on to carts and taken to the king's coffers in London. Papal reports subsequently put the number of wagons in the caravan of loot as between twenty and twenty-six and, although this was probably an exaggerated figure, there is no doubt that it was a massive plunder. The prize gem, known as 'the regale of France', was allegedly set in a ring for the king's plump finger.

A later decree ensured that there should be no visible reminders of the disgraced former saint or the objects of devotion associated with him: 'there should remain no memory of them in wall, glass windows, or elsewhere within churches.' The way in which this decree was implemented was often haphazard or opportunistic: for instance, the parishioners of Ashford in Kent did not obliterate the image of Becket in their church, but converted it with some ingenuity into an image of St Blaise – a considerably less controversial figure.

At some stage during Henry's visit to Kent, a number of plays by John Bales were performed which further served to undermine Becket's reputation as a martyr and saint; he was portrayed as a traitor to his king, Henry II, and a defender of the indefensible privileges extended to the clergy. It seems likely that the plays also depicted Becket's murder in such a way as to suggest that he was the aggressor and started the fight with the knights. By common consent the plays were more effective than sermons in debunking the prestige of the saint in his own diocese of Canterbury.

Becket had for so long been England's favourite saint that his image now had to be erased from all sorts of unlikely places. Peter Roberts (an historian at the University of Kent) has pointed out that not only did the scene of Becket's martyrdom appear – as well it might – on the Archbishop of Canterbury's seal, but it also had to be erased from the city's seal; it even appeared on the City of London's arms and seal. St Thomas's hospital in London had to be renamed, though it managed shortly afterwards to revert permanently to its original title by claiming to be named after the Apostle Thomas and not the martyr of Canterbury. Ornamental and illuminated books had to be purged of offending pictures at great artistic loss. One stained-glass window in Canterbury Cathedral only survived by being hurriedly painted over. Failure to spot and correct such things could result in the direst of penalties.

The desecration at Canterbury caused particular offence in Rome. Henry VIII had already been the subject of a bull of excommunication in 1535, but this instrument had been suspended; now it was reinstated and enormous efforts had to be made in England to prevent copies of the bull being smuggled into the country and causing embarrassment or disaffection.

With Becket's shrine at Canterbury gone, and its subject denigrated, the most popular pilgrimage in England was effectively halted in its tracks. No more could friars wanting to revive their faith, or yeoman farmers wanting to escape temporarily from the confines of their farms, or peasants wanting to see something of the world outside their masters' feudal estates, find a valid pretext for setting off to Canterbury. No longer could disparate bands of pilgrims, such as Chaucer's, find a worthy and commendable reason for making a spring jaunt to Kent. After 1538, for the moment at least, the pilgrimage was in abeyance. When Thomas Tyrell, a Suffolk parson, extolled the merits of Christian pilgrimage in his weekly sermon at the end of December that year, his congregation asked where they could go; Walsingham, Durham, Glastonbury and now Canterbury were no longer viable destinations. Rome, in the atmosphere of the English Reformation, was out of the question. 'Go to Jerusalem,' Tyrell replied. It was hardly a practical or helpful answer.

10

Erasmus: the Sceptical Pilgrim

IT FELL TO one who was perhaps the most celebrated and intellectually distinguished of all pilgrims to Canterbury to make the most critical and detached commentary on Becket's shrine. Erasmus visited Canterbury probably around 1515 with his friend Dean Colet. To understand the significance of his visit it is necessary to recall something of his career, and identify the point in his life when the visit took place.

Erasmus was born in the mid-fifteenth century into an age of transition, and contributed substantially towards that transition himself. Constantinople had fallen to the Ottoman Turks only thirteen years before, and in Erasmus's lifetime the militant forces of Islam were to threaten the gates of Vienna and the very heart of Christendom. Although the Moors had been finally expelled from the Iberian peninsula, it had long been recognized that the crusades had totally failed to dislodge the Levantine followers of the Prophet from the Holy Land. But these external threats were overshadowed by the internal dissensions which had recently begun to shake the foundations of Christendom at home.

Wycliffe and Huss, although persecuted for their supposed heresies, had initiated a process of criticism and questioning within the church which was to defy suppression. Wider access to the Bible, brought about by the fortuitous coincidence of translation and printing, was to undermine the formerly unquestioned authority of the Pope and his entire ecclesiastical establishment. And in many respects the church was its own worst enemy: corruption and abuse of power were everywhere apparent. Self-indulgent Medici and Borgia popes presided over a regime where indulgences were sold, where conspicuous wealth was accumulated, and where fresh knowledge and enquiry were denounced.

Indeed, as the Renaissance gathered strength in Italy, and as the wisdom of the ancient world was rediscovered and matched with new discoveries in astronomy and other sciences, an unprecedented mood of questioning of the old theological conventions began to emerge. Erasmus was to become a central figure in these new thought processes and – by extension – a controversial figure in the world of monasteries and relics, of abbeys and pilgrimages.

His own origins had been unpromising. Born in Rotterdam in 1466, he was early left an orphan under the guardianship of an uncle who systematically embezzled the money which had been left for his provision. Long before he was old enough to take monastic vows, he was put into a monastery, not in recognition of any early bent towards the spiritual life, but more as a convenient way of disposing of an impecunious relation. In the fullness of time, and almost as a matter of course, he became an Augustinian monk. The prior of his abbey, noticing how he gravitated towards the library and no doubt thinking he would benefit from wider knowledge, arranged for him to take up a post as secretary to the Bishop of Cambrai. The bishop in turn was impressed with Erasmus's scholastic potential and eventually agreed to release him to go as a student to the Sorbonne in Paris, granting him a small allowance to meet his living costs.

At the Sorbonne Erasmus first began to show his mettle: he established a reputation both as a scholar and as a wit. Soon he began to augment his allowance with earnings from teaching Greek; he

Hieronymus Bosch, in his triptych of 1480, gives an impression
of the hazards that await a pilgrim on *The Path of Life*

Erasmus was welcomed as
a scholar at Canterbury but
wrote very cynically about
the display of relics which
was shown to pilgrims there

The crusader castle of Krac des Chavaliers was a landmark and
haven on the overland route through Syria to the Holy Land

The walled town of Carcassonne was a stronghold of the
Cathar heretics who provoked the Albigensian Crusade

The sixteenth-century Hostel San Marco at León is now a
parador but still a staging post on the route to Santiago. A bronze
statue of a pilgrim sits at the foot of the cross in the foreground

The monastery square at
Montserrat: 'more like a
small market town'

The monastery of San
Juan de la Peña nestling
under a Pyrenean rock
face on route to Santiago

'Romerias', or local pilgrimages, in Spain have always been
the occasion for festive equestrian journeys and picnics

A pilgrim with his 'staff of faith' and 'bottle of salvation' as portrayed in a Pyrenean monastery on the route to Santiago

Fountain in the cloisters at the thirteenth-century monastery at Poblet

John of Gaunt is entertained by the King of Portugal on
the campaign which included his pilgrimage to Santiago

Fifteenth-century pilgrims paying their tolls at
the gates of Tyre on their way to the Holy Land

Sir John Mandeville taking leave of the King
of England before setting out on his travels

Prester John, the fabled Christian monarch of the Orient who
features in Mandeville's travels, is depicted honouring the cross

also embarked on his career as a writer, and managed to visit Italy where he acquired some awareness of the burgeoning Renaissance.

Among his pupils was a well-connected young Englishman who was the eldest son of Lord Mountjoy. In 1497, at the age of thirty-one, Erasmus made his first visit to England under the patronage of the Mountjoy family. They were well placed to further his career, and introduced him to other eminent scholars – notably Thomas More (later to be Lord Chancellor) and John Colet (later to be Dean of St Paul's and founder of St Paul's School). He studied at Oxford and went on to teach at Cambridge. Already – aided by the universal use of Latin among European scholars – he was becoming something of an international academic. But he was also a man of parts who could hold his own in the competitive world of Tudor English society. A letter from Faustus Anderlin in Paris indicates this:

> Your friend Erasmus gets on well in England. He can make a show in the hunting field. He is a fair horseman, and understands how to make his way. He can make a tolerable bow, and can smile graciously, whether he means it or not.

In fact, so successful an impression did Erasmus make in England at this time that his patrons presented him to the nine-year-old Prince Henry – later to become the formidable King Henry VIII – who was enchanted by Erasmus's elegant compliments. But despite offers of a church living in England from the future Archbishop Warham, Erasmus did not stay in the country or accept a position in the household of some prince, but preferred to continue studying and writing independently on the continent.

It was at this period in his life that he wrote *Adagia*, a collection of proverbs, epigrams, anecdotes and personal reflections, which first established him in print as a critic of accepted ideas and one who was capable of sarcasm to make his points – an unusual literary quality at the time. His subsequent *Encheiridion* – a sort of manual for a Christian knight – placed an unfashionable emphasis on good works

117

rather than outward forms of piety such as pilgrimages. Tyndale was to translate this work into English.

When Henry VIII came to the throne of England in 1509, Mountjoy wrote to Erasmus pressing him to return to England and telling him that the king would find a position for him at court. His friend John Colet had already been appointed Dean of St Paul's, and Thomas More had come out of enforced retirement to take on legal and public duties. Despite his natural disinclination for the fruits of office, Erasmus succumbed and indeed was disappointed to find on arrival in England that he was not offered a post as a royal ecclesiastical adviser, but merely passed on to Archbishop Warham and offered a comfortable country parish. This did not suit Erasmus, who needed the stimulus of erudite company and accessible libraries; he resigned, but managed to retain the parish stipend – thus ensuring a steady income to finance his further writings. These included two seminal works: a Greek translation of the New Testament with his own commentary, and his *Encomium Moriae* (or *Praise of Folly*).

Erasmus's translation and his commentaries on it turned men's minds towards the idea of making the teachings of the New Testament available in vernacular languages, with all the implications that entailed: no longer should services be remote from common people and accompanied by choristers chanting words they did not understand. Congregations could bring their own judgement to bear on texts they understood. The path was being opened up for Luther and a full-blown Reformation.

Equally explosive was Erasmus's *Praise of Folly*. In this work (which was largely written while he was staying with Thomas More) conventional scholars, grammarians, legal luminaries and, particularly, monks came under the whiplash of his sharp pen. The world of the cloister and pilgrim shrine was being quietly and wittily undermined, but not tackled head-on. Confrontation was not Erasmus's way.

But confrontation was becoming increasingly difficult to avoid. Erasmus hung on to the hope that Pope Leo X would effect reforms from within the church, and he avoided any open endorsement of Luther's more destructive doctrines. Luther and his supporters, on the other hand, could not explain Erasmus's failure to come out on their side except as an act of cowardice. When contemporaries remarked that Erasmus had laid the egg and Luther had hatched it, Erasmus replied that the egg he had laid was that of a hen, but what Luther had hatched was a fighting cock. He set out his position in a letter to Cardinal Campeggio saying:

> The corruptions of the Roman Court may require extensive and immediate reform, but I and the likes of me are not called on to take a work like that upon ourselves. I would rather see things left as they are than see a revolution which may lead to one knows not what. Others may be martyrs if they like. I aspire to no such honour.

Neither the entreaties of Leo X's successors for the help of Christendom's greatest scholar, nor the goadings of Luther's supporters, could move him.

This was the man who arrived at Canterbury around 1515. The king's desire to divorce his queen, Catherine of Aragon, in order to marry Anne Boleyn had not yet become an issue, but some of the factors that were to justify – at least in the king's own mind – his Dissolution of the Monasteries twenty years later were already in place. The obsession with relics was more of an obfuscation than an assistance to religious commitment, and the conspicuous and excessive wealth of the church – not only in land but in jewellery and other material valuables – was in marked contrast to the Christian doctrine of denouncing wealth in favour of giving to the poor and needy. Erasmus and Colet were therefore under-impressed by what they found as the focus and conclusion of their Canterbury pilgrimage.

Erasmus recorded his impressions of his pilgrimage with Colet, and recorded them in an unusual and somewhat devious way. The so-called *Colloquies* were a literary device enabling the author to conduct a dialogue between two imaginary persons, one of whom asks leading questions and the other of whom gives informative – and often provocative – answers. By using this device, Erasmus avoids the necessity of identifying himself directly with the views, innuendos and criticism that he puts forward; it was a formula well suited to one who wanted to remain ostensibly standing on the sidelines (as he would himself have said) or sitting on the fence (as his detractors would have said).

The *Colloquy* relating to Erasmus's visit to Canterbury with Dean Colet is a classic of its sort, and reveals his distaste for the relics which formed the focus for pilgrimages; it equally reveals his distaste for the way in which centres of pilgrimage – such as Canterbury – accumulated scandalously large wealth.

It starts with the questioner enquiring about the geographical and architectural aspects of Canterbury 'in a part of England opposite to France called Kent' and where 'the church dedicated to St Thomas raises itself to heaven with such majesty that even from a distance it strikes religious awe into the beholders'. The 'two vast towers' of the cathedral 'make the surrounding country far and wide resound with the wonderful booming of their brazen bells'. So far, so good: Erasmus is building up the prestige of the cathedral's environment in a way which seems innocent enough.

But almost immediately, the first snide remarks creep in. The questioner is told that Becket's assassins are commemorated by statues in the south porch, and he asks why 'so much honour is bestowed on the impious'. The answer is that they are perpetuated in the story – like Judas and Pilate in the Gospels – so that the guilt of their crimes shall not be forgotten: 'they are thrust into sight, that no courtier [the murderous knights could be described as courtiers] should hereafter lay his hands upon bishops, or upon the property of the Church.' In fact, Erasmus implies, the assassins are only commemorated so that the persons and possessions of churchmen should be safeguarded – a self-interested motive.

Worse is to follow. When the questioner asks what is to be seen in the cathedral, the reply is 'nothing, except the magnitude of the structure, and some books fixed to the pillars, among which is the gospel of Nicodemus'. There was nothing unusual about books being chained to pillars in churches in the sixteenth century, as their value was such that they might otherwise have been stolen. But the suggestion that the only Gospel available was that by Nicodemus, rather than those of the Evangelists, was an obviously insulting remark, since Nicodemus's so-called Gospel (which had been printed in London some five years earlier) was already generally believed to be spurious. An empty cathedral with a bogus book was how Canterbury was being presented.

The statue of the Virgin, erected on the spot where Becket died, is described as 'mean, and not remarkable in any respect'. When Erasmus goes on to tell how 'the sacred rust of the iron [on the sword with which Becket was killed] was religiously kissed' he is clearly showing distaste for the whole procedure. As he also is when he tells how the forehead of Becket's skull is 'left bare to be kissed, while the other parts are covered with silver'.

The tone then becomes sharper. Erasmus described how Becket's hair-shirts were hung in the gloomy crypt 'reproaching us for our indulgences and luxuries', and it is suggested that the people whom they ought really to reproach were the self-indulgent monks who were guarding the shrine. Their showmanship in delighting in the grisly relics – 'sculls, jaw-bones, teeth, hands, fingers, entire arms' – is contrasted with the more wholesome and normal behaviour of Dean Colet (here given the pseudonym of 'Gratian Black') who, 'when an arm was brought forward which had still the bloody flesh adhering to it, drew back from kissing it, and even betrayed some signs of disgust'.

Next came the showing off of the treasures kept under the altar — 'all most sumptuous; you would say that Midas and Croesus were beggars, if you saw the vast assemblage of gold and silver'. When they reach the sacristy — 'Good God! What a display was there of silken vestments, what an array of golden candlesticks!' But, Erasmus points out, amidst all this luxury there was no sign of the cross. On the other hand there was 'a sudary [a shroud], dirty from wear, and retaining manifest stains of blood'. Erasmus manages to make the whole sacred exhibition sound either inappropriately opulent or unpleasantly macabre.

Erasmus explains that ordinary pilgrims would not have been shown all these treasures. He and Dean Colet were only admitted because they had some acquaintance with Archbishop Warham who had given them an introduction. He goes on to extol the learning, simplicity of manners, and piety of life of the archbishop, which — by implication — is of a different order from the monks who are so proudly showing them round the evidence of their worldly wealth.

Dean Colet now leads the unfortunate monk into a moral dilemma. He starts by saying: 'Good father, is it true what I hear, that Thomas [Becket] while alive was exceedingly kind to the poor?' The curator monk assures him that was the case, and in answer to a further question agrees that if this were so when Becket was an archbishop on earth how much more must this be the case now that he is a martyr and saint in heaven. Then comes the awkward question:

> Since, then, that most holy man was so liberal towards the poor himself . . . do you not think, that now, when he is so wealthy, nor lacks anything, he would take it very contentedly, if any poor woman, having starving children at home, or daughters in danger of prostitution from want of dowry, or a husband laid up with disease . . . should first pray for pardon,

and then take from these so great riches some small portion for the relief of her family?

This went down extremely badly with the curator monk. He glowered at the visitors and then 'would have cast us out from the church with disgrace and reproaches, if he had not known we were recommended by the archbishop'. This was not the reaction which was expected of pilgrims in these pre-Reformation days.

Erasmus now philosophizes about the culpability of those who consume so much wealth in the adornment of buildings, in golden statues and in organs making 'a musical din . . . whilst at the same time our brethren and sisters, the living temples of Christ, are wasting with thirst and hunger'. He adds that while in former times bishops were admired for selling sacred vessels to provide for the poor, now they are 'applauded only . . . there is neither liberty nor inclination to imitate them'.

At this point the head priest came forward to meet the visitors. He had the title of prior (normally reserved for the second in command of an abbey) because the Archbishop of Canterbury was the titular abbot, but it was observed that he enjoyed the lavish trappings and income of an abbot. This prompts Erasmus to remark caustically: 'Forsooth, I could bear even to be called a camel if my revenue was suitable for an abbot!'

With the prior on the scene, more of the same sort of sightseeing is resumed: 'The Prior with a white rod pointed out each jewel, telling its name in French, its value, and the name of the donor, for the principal of them were offerings sent by foreign princes.' Some of the gems exceeded the size of a goose's egg. The monks stood around in veneration of all this wealth and 'we all worshipped'. Erasmus makes it quite clear that it was the jewels and not the deity or the saint which were being worshipped. And as before, grisly relics of Becket are again produced: 'torn fragments of linen . . . retaining marks of dirt . . . the runnings from his nose, or such other superfluities from which the human frame is not free.' Colet (alias Gratian) is again revolted, and when – as a signal honour – he is offered one of the soiled pieces of linen 'Gratian, not sufficiently grateful, drew it together with his fingers, not without some intimation of disgust, and disdainfully replaced it. The Prior, like a sensible man, pretended not to notice.'

Erasmus concludes his account of his visit to Canterbury with a description of the hazards of the road to London which is 'very hollow and narrow, and moreover the banks on either side are so steep and abrupt, that there is no possibility of escape; nor can the journey be made by any other way'. He goes on to describe how, in these trapped conditions, pilgrims are set upon by rascals who try to enforce a charge for showing them entirely spurious relics of Becket – an old piece of a shoe which they insist must be kissed and a toll paid for doing so. It is, Erasmus reflects, better than being set on by a band of robbers – but not much better.

Twenty years later, when Henry VIII had pushed through his divorce from Catherine of Aragon, had fallen out with the Pope and had established himself as supreme head of the church in England, he was to use the very arguments that Erasmus so deftly deploys in his *Colloquy* – the invalidity of relics and the excesses of wealth – to justify his brutal disbandment of the monasteries throughout the realm. Erasmus would never have wished this: for him, reform and not revolution remained the objective. But his snide comments had fallen on ready ears. The harm was done. In receiving the most eminent Christian theologian of his time, the unfortunate Prior of Canterbury was to find that rather than entertaining a devout pilgrim, he had been sheltering a veritable snake in the grass.

11

Less Frequented Pilgrimages: Mount Athos, Glastonbury, Durham, Walsingham

APART FROM THE great celebrated pilgrimages to Jerusalem, Rome, Santiago and Canterbury, there were a host of destinations that attracted pilgrims from all over Europe in the Middle Ages. Mount Athos, with its community of Orthodox monasteries, attracted visitors from many parts of the Byzantine empire; the Spanish had always indulged in local pilgrimages to a multitude of national shrines, many of them connected with the Reconquest from the Moors; in England – although Canterbury was the pre-dominant draw – there were other well-established destinations, among which Glastonbury, Durham and Walsingham were perhaps pre-eminent.

In the case of the great pilgrimages, there were numerous accounts written by pilgrims, partly because they attracted the great and the scholarly, who were literate, and partly because the time and risk involved in such pilgrimages made them a memorable – often the most memorable – event in a lifetime. But in the case of the less frequented routes, it was a different story. There are numerous references to the journeys, but almost no diaries or other detailed accounts. One reason for this is that a very large majority of these local pilgrims were illiterate and so unable to record their experiences; another reason is that to the more sophisticated – and therefore literate – pilgrims these journeys within their own county, or at least their own country, were not sufficiently remarkable to warrant writing long accounts, as they would have done of foreign ventures.

And yet these lesser destinations were an important part of the medieval pilgrim scene, and without some account of them any chronicle would be incomplete; collectively they probably attracted more visitors than the famous sites. Of course, just occasionally a 'lesser' destination was more challenging than Rome or even Jerusalem, such as a journey to Mount Sinai, which was fraught with danger. But even when they were a quieter experience, these lesser pilgrimages impinged on the great sites by being rival attractions and by instilling a zeal into their participants which often led them on to undertake something more adventurous later in life: Durham could open up a vista of Santiago, or Walsingham of Bethlehem.

However much distant travel, with its freedom from social and geographical constraints, might be for many the main attraction of medieval pilgrimage, there were others who were content to undertake much more modest journeys to purge their sins at the shrine of some local saint. Eamon Duffy, the Cambridge theologian and historian, has pointed out* that all over England in the later Middle Ages parishioners were setting out on limited excursions to nearby shrines to seek healing or absolution for their sins. Bishops or magistrates would send minor transgressors to do penance within

* In his essay in *Pilgrimage*, edited by Morris and Roberts (see bibliography).

their own diocese or county. The local saint was the obvious destination of first resort. Such use of local facilities also helped to consolidate the reputation of parish and regional religious assets, and to swell local funds.

The practice of such short-haul pilgrimages was certainly not confined to England. In fact, it reached its greatest popularity in Spain with the emergence of the *romeria* – a pilgrimage to a relatively local shrine, abbey or monastery where healing and absolution of sins could be hoped for in return for devotion, gifts and prayer. However steady the stream of long-distance pilgrims to Santiago de Compostela from all over Europe might be, it did not deter an even larger number of Spaniards setting out from their local *pueblos* to such favourite regional centres in Catalonia as Montserrat or Poblet, or in Aragon as Zaragoza, or in Andalusia as El Rocio (traditionally, and to this day, a pilgrimage usually performed on horseback). Local associations or clubs still form up to complete these regional acts of piety in a tradition that reaches back to the Middle Ages.

'We therefore gladly urge Your Holiness that, by your prompt solicitude, there be afforded him everywhere a courteous reception and treatment' – from a standard letter of introduction supplied to pilgrims to Mount Athos by the Patriarch of Constantinople

Although Mount Athos has not generally been considered as one of the principal pilgrim destinations of Christendom, there has always been a steady trickle of male visitors who made their way to this inaccessible promontory reaching into the Aegean from northern Greece. It has been a retreat for the dedicated few rather than an objective for the penitent many. And the reason is that this peninsula has since time immemorial been sacred territory, and has – since at least the ninth century AD – been the site of a cluster of monasteries or *lavras* claiming special status within the eastern Orthodox church and thus confirming Athos as 'the Holy Mountain'.

The Christian connection was, according to legend, established at a very early date indeed in the Christian calendar. The Virgin Mary is believed to have been invited to Cyprus towards the end of her life by Lazarus (he who had been raised from the dead) who was then a bishop there, because – in the memorable phrase of John Julius Norwich – 'he wanted so much to see her before he died again'. (An over-vigilant copy-editor of Norwich's book altered the phrase to 'see her again before he died', but happily the author spotted and re-corrected the alteration.) The Virgin Mary's ship was deflected by a storm and landfall was made not on Cyprus but on the densely wooded mountain range of Athos. Immediately on landing, Mary declared the peninsula holy ground and the place where she wished to end her days; she personally baptized the entire – if meagre – population.

For some reason that has never been fully explained, the Virgin Mary also decreed that Athos should be forever closed to other women; when the Empress Pulcheria landed at Vatopedi monastery in the fifth century she was allegedly confronted by an icon of the Virgin and the words: 'Go no further; in this place there is another Queen than thou!' And in the fifteenth century when the widow of an Ottoman sultan came to the promontory, supposedly to deliver an incomparable treasure – no less than the gold, frankincense and myrrh given by the Wise Men to the infant Jesus – she too was abruptly turned away. A few other women have, over the centuries, managed to penetrate the Holy Mountain: the wife of the Emperor Steven Dushan in the fourteenth century and Lady Stratford de Redcliffe, the wife of the British Ambassador to the Porte

(Constantinople), in the nineteenth century were among those whose curiosity overcame their sensitivity.

Mount Athos took a great step forward during the heyday of Christian pilgrimage in the later Middle Ages. Of the twenty-one monasteries that survive today, eight were built in the eleventh century, two in the twelfth, one in the thirteenth, four in the fourteenth and one in the sixteenth century. Not only did this signify a quantum leap in the number of monks on the peninsula, it also resulted in a notable increase in the number of pilgrims visiting the Holy Mountain. But there were also set-backs during this period. At the end of the eleventh century the local shepherds, who supplied the monks with milk, eggs and wool from their farms north of the peninsula, were found also to be supplying them with the sexual services of their wives and daughters. The Patriarch reacted sternly: he took the rather extraordinary precaution of decreeing that in future monks should be full-bearded to ensure that there was no confusion with women. (Most Athos monks still observe this rule.) But still, despite the scandal, pilgrims and devotees continued to arrive. As well as being drawn by the holiness of the environment, they came from a variety of other motives.

The lure of holy relics had always been a factor. Even before the arrival of the Wise Men's gifts, there had been a huge influx of Christian relics after the sack of Constantinople by the western crusaders in 1204; and an even greater influx was to come after the final fall of Constantinople to the Ottoman Turks in 1453. John Julius Norwich describes being shown 'a great splintery stew of skulls and jawbones, of fingers and feet and fibulas, and endless successions of desiccated teeth' and concludes that where relics are concerned Mount Athos must stand supreme among all the shrines of Orthodox Christendom.

Apart from the relics there are also libraries and frescoes and icons of extraordinary richness which have drawn scholars and art critics to the Holy Mountain. They have done this from the earliest times, throughout the Middle Ages, and up to the present. When the Hon. Robert Curzon visited the monasteries in the 1830s he managed – by fair means or foul – to make off with a remarkable selection of medieval illuminated manuscripts; when David Talbot Rice accompanied Robert Byron to Athos in the 1930s, his main objective was to photograph the frescoes; Robert Byron himself was obsessed by the icons, as well as other aspects of Byzantine art; when William Dalrymple was writing his book *From the Holy Mountain* in the 1990s it was here that he found the original manuscript of John Moschos's book which was to prove the inspiration for his journey around the monasteries of the Levant. Treasures that have nothing to do with the objects found in reliquaries have always been an additional draw.

But even more than the contents of the monasteries, it is the buildings themselves that thrill the visitor. Constructed like fortresses, they crown the craggy headlands. And their sheer walls and lofty towers are no affectation: for many centuries, and particularly after the ravages of the Fourth Crusade and the later Ottoman seizure of Constantinople, the monks feared that they were the next in line for assault and pillage. In fact, the Turks left the monasteries of Athos to their own devices, and the conglomeration of disparate buildings – growing indigenously from the hard soil like Italian Renaissance hill-towns – remain a glory in themselves.

Relics, treasures and buildings have all added to the allure of Athos. But there is another possibly more potent attraction. For those who seek tranquillity and a total escape from the material world, Athos is a unique environment. The rough paths that lead between the score or so of monasteries and the plethora of smaller *sketes* and hermit caves that make up the religious framework of the forty-odd-mile-long peninsula are eternal pilgrim routes, worn bare by the feet of the faithful over a millennium. Medieval clerics trod these paths, unthreatened by piracy, robbery or charlatans;

there was no risk here of encountering Margery Kempe with her tiresome fits, or the Wife of Bath and her scurrilous tales.

The beauty of the landscape, though perhaps not a reason for coming in the first place, has also been a factor in encouraging the pilgrim to Athos to linger or to return. Largely because of the total absence of all female life (exceptions are sometimes made of cats) the scenery, dominated by the austere peak of Athos, is softened by a landscape of woodlands undamaged by deer or goats, of pastures uncropped by cattle and sheep, of vineyards unregimented by commercial considerations, and of monastic courtyards uncluttered by hens. To the medieval traveller, as surely as to the contemporary visitor, Athos has an almost eerie quality of otherworldliness. Unlike most pilgrim destinations, this is a place essentially to appreciate for itself rather than for the excitements or rigours of the approach march. To visit Mount Athos is to become a monk oneself for some tiny chapter of one's life – and it was ever thus.

'Sothely Glastenbury is the holyest erth of england' – Vernon MS *c*.1350

In terms of antiquity, sanctity and, it has to be admitted, incredibility Glastonbury stands supreme among the pilgrim destinations in England. Its claim to be a Christian Holy Place dates back to before the earliest Christian associations of Rome, and rests on the legend that St Joseph of Arimathaea came here with the holy grail from France, some years after he had arranged the burial of Jesus in the holy sepulchre outside Jerusalem. Alleged evidence of this was he had planted a thorn which bloomed once a year at Christmas. And as if this legend were not enough, there is also the belief that

King Arthur's Avalon was also at Glastonbury and that his romantic campaigns in the sixth century AD to preserve Christian and knightly values in England culminated here.

Even before the first reputed Christian connection, Glastonbury was a sacred place, and indeed this would have been one of the reasons why Joseph of Arimathaea may have chosen to plant his cross here, since wherever practicable the early Christians preferred to build their shrines on ground which was already hallowed. According to William of Malmesbury, the twelfth-century chronicler of Glastonbury, the first Christian church was built here in 166 AD. Other notable events followed: St Patrick, hot-foot from his conversion of the Irish in the fifth century, is reported to have spent his last years here and to be buried at Glastonbury; a century later the same was alleged of St David of Wales. There was already an Abbot of Glastonbury in the eighth century, indicating that the church had already become an abbey by then. But the great consolidation of Glastonbury took place in the tenth century, and was the work of one man, St Dunstan.

Dunstan was a remarkable figure by the standards of any age – a Renaissance man before the Renaissance. He held the torch for Christianity between the dark days of King Alfred's struggles with the Danes and the equally gloomy period that preceded the Norman Conquest. He was born near Glastonbury in 909, became a monk and was appointed Abbot of Glastonbury in 939 by King Edmund, moving on eventually to become Archbishop of Canterbury in 959 in the reign of King Edgar. But his progression was not smooth or untroubled. From an early age Dunstan's multiplicity of talents – he was a scholar, teacher, musician, metal-worker and statesman – incited jealousy in his contemporaries. At different times he was accused of sorcery and of treason; he was banished and attempts were made to drown him in the marshes around Glastonbury. King Edmund recognized (at one of the periods when Dunstan was out of favour at court) that he had dealt unfairly with him and this appears to have weighed on his conscience. One day when the king was out hunting near Cheddar Gorge in Somerset his hounds gave chase and followed a stag over the edge of the gorge. The king's horse was galloping out of control and appeared to be about to follow the hounds into the chasm. Edmund instantly vowed that if he survived he would make amends to Dunstan. The horse stopped in its tracks and Dunstan was made Abbot of Glastonbury. It was the start of a period of architectural and spiritual reconstruction: Dunstan completed the abbey church and he installed the Benedictine Rule in such a way that made the place a model as a house of learning and godly living. When he died he was made a saint with unusual rapidity, and miracles promptly began to characterize his tomb (although both Glastonbury and Canterbury were later to claim his body rested with them). He had put Glastonbury firmly on the emerging medieval church map – at this stage in its history without any legendary or other link with either Joseph of Arimathaea or King Arthur. That was to come later.

Although Dunstan's spiritual achievement remained inviolate, almost all his architectural work was destroyed in a great fire at the monastery in 1184. Possibly by way of compensation for the material set-back, the legends of St Joseph of Arimathaea and King Arthur started to take practical shape at about this time. The legend of St Joseph appealed particularly to King Henry II who, despite his long and fatal controversy with Thomas Becket, was still anxious to curtail the influence of Rome and the papacy within England; to Henry therefore, the existence of an abbey which predated in its Christian associations even Rome itself was an asset not to be lost. He set about rebuilding the abbey without delay and the new church was completed and consecrated in 1186.

The monks were then granted the king's consent to search actively for the tomb of the fabled King Arthur. This idea appealed to Henry II because, just as the St Joseph legend was seen as a curb on Rome, so the King Arthur legend was seen as a curb on the tiresome

Welsh who had persistently claimed him as their own sleeping champion. Not altogether surprisingly, five years later the monks succeeded in finding Arthur's skeleton in the hollowed trunk of a buried oak tree, complete with a leaden cross bearing an inscription linking the body irrevocably with Arthur. Now Glastonbury had two fresh and powerful attractions for pilgrims.

One of the many happy aspects of these new discoveries was that they were linked by a potent symbol of sanctity – the holy grail. St Joseph was reputed to have brought this chalice, from which Christ served the wine at the Last Supper and in which St Joseph collected his blood from the cross, when he came to England; and the manifold legends of King Arthur's knights of the round table featured their search for this holy grail. Glastonbury was to ensure that one of its nearby hills was to be called Chalice, to register the connection.

Indeed it was the policy of Glastonbury to demonstrate its links to these holy connections as explicitly as possible. With this in mind, an unusual work called the *Magna Tabula* was produced – a set of huge wooden pages, lined with parchment, telling in Latin the story of the connection of St Joseph and other saints to the abbey. The whole contraption was fixed to the wall where its wooden leaves could be turned by pilgrims – or at least by those of them who could read: it was in fact the earliest tourist guidebook. (The fourteenth-century *Magna Tabula* is still extant and was acquired by the Bodleian Library in Oxford in 1947.)

With its credentials established, and a steady flow of miraculous healings to confirm them, Glastonbury was riding high in the fifteenth century. The buildings were famed far and wide for their splendour; the treasure and vestments were among the most magnificent anywhere; the lands and estates increased in size and rents; financial practices of dubious morality – the marketing of annuities and loans – were introduced to augment the income of the high-spending abbots. And throughout it all the income from pilgrims' donations escalated. Successive abbots of Glastonbury claimed precedence over other lesser abbots and prelates at various councils of the church. There may have been those who predicted that pride would be followed by fall, but none could have forecast how gruesome that fall was to be.

Violence had over the centuries been an unhappily recurring feature of life at Glastonbury. In 1083 there had been a particularly bloody incident when a newly appointed Norman abbot tried to introduce a new form of chanting in the mass – not, one would have thought, the most explosive of reforms. However, the monks resisted hotly and the abbot called in French soldiery to bring them to heel; this involved the Norman archers climbing to the upper floor of the church and shooting down into the nave until 'the wretched monks lay around the altar, and some crept under . . . and they smote some of the monks to death, and many they wounded therein, so that blood flowed from the altar upon the steps'. After this, it appeared the abbot had made his point, and the new chants were obligingly adopted.

Another violent incident occurred a century later when Bishop Savary of Bath decided that he should be appointed abbot and that Glastonbury should be given cathedral status, thus enhancing the status of the abbot/bishop but diminishing the independence of Glastonbury. Once again the monks resisted. The bishop – by using family connections with the Holy Roman Emperor – managed to make the fulfilment of his plan a condition of the release of Richard Coeur de Lion after the latter's imprisonment on the continent on his return from crusading. But once freed and back in England, Richard decided that his promise had been extracted under duress and reneged on it. The bishop and the monks continued to argue the toss, appealing to Richard's successor, King John, and even to the Pope. At one stage the bishop had the doors of the great church broken down, and forced through the ceremony of his own induction; later four of the monks who had been imprisoned for their pains died mysteriously and simultaneously of poisoning. So the terrible events at Glastonbury in connection with the Dissolution of the Monasteries by Henry VIII were not totally unprecedented horrors.

Over the preceding five centuries, despite these aberrations, most of the abbots of Glastonbury had been dedicated and often holy men. It was ironic that possibly the most dedicated and holy since St Dunstan should have been in office at the time when both he and his monastery came under the most brutal attack in its long history. Richard Whyting became abbot in 1525. A doctor of theology, he was an able administrator and austere in his private life. He had watched with concern Henry VIII's breach with Rome: the fall of Cardinal Wolsey, the rise of Thomas Cromwell, the Act of Supremacy and the trial and execution of Sir Thomas More. Whyting was not provocative: like More, he rode with the new doctrines and the new legislation as long and as far as he could. But the king and his greedy chancellor, Thomas Cromwell, were determined to lay their hands on the riches of Glastonbury. First the treasures were requisitioned by the crown: the 'great sapphire of Glastonbury' and the gold and silver altar pieces were declared 'superfluous' and seized. Then first one and later another Visitation was made to the monastery. Whyting was declared to have 'a cankered and traitorous mind' and was removed to the Tower of London. The monks were dispersed and the abbey looted of its remaining possessions.

Not satisfied with having forcibly acquired the long-accumulated wealth of Glastonbury, the king and his chancellor determined on making an example of the abbot, presumably to deter others (if others remained) who might resist the ravages of the crown. In November 1539, Whyting was sent from the Tower to Wells where a show trial was set up on 15 November; false witnesses were not subjected to interrogation; the jury was packed with those who had deserted the abbot to curry favour with the crown; the sentence of death for high treason was a foregone conclusion. On the very next

136

day, the abbot was bound to a hurdle and dragged through the streets of Glastonbury to the summit of Glastonbury Tor – a place overlooking the sites that had been held sacred for so many centuries. There the full rigours of a brutal Tudor execution were performed on him and two fellow monks. The abbot's quartered body was distributed between the neighbouring towns of Bath, Wells, Bridgwater and Ilchester and his head put on a spike over the entrance to the by then deserted monastery.

Sacred places retain their sanctity in adversity and even in desolation. Although less and less remained of the great abbey as the subsequent centuries rolled by, the ruins are still there as a focus of devotion. St Michael's Tower looks down from Glastonbury Tor; the abbot's kitchen, the lady chapel and the gatehouse stand as lonely monuments to its past splendour, and the surviving columns – taken with these other monuments – show that the length of the nave must have been greater than any other church then or now in the whole country. The medieval pilgrimage, the incessant tramp of weary feet over the surrounding marshlands, ceased overnight at the Dissolution and the grim execution. But among the vast throng who attend the current Glastonbury festivals there are not a few who feel some touch of the shades of St Joseph of Arimathaea, King Arthur and Saint Dunstan. The holy grail is still an evocative concept.

'*Lord, make me an instrument of Your peace!*' – St Francis of Assisi (1181–1226)

Three centuries before St Dunstan had done his great work in establishing the abbey at Glastonbury, a boy born in the Scottish borders was displaying a marked vocation for the priesthood. St

Cuthbert (as he was to become) started life as a shepherd, but by the age of sixteen he gave up looking after sheep and took to looking after souls. He entered the Abbey of Melrose in 651 AD and was in due course to take over as Prior and later as Bishop of Lindisfarne (Holy Island) and then, after his death, to become the focus of one of the great British pilgrimages – to Durham Cathedral.

Saint Cuthbert, both during his life and in the three centuries following his death, was associated with travel and by extension with pilgrimage. He had been reluctant to move from Melrose Abbey to Lindisfarne and, having done so, spent much of his time walking the hill tracks across the Scottish borders between the two abbeys and tending to his scattered flock. The route he took is now a signposted path, traversing some of the most lovely countryside along the River Tweed and through the Cheviot Hills, and takes some four or five days to walk. When not walking the hills, Cuthbert preferred to retire for meditation to a smaller island off Lindisfarne, and then to the remote and uninhabited Inner Farne islet where there were even fewer diversions and more opportunity for the contemplative life. The monks helped him to dig out a cell in one of the caves, but even here people beat a path to his door seeking Christian counsel and healing.

It was a difficult time for the peoples of north Britain. Not only was the traditional practice of cattle rustling already rife in the region, but the teaching of the church had been disturbed and confused by the controversies that had surfaced at the Council of Whitby in 664. Also there was an outbreak of the Yellow Plague that had taken a heavy toll. Support from an itinerant priest of proven sanctity was an inspiration to some and a comfort to many.

Cuthbert, as well as being a self-evident holy man, was arguably the first 'green' saint. Five centuries before St Francis of Assisi, he established a reputation for an affinity with birds and beasts. There were reports of seals coming out of the sea to romp with him on the beach, of otters coming out of the rivers to warm his feet, and of eider duck flying happily into his outstretched hands (and hence being known as Cuthbert or 'Cuddy' ducks). His life on Farne was as closely in unity with nature as St Francis's in his grotto in Umbria.

So great was Cuthbert's reputation that in 685 King Egfrid and Archbishop Theodore of Canterbury persuaded him to take on the bishopric of Lindisfarne. Reluctantly leaving his windy island of Inner Farne behind him, he resumed his travels through the Borders until ten years later he again went into retreat on Farne and died there. The monks brought his body back for burial on Lindisfarne, where it rested peacefully for almost a hundred years. Then the travels began again.

In 793 Viking raiders from across the North Sea sacked the abbey at Lindisfarne, slaughtered some of the monks and carried off whatever treasure they could find. They did not, however, desecrate the tomb of St Cuthbert because they appear not to have found it, and the monks who had escaped returned to reconstruct the abbey. But Viking raids were to become ever more frequent and menacing along the coastline, and by 875 the monks had decided that it would be wise to evacuate Lindisfarne altogether and, of course, to take their most holy relic, the body of St Cuthbert, with them. For the next century and a quarter the saint's coffin was moved from place to place, seeking a safe haven in a stormy and violent world.

Their travels took them through Northumberland and Galloway, and chapels or churches were erected (and many still stand) at the places where they halted. While the Vikings continued their pagan raids and destroyed the great northern monasteries at Lindisfarne, Wearmouth and Jarrow, the little cavalcade of monks with their precious load continued to elude them. Together with the saint's coffin they had rescued one other prized possession: the richly illuminated manuscripts that constitute the *Lindisfarne Gospels* (now in the British Library); this too had its adventures, being swept overboard and retrieved from the sea.

139

Just as in his lifetime healings and conversions had attended Cuthbert's progress through the Borders, so on his death miracles and wonders attended the progress of his body, which had – according to many witnesses at different times – remained undecayed ('uncorrupted') by the passing of the years. In a land of forests and famine, racked by plague and violence, somehow the fragile bearer-party continued to keep going. These were the years in which King Alfred the Great was trying to consolidate his kingdom farther south, but in the north disorder and anarchy still prevailed. As the journey continued there were longer halts at Crayke and at Chester-le-Street, until finally the coffin came to rest – following a slightly equivocal revelation by a milkmaid and cow – on a bluff above the River Wear at Durham.

By 995 a wattle church had been constructed to house the saint's remains, and soon this was replaced by a stone edifice. Following the Norman Conquest, Durham was quickly recognized as a strategic site and a castle was erected close to the church. A decade later both the English king and the Pope approved the installation of a Benedictine community to take over the religious establishment, and in 1093 the construction of the building that was to result in the present magnificent cathedral was begun. From its earliest days in 1104, the shrine of St Cuthbert was a prominent feature of the cathedral: the scene was set for one of the greatest pilgrimage destinations in Britain.

The twelfth century was the golden age of pilgrimage and thousands flocked to Durham. Soon it was to become (according to the sixteenth-century *Rites of Durham*) 'one of the most sumptuous monuments in all England, so great were the offerings and jewels that were bestowed upon it'. Not only were the pilgrims overawed by the mighty Romanesque cathedral with its marble and gilt shrine, but they also reported miracles and healings. Extensive lands and properties accrued to the cathedral. With its prince bishop, Durham became a monument to the power and wealth of the church.

The shrine also became a beacon for sanctuary — with all the moral and legal complications that that involved. The great sanctuary knocker on the north door of Durham Cathedral (which is still to be seen) would summon an ever-watchful monk to admit the fugitive seeking sanctuary and take him for examination by the prior. Provided he confessed his crimes in full — and most were murders — the fugitive would be granted up to forty days' asylum, after which he would be escorted to the coast and put on a ship for foreign parts — in effect, exiled. If no ship were available to give him passage, he would be obliged to walk into the seas and pray for one to come and take him off. Despite the sheriff's escort, some fugitives would be waylaid by friends or relatives of the victim, and killed in revenge before they could embark. The penalties for those taking the law into their own hands in this way (particularly if they broke into the cathedral) were more dire than those meted out to the original murderer: for them there was no sanctuary, but excommunication and torture before execution. Even hunted stags would be granted refuge in the cathedral which housed the remains of the animal-loving saint. The sanctuary of St Cuthbert's shrine was to be ignored only at risk of grievous suffering in this world and damnation in the next.

Apart from the complications of the sanctuary laws, the shrine of St Cuthbert also had its security problems. The monks took it in turn to guard their treasures round the clock as there was an active market in saintly relics, and the most predatory raiders were often clerics from other institutions which were themselves short of relics — and therefore short of appeal to profitable pilgrims. (Jonathan Sumption in his book *Pilgrimage* illustrates the point vividly by recalling how St Hugh of Lincoln when a guest at Fécamp Abbey had horrified his hosts by biting off a finger from a preserved arm supposedly of St Mary Magdalene.) Rowdiness was a problem as well as security at Durham: pilgrims often became overexcited and sang secular songs which were vulgar and offensive to more sedate pilgrims. The cathedral employed robust lay brothers – in effect bouncers – to evict any pilgrims who got too carried away with the elation of achieving their goal.

But, if they caused expense and problems, the relics at Durham also had positive practical aspects as well as being a source of income. On account of their wooden buildings, medieval cities were always vulnerable to fire and Durham had had more than its share of conflagrations. Whenever these occurred the monks at the cathedral uncased their relics and took them into the town with the fire-fighters as a potent weapon against the fire spreading to the cathedral precincts.

Durham also had one brand of pilgrim peculiar to itself: Scottish penitential pilgrims who would be sent from north of the Border to expiate their crimes. Many of these would be instantly recognizable by the fetters in which they were obliged to perform their penance, as this remained a practice in Scotland after it had ceased to be common in England. But even at Durham some such convicts caused widespread curiosity and awe: in 1164 one murderer appeared wearing an iron belt made out of the sword with which he had murdered his victim. In fact, these penitents were often glad of a chance to come to Durham as St Cuthbert had a reputation for absolving them from their sins in a very practical way: their chains would sometimes dissolve and drop away at his shrine. The chronicler Reginald of Durham interpreted this as evidence that St Cuthbert could both free the body as well as the soul from the stigma of sin. But others were more sceptical and attributed the disintegration of the fetters to rust rather than divine intervention; as Sumption comments, it is difficult to know what to make of these stories.

Durham also attracted an unusually large collection of grisly votive offerings. Even if nothing quite as macabre as the tapeworm left at Canterbury was visible, there were some fairly grotesque offerings: a withered finger, for instance, was left on the altar at

Durham by a shepherd who trusted that St Cuthbert would replace it by a new one. Such offerings were – not surprisingly – discouraged by the monks who had to live with them.

Even more uncertain than the reception accorded to criminal pilgrims or donors of macabre relics at Durham was the reception of women. Before the fourteenth century, female pilgrims were relatively rare: Margery Kempe and the Wife of Bath would both have been even more unusual a hundred years earlier. But Durham appears to have had a long-standing and peculiar aversion to women pilgrims: Symeon of Durham proudly declared in the early 1300s that no woman had ever been allowed to enter St Cuthbert's sanctuary. It was not clear whether the ban resulted from the misfortunes of female pilgrims who had tried to penetrate the shrine, or whether the misfortunes had resulted from ladies trying to enter a world which was closed to them. Countess Tostig had been struck with paralysis at the entrance to the shrine. More deservedly perhaps – in the opinion of the times – a maid who disguised herself as a monk and entered the sanctuary in the suite of the Scottish King David was also instantly paralysed. Hardly surprisingly, the belief grew up that St Cuthbert was averse to women. But the absence of women did not seem adversely to affect the pilgrims' financial contributions which remained consistently high.

Such a wealthy ecclesiastical establishment might have been expected to feel the full rigours of Henry VIII's Dissolution of the Monasteries. Its dependent monasteries and abbeys, including Lindisfarne, were early victims of the purges. When Thomas Cromwell's 'Visitors' came on Henry's orders to supervise the Dissolution of Durham, they naturally seized the precious stones and jewels in the shrine of St Cuthbert, and seemed determined to desecrate the grave and burn the bones of the saint whose remains they condemned as a 'papist icon'. But the long tradition of St Cuthbert being a survivor was not over: the monks managed to rebury their saint with dignity and even arrange for their Prior to become Dean of the cathedral. There was none of the viciousness of the savage executions at Glastonbury. The mighty cathedral remained intact and, if pilgrims were henceforth to be discouraged, at least they were not to be persecuted or totally banned. It seemed that the gentle Cuthbert's greatest miracle was to draw the venom from his enemies in death as he had done in life.

'As ye came from the holy land of Walsinghame . . .' – from a sixteenth-century anonymous ballad

Of all the pilgrim destinations in England, Walsingham was the most intensely focused on a single image and the most patronized by royalty and the aristocracy: as such, it appeared to supporters of the Reformation as offensively 'papist', and to many of those who went on humbler journeys as (in more modern parlance) a 'toffs' pilgrimage'. But it was well founded in antiquity.

Although less ancient as a focus of pilgrimage than Glastonbury, and post-dating the remarkable events surrounding the life and death of St Cuthbert, Walsingham also dated its attraction for pilgrims from prior to the Norman Conquest. But only just: the vision which appeared to the pious Richeldis de Faverches occurred in 1061 (and was repeated three times to ensure, it seems, that the lady was left in no doubt about its significance).

In summary, the vision consisted of a visitation by the Virgin Mary who transported Richeldis in a dream to Nazareth to show her the very spot where the Annunciation had taken place. Richeldis was then invited to measure the building where the Angel Gabriel had appeared and to reproduce it in her home village of Walsingham – a surprising request which inspired Richeldis to immediate action.

There are various stories relating to the building of the shrine, though most of them only surfaced long after the event. The most celebrated – in *Pynson's Ballad* of 1496 – tells how there was doubt about the correct site on which to build and the carpenters, having started on one site, found that their joinery was all awry; but when they retired for the night their material was mysteriously moved to a different site and miraculously put together in an elegant and durable form. The shrine had therefore been created with divine intervention, and from the start it attracted widespread attention.

That this should have been so is the more remarkable because Walsingham was on the way to nowhere. Situated only a few miles from the north Norfolk coast, it was not like Canterbury: a staging post for the Channel, nor like Glastonbury: conveniently close to such cities as Bristol and Bath and en route for the Welsh Marches. It rises alone: a free-standing destination in the rolling plains of East Anglia, and despite this it generated its own 'Walsingham Way' which was as famous in its day as the 'Pilgrims' Way' from Winchester to Canterbury.

Despite its isolation, royal visitors in particular made their way to Walsingham regularly over the five centuries of popular pilgrimage. The Augustinian canons who during this long period guarded and cherished the shrine received in succession the brother of Henry II who gave an endowment, Henry III who became a regular and generous visitor, Edward I who came some dozen times, Henry VI (not surprisingly in view of his religious propensities) who came frequently, and most of the troubled monarchs of the Wars of the Roses – as well as the celebrated Warwick the Kingmaker – came at least once. Where kings had led the way, the nobility followed, making their own contributions to the funds of the shrine. In fact the collection of jewels which had been left by well-endowed pilgrims was so valuable that the monks decided they had to close and bolt the priory gates at nightfall and keep plebeian pilgrims waiting outside until their treasure house could be opened with a suitable degree of security. One overambitious prior – with the unfortunate name of Prior Snoring – even attempted to get his priory independence from the authority of the Bishop of Norwich and make it directly answerable to the Pope, an attempt which both the bishop and the king managed to frustrate.

The wealth and arrogance of the monks at Walsingham naturally attracted criticism, particularly from reformers and those who wanted to see the role of the church modified by the translation of the Bible into English and by the enhanced role of the individual's conscience as a direct link to God. The Lollards in the fourteenth century were predictably outspoken in their hostility to Walsingham. The sacred image of the Virgin which had been the focus of much pilgrimage and prayer was decried by them as 'the wyche of Walsingham' – a virulent symbol of the superstitions which they wished to discard. But it was the Lollards who lost out, and not the established church and the monks: Sir John Oldcastle, the Lollard leader, was hanged, and the prosperity of Walsingham went on unabated.

Ironically, Walsingham's popularity was at its height immediately before its fall: its income from pilgrims alone was £260 in 1535 – a very substantial amount by the values of the day. The early Tudors followed the example of their predecessors: Henry VII came often, and in gratitude for divine assistance in putting down the uprising of Lambert Simnel (the kitchen-boy imposter who posed as a claimant to the throne) he sent his royal banner to grace the shrine. In fact, so significant was Walsingham at this period that when Henry VII decided to commission devotional statues of himself he donated them to three places only – Canterbury, Westminster and Walsingham.

Henry VIII, in his early years, while earning the title of Defender of the Faith from the Pope and still married to the intensely devotional Catherine of Aragon, followed in his father's footsteps. Indeed he followed them so literally that on one occasion he walked

146

the last two miles to the shrine barefoot to pray for a male heir. When the short-lived Prince Henry was born, the king made a thanksgiving visit; and Catherine later went there, no doubt hoping for a more long-lived male heir. Henry VIII endowed a 'king's candle' to burn in perpetuity at Walsingham; but this too, like Catherine's son, was to prove not very durable. Even Cardinal Wolsey, who was notorious for failing to appear at abbeys, like Bayham, and priories from whose wealth he had drawn a steady income, found time to go to Walsingham.

But none of this royal and aristocratic favour was to save Walsingham when Henry VIII's rift from Rome occurred. The monks gave an easy opening to their enemies and would-be despoilers: a Visitation by an independent bishop in 1514 found that the prior was embezzling the funds, keeping a mistress, selling off the priory's lands and – worst and most profane of all – keeping a Fool and allowing him as such to take part in services. With such an example set by their spiritual leader, it was little wonder that the rest of the monks had gone off the rails too, one of them protesting (according to the *Visitations of the Diocese of Norwich 1492–1532*) that 'I doo noo wors than oure fader priour doithe'. None of this misbehaviour seems to have affected the steady flow of pilgrims and donations.

It was only the Dissolution of the Monasteries which was to do that. This process was under way by 1536 when the uprising against Henry's anti-monastic policies (as implemented by Thomas Cromwell) reached its climax in the so-called Pilgrimage of Grace. This revolt was dangerously threatening to the royal power, but confined essentially to the north, more particularly Yorkshire and Lincolnshire; the only community to declare for the rebels in the south or in East Anglia was Walsingham. From then on, the writing was on the wall as far as they were concerned.

Already in 1535 there had been an inquiry made into the state of affairs at Walsingham, and especially into their finances and hoard of jewels. By May 1537, there were more explicit reports of plotting at Walsingham. One canon was hanged, beheaded and quartered there, and others met a similar fate in nearby towns. The prior – the successor to the disgraced patron of the Fool – concluded that this was no time for heroics. He allowed Thomas Cromwell's visitors to carry off the carved figure of the Virgin and this was burnt, together with other formerly sacred and now discredited images, at Smithfield market in London, in what Bishop Latimer (himself to be burnt at the stake by Queen Mary eighteen years later) described as 'a jolly muster' of such objects. Even the destruction of the Virgin's image did not apparently completely end her efficacy as a focus of pilgrimage. An old woman from a village near Walsingham claimed that the image was still performing miracles in London several years after it had been burnt; she was put in the stocks at Walsingham in a paper hat declaring she was a false witness; nothing daunted, she stuck to her story and was dragged round the town in an open cart while local boys were encouraged to throw snowballs at her.

Meanwhile, whatever the tenacity of local belief, the Prior of Walsingham knew where his future lay. He was busily in correspondence with Thomas Cromwell about being allowed to keep some of the priory silver and negotiating a good pension and parsonage for himself, and lesser benefits for some of his brethren. The spectre of their quartered brother monk must have haunted them all. By August 1538 the surrender of Walsingham and all its treasures was completed; even Henry VIII's own candle was allowed to go out.

The centuries of patrician pilgrimage were over, and not to be resuscitated – in a modest form by both Protestant and Roman Catholic pilgrims – for nearly another four hundred years. Walsingham had always been an unusual destination, not only on account of its aristocratic associations but also on account of its expensive nature. One aspect of this was that many were encouraged to bring effigies of themselves to be lodged at the shrine; these might be complete statues (sometimes life-size) or models of particular limbs or physical features – legs and noses were not uncommon – which were in need of repair or improvement. John Paston (from the famous family of fifteenth-century letter writers) was one who brought such an effigy.

Although high on expenses, the journey to Walsingham was low on danger. The rich, flat arable land of East Anglia held fewer perils for the traveller than the wooded or forested terrain of Kent or the west country, or the strife-ridden borders of England and Scotland. So fewer wrote accounts of their adventures; 'pilgrimage was too common to be noted unless linked with the movements of an important person', the historian Donald Hall remarked of Walsingham. In fact it could be concluded that Walsingham, as well as being a pilgrimage for grandees, was also a pilgrimage for those who preferred to risk their pockets than their persons: the adventure in this case was more financial than physical.

St Cuthbert, who spent much time walking through the Scottish Borders, has his knee healed by an angel, as depicted in the Venerable Bede's account of his life

12

Brother Felix: the Popular Pilgrim

To go on pilgrimage to Jerusalem and the Holy Land was a great achievement in the Middle Ages which was nevertheless accomplished by substantial numbers of pilgrims. The exploits of Canon Casola and others on this route have already been described. It was no small undertaking. But to go farther south across the desert and into Sinai – one of the bleakest wildernesses of the Near East at any period – to reach the fabled Mount Sinai, where Moses received the Ten Commandments, and to visit the nearby Monastery of St Catherine was a quite remarkable feat realized by very few. One who did achieve this, and survived to record in detail his impressions and adventures, was Brother Felix Fabri from the Dominican monastery of Ulm in Germany.

It was not Brother Felix's first trip to the Holy Land. He had made a pilgrimage in 1480 as far as Jerusalem. Although he obtained permission from the Pope and all the appropriate church authorities, he was none-the-less very nervous about the prospect of such a journey: he knew it was a hazardous undertaking and feared for his life. In particular he was afraid of the sea 'which I had never yet seen'. So he sought advice from 'the illustrious Prince Count

Eberhard of Wurtemburg' who had himself made the journey and who was renowned for his wisdom and good sense. In fact the count was much too sensible to push Brother Felix either way, and told him there were three things in life which no one should advise another to do or not to do: to get married, to go to war or to go on pilgrimage. So Brother Felix had to make up his own mind and decided to go ahead. He had been fortunate enough to have entrusted to his care a young aristocrat, whose father wanted to send him on a pilgrimage to acquire a knighthood of the Holy Sepulchre in Jerusalem, and this met most of his expenses. But in the event the trip had not come up to his expectations: everywhere he had felt rushed as 'we ran round the holy places without understanding and feeling what they were'. Although the phenomenon and the term were not to emerge for several centuries later, he had in fact had the sensation of being on a package tour. So while for most pilgrims one visit to the Holy Land in a lifetime was an outstanding and more than sufficient achievement, the eager Brother Felix set about trying to go on a second one in 1483.

He went through all the hoops of seeking permission again, and this time he was taken on as chaplain to a very exclusive little group of German grandees. The group comprised four noblemen (who were also dubbed as knights): the Lord John Werner, 'a man handsome and wise, remarkable for the grace of his manners, and learned in the Latin tongue'; Lord Henry von Stoeffel, 'a strong and active man, of a manly character'; Lord John Truchsess von Waldpurg, 'a nobleman of tall stature, a man of remarkable and lofty character, serious, and deeply concerned about the salvation of his soul'; and the Lord Ber von Rechberg, 'the youngest of them all, and the liveliest, bravest, tallest, most cheerful, kind and liberal of the party'. These four were supported by seven others (in addition to Brother Felix, their chaplain): an adviser whom they regarded as a father-figure, a barber who was also a competent musician, a man-at-arms who was both bodyguard and soldier-servant, a manciple or steward who was responsible for supplies and finances, a cook who was 'a good simple fellow, patient under hardships', an interpreter and former merchant who had been captured and forced into being a galley-slave where he had learnt his Arabic, and finally a schoolteacher who was 'a man of peace, eager to serve their lordships'. The four grandees paid all the expenses of the whole party. With such a high-minded group of aristocrats and such a competent supporting staff, it was surprising that they were all to become so dependent for survival on the diplomatic skills and kindly good sense of their chaplain. As we shall see, it was Brother Felix who was to become the anchorman of the whole party.

From the outset, while they were still in Venice awaiting their ship, the four lords (or knights as Brother Felix prefers to call them) seem to have recognized their dependence on him, because when he tried to arrange separate accommodation for himself in a local Benedictine monastery 'where he could sleep, pray, read and write, and escape from all the noise of the inn', they would not hear of it: 'indeed, it displeased them very much, nor would they on any terms consent to my leaving them'. The chaplain was needed for much more than just administering divine service.

He also had another role which was from our point of view the most valuable of all: he was the expedition's scribe and chronicler. He had promised his fellow monks at Ulm that he would record as fully as possible what he did and saw; in the event he also recorded the stresses and strains of relations between the pilgrims. This was no Chaucerian band of genial storytelling fellow travellers, but a surprisingly prickly, quarrelsome and easily frightened group whose health and morale was under constant strain. In fact, probably a very typical pilgrim party.

Many of the features of the journey by Venetian galley from Venice to the Holy Land, and their tour of the Christian sites – a much more thorough one than on his previous trip – followed in a pattern not dissimilar from the journey to be made by the Italian Canon

Casola eleven years later. From Venice they put in at Cyprus and sailed on to Jaffa and went overland to Jerusalem, Bethlehem and the River Jordan. We can pick up the story from the point when the party leaves the Holy Land to venture into virtually unknown territory further south – what is now the extreme south of Israel and the deserts of Sinai. From here on the pilgrimage was taking on a new dimension: it was a desert expedition which required a whole new approach – a caravan of camels and asses, of carefully selected and preserved supplies, of newly engaged and often stroppy hired hands. The party was eventually to amount to twenty-five camels, thirty asses, seven camel-drovers, six ass-drovers, two Arab captains and guides – making a total in all of some thirty or more persons and fifty-five animals. This was a sizeable expedition by any standards and would have lessons and implications for any subsequent pilgrims on this route.

Like the good Boy Scout he is, Brother Felix gives plentiful and practical advice to any who might wish to follow in his footsteps. He spells out how a contract must be made with a dragoman (interpreter and guide) who should supply camels and camel-drovers for the baggage, and asses for the pilgrims to ride. Wisely, and rather pedantically, he emphasizes that pilgrims must be precise about departure dates and quantities of baggage. He insists the 'many jars full of wine' must be covered up with sacks made of hair so that the camel-drovers are not either shocked at these signs of non-Islamic indulgences, or – more likely – tempted to steal them. He recommends, as well as normal provisions, packing 'coops with live cocks and hens'. He also sensibly suggests that for a desert journey of this sort some extra provisions should be included – biscuits, smoked meat and cheese – to give to the Arabs and Midianites encountered en route 'as this soothes their rage'. No wonder the party needed twenty-two pack animals.

Being a considerate travelling companion, Brother Felix does not join the scramble to choose the best riding ass for himself, but is content to accept the ass that all the others had rejected. No one seemed to resent the fact that, in the event, he turned out to have the safest, most reliable and least vicious of all the animals offered.

Despite all the wrapping and concealing of the wine jars, even before they were off one of them got broken and evoked 'the fury of the Saracens' who, when they smelt the wine ('very good wine bought at a great price'), threatened to rush on the pilgrims and break all the other jars. Fortunately this disaster was averted, because Brother Felix records that 'had we been deprived of our wine, we should not have attempted the pilgrimage to Mount Sinai'. He even managed to catch some of the spilt wine in his own bottle. Clearly conviviality was to be an essential ingredient of this desert journey.

Loading the camels was to be a stressful experience for many days to come. The Arabs understandably preferred to dump all the pilgrims' kit together and to distribute it in an even division between the camels; the pilgrims on the other hand much preferred to have each one's personal possessions and supplies loaded on to one camel, so that at the end of the day each individual's luggage was all in one place. Brother Felix tried, as always, to sort it out and avoid 'many quarrels and much trouble'. Similar disputes arose when the caravan was under way. The pilgrims wanted to rest and lunch in the shade of any trees they found, but the dragoman insisted that the camels could not be halted without being unloaded, and to unload and reload them in the middle of the day's march was an unreasonable request. Brother Felix prevailed on his companions to accept this.

Throughout the journey these disputes between camel-drovers and pilgrims were to recur. Several weeks into the desert crossing, the former were to try to insist that the latter threw away their non-essential gear, or else paid for extra camels to carry it; the pilgrims complied and hired three more camels rather than cut down on their comforts and wine stocks. Another particularly mean trick which the camel-drovers practised was deliberately to leave unpacked some item of personal equipment belonging to a pilgrim and then, when all the camels were fully loaded and the pilgrim discovered his package left on the sand, demand an extra tip for making the necessary reloading to include the missing item.

Everywhere they stopped, the pilgrim party was a focus of curiosity and attention 'because there had been no Latin pilgrims [south of Jerusalem] for many years'. From time to time they were stoned. Their behaviour must indeed have seemed quite weird to the local Arabs. At one point, for instance, they all vaulted over a dry stone wall into a barren field and kissed the ground. It was – they believed – the plot of land from which the clay was taken by God to make Adam. At another point they all trooped into a small dark cave to celebrate the fact that it was here that Adam first had intercourse with Eve. The Saracens (as Brother Felix preferred to call them) were at once mystified and suspicious of such bizarre behaviour – the excuse for which did little to reassure them of their visitors' bona fides.

Indeed, the eager and uncritical Brother Felix was forever identifying – for the enjoyment of his travelling companions – more and more places of biblical significance in this barren land of the Levant and Sinai. As well as the somewhat intimate connections with Adam and Eve, he was able to point out the sites of Cain and Abel's quarrel and of Samson's destruction of the temple of the Philistines. He also had a propensity to sing psalms when he was on night sentry duty, but his companions do not seem to have held this against him.

Brother Felix was very conscious that in continuing their pilgrimage south of Jerusalem and into Sinai the party was retracing the route of Joseph and Mary's flight into Egypt with the infant Jesus to avoid their child being involved in Herod's slaughter of the innocents. He finds some unidentified 'traces' of this historic journey: 'for instance, the place where they were attacked by robbers' according to St Anselm. He recounts the story of this incident and how 'a certain youth, who was the son of the chief of the robbers, when he saw the child on its mother's lap, was miraculously seized with a wondrous love towards it'; the young robber then insisted on freeing the Holy Family and 'pointing out a safe road to them'. The story ends with explaining how the young robber was to end up as the 'good' thief who was crucified alongside Jesus and who said to him, 'Lord, remember me when Thou comest into Thy kingdom.' Brother Felix's ability to conjure up a direct link between a barren and featureless stretch of desert and such a moving Christian tale must have greatly added to the quality of spiritual tourism inherent in such a pilgrimage.

Brother Felix's robust Christian enthusiasm had its down side in an equally robust distaste for and condemnation of everything to do with Moslems and Jews. Saracens are declared to 'emit a certain horrible stench' and Jews to 'stink even worse'. When he encounters cairns of stones and 'dangling rags' put up to mark places sacred to Islam, he 'plucks away all these rags . . . and puts crosses in their place'. Even when some of their own Moslem guides put themselves at risk to stop two of the Christian knights fighting each other, he attributes this 'not to their courage, but to the false doctrines of the faith': the theory of predestination led them to believe that they would not die ahead of their time as a result of taking such risks. There are gratuitous references to 'the accursed Mohammed', and a long diatribe claiming that the Prophet's coffin in Mecca is suspended in the air by magnets and not, as suggested, by some divine power: 'and so the besotted people are confirmed in their error'. These attitudes which might appear chauvinistic – if not positively Fascist – in the twenty-first century, also extended to gypsies, who come in for denigration as 'the subtlest of thieves'.

Brother Felix contrasts his own Christian pilgrimage with those who go 'to the sepulchre of Mohammed, the son of the devil, and seek to serve that most wanton harlot Venus'. He also mocks the Moslem fast of Ramadan as 'a strange unnatural fast, fit only for carnal and beastly men!' He claims that after the fast comes 'lust, gluttony, drunkenness and revelling . . . indulging all their basest desires'. In fact, Brother Felix reveals in his attitudes some of the worst of the legacy of the crusades – a disrespect for Islam and a vicious attitude towards Moslem practices, especially in all matters sexual.

His Christianity is also exclusively Catholic (a contradiction in terminology in which he would have seen nothing odd). Orthodox Christians, 'Greeks', were roundly condemned whenever encountered. When turned away from one Orthodox chapel, he ascribed the rebuff to 'Divine goodness, which would not suffer us to celebrate Mass in a schismatical or heretical church'. And when he eventually reaches St Catherine's Monastery on Sinai he is vitriolic about the Orthodox monks there, whom he describes as 'excommunicate, schismatic and heretics . . . who will not open their church door to a pilgrim unless they see his money, and will not give one drink of water without taking money for it'. This was in marked contrast to the hospitality expected and usually supplied by western monasteries along the lesser known as well as the well-trod pilgrim paths of Europe and the Levant.

Despite these extreme and belligerent attitudes, Brother Felix was good at heading off trouble with the locals by such simple ploys as giving biscuits to the children of potentially hostile Arabs. Often access to a remote and vital well was only made possible by such tactics. He encouraged his companions to make similar gestures: 'our young knights danced with their young men upon the plain, ran races with them, lifted great stones, and strove with one another in all good fellowship.' Brother Felix was instrumental in initiating all such jollifications.

In fact, Brother Felix was the pilgrim whom other pilgrims wished to be with. When two of the knights – Baron von Warno and Lord von Braitenbach – fell sick, Brother Felix, although suffering from a fever and dizziness himself, was the one who attended to them. When the pilgrims quarrelled among themselves about the route they should take, it was he who helped reunite the party and stiffen their resolve 'not to leave any sick man behind us, but to carry in baskets on camels all who were unable to sit upon asses'.

He was also consistently thoughtful and considerate towards those weaker and ailing members of the party. Having succeeded in establishing that the sick knights should be carried in wicker panniers on the camels, he none-the-less was one who insisted on taking the sick out of their panniers and persuading them to walk down any really steep or dangerous section of the path. The wisdom of this was proved when one camel slipped and his entire load went crashing down the hillside: 'had the sick lord stayed in his pannier, as he would have preferred to do, he must have been dashed into a thousand pieces; had he a thousand necks, they would all have been broken.'

If we have any doubts about Brother Felix's popularity with his fellow pilgrims, a couple of lines in a poem composed by one of the groups confirms his status:

> Next Felix comes, the glory of Ulm's land,
> Who, doubly learned, to God gives all his lore

Doubtless his popularity was enhanced by his action on the descent from Mount Horeb when he turned out to be the only pilgrim who had brought an adequate hamper of food: biscuits, hard-boiled eggs, smoked meat and cheese. He declined requests for scraps from his basket, but instead tipped the whole contents on to a rock and invited everyone to help themselves. 'At this invitation all of them came, and right merrily ate all that we had . . . at this feast of mine were present counts, knights, priests and monks'. Once more, Brother Felix was everyone's favourite.

Like so many fifteenth-century travellers, Brother Felix some-what mars his credibility by including fantasy with fact. For instance, he accurately describes the contrasting desert heat of the days and cold of the nights; he describes the snakes and scorpions and occasional crocodiles encountered; but then he includes references to dragons, fauns and satyrs in the same passage. On another occasion he indulges in a long explanation about the appearance and habits of unicorns. Other natural hazards sounded more convincing, such as the packs of wolves that used to howl around their camp at night and alarm Brother Felix when he was on sentry duty (although on one occasion what he took to be wolves turned out to be a particularly noisy Saracen at prayer).

Of all the hazards in the desert, the one which particularly seems to have disturbed Brother Felix were the snakes. He had an understandable horror of sleeping in a camp riddled with snake holes, and he found the huge dead serpents in the cisterns and wells much detracted from the joy of finding water. Sometimes the progress of the caravan was impeded by 'the whole ground being honeycombed with the holes of asps and serpents'. He also disliked the requirement to walk between the two halves of a snake which had been cut in two by a sword; but it was believed that the halves would join up again 'unless men passed between them', so this ritual had to be observed.

As well as natural hazards there was always the threat of robbery. When in camp, the pilgrims snuffed out their cooking fires at night, kept silent and posted guards. When at an inn or a manger, they would roll stones in front of the door to keep out intruders. Often however, Brother Felix confesses that 'in sooth, those watches were more needed by us on account of our own servants – the camel-drovers and ass-drovers – than of strangers . . . these men stole our biscuits, eggs and everything they could'. When they saw approaching camel caravans, the knights drew their swords and prepared to join battle. Frequently they would encounter armed bands of Arabs who would demand a toll for allowing them to cross the land of 'the lords of the wilderness'; if however these marauders decided that the pilgrim group was better armed than they were, they would change their demand for tolls to an entreaty for alms. Sandstorms encouraged robbers to approach and escape under cover of darkness. Alternatively, clear visibility often enabled robbers to see where a caravan was camping and to sneak up and steal camels or provisions during the night. On one occasion Brother Felix's camp was penetrated by such Arab thieves who made off with a camel; but they were tracked down to a cave by the camel-drovers and one was speared to death. The law of the desert was a harsh one.

One quality which added to Brother Felix's stature among the aristocratic pilgrims with whom he was travelling was his taste for adventure. On some occasions he would go off alone to explore a high sand-dune or a distant landmark, and he sometimes got badly lost in so doing, having to retrace his way by dint of finding his own rapidly disappearing footsteps in the sand.

Just how dangerous and deceptive such exploits in the desert could be became clear when a group of the pilgrims – four knights, two clergy (including Brother Felix), and one servant – detached themselves from the main party, against the advice of the dragoman, to go down to the Red Sea for a swim. The distance was far greater than appeared to the untrained eye, and night fell leaving them stranded and unable to retrace their steps because they could not see their footprints. It was so dark they couldn't even see the sea any more and they 'wandered on an uncertain course, now to the right, now to the left . . . at one time following this man's advice, at another that one's'. They shouted; they looked for the camp fire of their comrades; and, inevitably, 'they fell a-quarrelling, for one man wanted to go this way, and another that'. Two knights in particular, who were old enemies it seems, looked like fighting until Brother Felix, the peacemaker as always, 'put myself and my ass between them'. In fact he held the whole party together: 'I took great pains to quiet those who were wrangling, and to call back those who

161

would have strayed away.' After midnight they rested fitfully on a sand-dune and Brother Felix went up a small hillock to see if he could get his bearings, and silently to call on the assistance of the Blessed Virgin. None of this helped, and soon he found he had lost the others who were themselves lost and was quite alone. He had failed to take his own advice, and when eventually he rejoined the lost knights they chided him with his irresponsibility. Eventually the whole group were saved by hearing the camels roaring as they awoke in the pilgrim camp and – after some apprehension as to whether they were approaching the wrong camp and falling into an Arab ambush – they were all reunited. Brother Felix's Boy-Scout skills had proved less effective than his peace-keeping ones.

The climax of the whole expedition was of course the arrival at St Catherine's Monastery, at the foot of Mount Horeb and St Catherine's Mount – all part of the Mount Sinai range – and the ascent and descent of these summits. Here again were sites of special biblical significance, notably 'the very place that Moses saw the bush that was burning' without being consumed by the fire. Brother Felix also relates at length the story of how angels carried Catherine's body from the place of her martyrdom in Alexandria to the summit of the mount that bears her name on Sinai, and how they stood guard over her body for several centuries. This was a shrine as holy as any in Compostela or Rome, a worthy objective for an arduous pilgrimage. Brother Felix proudly recalls that a previous Pope had forbidden pilgrims to attempt to reach this destination, not because the Saracens had occupied the region (as was the case when for periods Jerusalem was out of bounds to Christians) but purely because of 'the difficulty of the journey and the dangers thereof'. Sinai, he argues, was the ultimate achievement of medieval pilgrimage.

The climb to the summit of Mount Horeb was physically very taxing for some of the pilgrims. A number of them felt faint and turned back. Others persisted – 'through a darksome and frightful cleft in the mountain . . . with a precipice on either side' – often on all fours. Most of the pilgrims found that their shoes fell to pieces during the climb. At one point they passed under a stone arch and here Brother Felix – never one to pass up an opportunity to tell an anti-Semitic tale – relates that any Jew attempting to pass under this arch in order to reach the place where Moses received the Commandments is 'driven back by Divine miracle'. Having ascended Mount Horeb, a number of the pilgrims went on to climb St Catherine's Mount on the same day. Brother Felix – ever helpful to his companions – found himself struggling to aid one of the weaker knights by 'tying a long towel to his girdle, by which some of us dragged him, while others held his hands and pulled by his arms, and others stood behind and pushed him along; so we had a wondrous deal of work with that pilgrim!'

The journey home was also full of adventures and incidents. The party crossed over from Sinai into Egypt west of the Red Sea, went down the Nile and ended up in Alexandria, which had a particular significance for them as the scene of St Catherine's grisly martyrdom – torture on her Catherine's wheel followed by decapitation. (Her crime had been trying to convert the Emperor Maximianus I to Christianity in the fourth century.) From there they embarked with a Venetian fleet to Venice and eventually Brother Felix reached his home monastery at Ulm. He arrived as the monks were at vespers. But the monastery dog recognized his footfall and set up such a barking and scratching at the door that the monks had to break off their prayers to open up. He was 'welcomed as one back from the dead'.

And not without reason. For all his vitriol towards the exponents of other faiths, Brother Felix had achieved a considerable feat; he was a stout-hearted pilgrim, a considerable biblical scholar and, above all, a good travelling companion. Although he would have been a less stimulating companion than Erasmus, a less influential one than John of Gaunt, a less pushy one than Canon Casola and a less provocative one than Margery Kempe, one would have felt that with Brother Felix in one's caravan one's chances of survival would have improved. The natives would have been placated, the internal dissensions modified, the appropriate saints invoked and the journey enlivened with frequent convivial evenings. Chaucer would have appreciated a character who knew when to bundle a sickly knight into a wicker pannier, and when to pull a fat one up a hill by his girdle.

13

Armed Pilgrimages: Crusades to the Holy Land; the Albigensian Crusade; the Pilgrimage of Grace

CHRISTIANITY WAS, AT its inception, a religion of peace: Jesus restrained his followers – notably Peter – from armed intervention on his behalf. And if they should not take up arms in defence of Christ himself, what other earthly cause could possibly justify so doing. The Early Fathers of the church were firm on the subject: war was murder. Long after the western church – based on the militaristic Roman Empire – had abandoned these principles, the eastern church of Byzantium stuck to them: St Basil, the founder of eastern monasticism, maintained that soldiers who had killed, albeit in legitimate battle conditions, were none-the-less debarred from receiving communion for three years. Gradually the rules changed, even in Byzantium: campaigns undertaken to defend the frontiers of Christendom, or to rescue Christians from pagan or infidel oppression, were legitimized. But still, for the first centuries after Christ, his followers generally deplored resort to force.

All that was to change in the Middle Ages with the development of the concept of chivalry. As Christendom came under attack from barbarian intruders, so the church actively encouraged its members to defend it: orders of chivalry combining religious precepts with martial arts proliferated; Pope John VIII declared in the ninth century that soldiers who died in battle for Christendom were holy martyrs; art, poetry and romance combined to glorify the knightly virtues of daring and courage and to denigrate pacifism.

The most notable outcome of this was the crusades, starting at the end of the eleventh century. A book about pilgrimages is no place for another history of crusades to the Holy Land. But it must be remembered that the First Crusade, as preached by Pope Urban II and by Peter the Hermit, was presented as a campaign to reopen the pilgrim routes to Palestine and to protect the peaceful pilgrims on their innocent and vulnerable journey. It was Islamic interference with this pilgrim route in the first place that provoked the whole series of bloody campaigns with their indefensible atrocities.

And it was not only in the Holy Land that Christians were under threat. Throughout the Iberian peninsula, Moorish rulers practised and spread the ways of Islam; at any moment, the warriors of the Prophet might cross the Pyrenees and come flooding into France and beyond. This was no time, church leaders felt, to be reticent about the use of force: those fighting the Moors in Spain, like the crusaders in the Holy Land, received special absolutions and recognition. When the King of Aragon – setting out to attack the Moors – was cut down by a Moslem assassin in 1063, Pope Alexander II immediately granted a formal indulgence to all who fought against the infidels in Spain.

The new formed Cluniac order of monks had always had a preoccupation with pilgrimage. They were the great organizers and protectors of the route to Santiago. From their far-off base in central France, they recruited and blessed knights from Burgundy, Normandy and other chivalric regions who would participate in the Reconquest, the *Reconquista*, in Spain. The pilgrim route to Santiago de Compostela was to be reopened as surely as the pilgrim route to Jerusalem: by the twelfth century, on the frontiers of Christendom pilgrimage was the pretext for holy wars. To the churchmen of the day, this did not seem a paradox, as it would have done to the early church Fathers.

There were other inducements too to persuade Christian knights from western Europe to take to the battlefield on the frontiers of Christendom. Land hunger was one. Whether estates in France, Germany or England were split up between a nobleman's sons, or whether they passed entire to the eldest, in either case there was shortage of land to go round. Fresh lands, new estates and uncharted territory were all available as the fruits of a successful crusade. And with papal blessing, glory as well as wealth was to be gained by the acquisition of such land.

But perhaps the most powerful inducement of all was the same inducement that had always led people to go on pilgrimage: the thrill of adventure, and the possibility of breaking out of the strait-jacket of medieval provincialism. To portray a crusade as a pilgrimage was a distortion of the truth; but the fact remained that the motivation overlapped and it was a convenient and reassuring distortion.

To these recurring inducements were added two others in 1095 when the First Crusade was being preached. A year of plague and floods had been followed by one of drought and famine: a foreign expedition might well open up opportunities for emigration to a more stable climate. There were supernatural inducements to add to the economic ones: a shower of meteorites in 1095 led to the widespread belief that the end of the world was at hand or a Second Coming of Christ imminent, and surely, it was argued, the Holy Land should be restored to Christian hands before such a Second Coming on earth? Haste was necessary.

No pilgrimage had ever been promoted with the intense enthusiasm with which the First Crusade was preached; the message reached a wider audience than ever before, but one which was similarly socially diverse: peasants and guild craftsmen, robbers and social delinquents, squires and aspiring knights . . . all joined the throng to seek glory, absolution, wealth or escape from drudgery. In the euphoria evoked by Peter the Hermit – and encouraged by Urban II – there was an element of deliberate obfuscation about the destination: to all it was Jerusalem, but while to some it was the city of that name in Palestine, to others it was the New Jerusalem – a city flowing with milk and honey, a divine destination, an ethereal conglomeration of spiritual qualities anchored in the clouds of heaven rather than the sand-dunes of the Middle East.

It is unnecessary to trace the course of the First or subsequent crusades to the Holy Land to see how quickly and how sharply they deviated from the pilgrimages which they had been their *raison d'être* and on which they had claimed to be based. The sack of Jerusalem in 1099 and the subsequent massacre of its inhabitants was only one, though perhaps the worst, of the reversals of that spirit of Christian humility and charity on which the early pilgrimages – and indeed the whole Christian faith – had been based.

But in one respect at least the First Crusade used the props, if not the spirit, of pilgrimage. Holy relics had always been a major component of the appeal of pilgrim destinations: bones of the saints, blood of the martyrs, pieces of the True Cross . . . again and again it was these that had been the focus of the pilgrims' shrines. Now, when the First Crusade faltered on the road to Jerusalem at Antioch in 1098, the ultimate relic was revealed to encourage them. Peter Batholomew, a poor and none too reputable peasant in the crusaders' army, presented himself at the tent of Count Raymond (one of the military leaders) declaring he had been shown in a vision the whereabouts of the lance that had pierced the side of Christ on the cross – an incomparable relic the discovery and possession of which would inspire the whole crusading force. After much argument and after other visions had been reported, Peter Batholomew was somewhat reluctantly conducted to the cathedral of Antioch (now recaptured from the Turks). Here Batholomew and others witnessed a party of workmen failing to discover the lance at the place which he had identified. To everyone's surprise, Batholomew than leapt into the trench and almost instantly drew out a piece of iron which was immediately recognized as the Holy Lance.

The discovery was not greeted without some scepticism: there were those who reminded the crusaders that there was already an authenticated Holy Lance in Constantinople; others recalled that Batholomew had been involved in a clearing-up operation in the cathedral a few weeks earlier and would have had an opportunity to 'plant' the lance head. The Bishop of Puy was suspicious of the liturgical detail of some of Batholomew's alleged instructions from his visionary interlocutors and, suspecting he had read these up, enquired whether he was literate; Batholomew assured him he was not, but his friends recalled otherwise. All in all, it was not the most convincing of revelations. But good news was not to be discounted: Batholomew and his find were taken at face value, and the crusaders' morale revived.

Even before they reached Jerusalem however, internal dissention had led to further doubts about the validity of the Holy Lance and the honesty or otherwise of Peter Batholomew. These doubts had been fed by Batholomew's maddening tendency to have further visions which resulted in strategic advice – 'straight from the mouth of the Apostles' – to the crusaders' commanders. A supposedly illiterate peasant was, it seemed to many, to be dictating the course of the campaign. At this stage Batholomew took a step which seemed to prove his own conviction in the integrity of his discovery – or else a quite exceptional degree of foolhardiness: he announced he would undergo trial by fire; he would run the gauntlet between bonfires of burning faggots, carrying only his Holy Lance which would protect him from the flames. He was put to the test and failed miserably, emerging from the flaming pathway so badly burnt that he died of his injuries shortly afterwards. Courageous he may have been; credible he was not. The crusaders' attempt to find and deploy their own pilgrim relic had backfired; it was yet further evidence of how difficult it was to establish any real link, or any real claim that a crusade was indeed a pilgrimage.

But others were to try to link the two more successfully. The key to so doing – as always – was keeping open the pilgrim routes. Not only were the Arab rulers of Palestine beginning in the eleventh century to make difficulties for Christian pilgrims when they reached Palestine, but the Turkoman invaders of Asia Minor from Central Asia were cutting off the land routes before pilgrims could even reach the Levant overland at all. Two things were necessary: a standing force to fight off military or brigand assaults on the pilgrims, and a chain of defended hostelries to shelter the pilgrims at the different stages on their journey. These twin objectives were the perceived role of the twin orders of chivalry specifically brought into being to cope with the problems.

The Order of Knights Hospitaller had its origins in the hospital of St John in Jerusalem before the First Crusade, but after the capture of Jerusalem in 1099 they converted themselves into a more ambitious order aimed at providing a whole network of hospitals and hostelries along the pilgrim routes across Asia Minor and the Levant; they even adopted a more ambitious patron saint – St John the Baptist in place of the little-known St John the Almoner. But there was an in-built commitment to charity among the Hospitallers: their hospitals did indeed tend to the sick and dying and (with some notable exceptions, such as Krac des Chevaliers in Syria) were not primarily fortresses; the monastic rigours and military conduct of the knights was modified by the presence of doctors and nursing nuns among them.

The Order of Knights Templar was always the more high-profile and aggressive of the twin orders. It was only founded after the First Crusade to fight off threats to the newly reopened pilgrim route. The assumption that, once the Christian kingdom of Outremer was established in the Holy Land, pilgrims would be able to move freely to their destination was found to be unsound. As early as 1103, an

English merchant named Saewulf was complaining about the hazards and discomforts of the journey; a German abbot named Ekkehard recorded robberies and murders along the route; others reported that any Christian travelling alone on the final stretch through Galilee risked being kidnapped by local Moslems and sold into slavery. This was not the state of affairs for which the crusade had been fought and won. The route had to be policed, and how better than by Christian knights – combining the elements of chivalry and monasticism – stationed in formidable castles punctuating the road to the Holy Land.

The success of the orders was almost immediate. Donations flooded in and they were granted special privileges. The Master of the Templars was independent of the authority of local bishops and answerable only to the Pope. St Bernard declared that to kill a pagan was to win glory; successive popes reinforced the promise of redemption to those who died in battle against the infidel, and some twenty-thousand Templars were killed in action during the two centuries of the order's activity. They were the storm troopers of Christendom – always at the front of the battle, always proud of their prowess, always jealous of their reputation for bravery. But like other elite troops, they also attracted the particular venom of their enemies: Saladin was normally humane in his treatment of Christian prisoners of war, but he always made an exception of Templars who were summarily executed (in the same spirit in which Saddam Hussein nearly a millennium later might torture or kill captured members of the SAS).

The fortunes of the twin orders reflected these different characteristics. The Hospitallers built up a groundswell of goodwill throughout Christendom by their good works, so when they were forced to move on from one location to another new homes were found for them. As the traffic to the Holy Land became increasing seaborne rather than overland (both Templars and Hospitallers had their own pilgrim ships in due course), so they found natural bases first in Cyprus and then in Rhodes and Malta. They endured sieges and assaults from Saracens and Ottoman Turks alike, but they survived to become a permanent charitable institution within the western church. They outlived the medieval world and the great age of pilgrimage.

The Templars did not. Their pride in their military prowess bred arrogance. And as their wealth increased, and their manors and lands spread throughout western Europe, so did the envy and hostility with which they were viewed. The process was compounded by the treasure they amassed and secreted in their castles, and by their practice of usury. Kings and nobles who borrowed money from them developed a vested interest in the destruction of their creditors and the abolition of their debts. The Templars also made the mistake of deliberately cultivating an aura of mystery around themselves and their practices; it was not difficult for the suspicious or the ill-intentioned to attribute sinister reasons for this secrecy: black masses and sodomy were among the more bizarre allegations (as they had been about the Cathars). Their ultimate enemy emerged in the person of King Philip IV 'le Bel' of France who in 1307 arrested the Grand Master of the Templars. He and members of the order were horribly tortured and the Grand Master himself was eventually condemned to be burnt to death over a slow fire. Only in Portugal – a country still deeply grateful to the Templars for their recent part in the liberation from the Moors – did the order survive under the name of the (still existing) Military Order of Christ.

The twin orders that had arisen to protect and succour the pilgrims en route for the Holy Land had both outlived their original purpose long before the conclusion of the age of medieval pilgrimage. But elsewhere other armed movements claiming to be pilgrimages were to get underway. Almost all were disastrous.

If the crusades to the Holy Land had certain pilgrim associations, this was even more the case with the Albigensian Crusade of the early thirteenth century in the Languedoc region of southern France. The crusade or crusades (there was more than one military campaign) were ostensibly to stamp out the Cathar heresy which had taken hold there. The Cathars, who had forgathered in a steady trickle over several decades, particularly in Albi, Carcassonne and Béziers, viewed their journey there partly as a flight from persecution elsewhere, and partly as a pilgrimage to enrol at the feet of the leaders of their movement. The crusaders, on the other hand, who set out to destroy the Cathars root and branch, viewed their march into Languedoc as a way of obtaining absolution from their sins, as they would do on a major pilgrimage or crusade blessed by the Pope. For neither party – Catholic knights or Cathar peasants – was this a real pilgrimage: but both had some reason for feeling that it was and some motive for maintaining that it was.

To understand the ferocity and brutality that attended these crusades, it is necessary first to understand something of the nature of the Cathar heresy itself. It was a form of dualism, that is a belief that, rather than one divinely controlled creation, there are two creations: one a spiritual world controlled by a benevolent God, and the other a material creation dominated by the devil and evil forces. Thus material and physical experiences were all to be discounted and regretted, notably eating meat, drinking alcohol, carnal pleasure and even marriage: man should aspire to spirituality through asceticism. These ideas were not new: they had been the core of earlier cult beliefs, mostly originating in the East. But, as

Jonathan Sumption (the historian of the Albigensian Crusade) has said 'Heresy, like Christianity, tends to move from east to west.'

Dualism had taken root in Armenia in the tenth century, and had spread to Bulgaria and other parts of the Balkans before the time of the crusades to the Holy Land. Soon it had crossed the Adriatic to the east coast of Italy. By the twelfth century it was moving further westward, carried by confused returning crusaders and pilgrims, and even more frequently by traders. It was a migration of ideas as much as of people. First Flanders, the Champagne country and the Loire valley harboured cliques of these heretics. The first dualists to be called Cathars appeared in Cologne in the 1140s. Elsewhere well-educated and rich supporters tried to suborn the Archbishop of Reims. Catharism appeared to the church to be a pernicious infection which contaminated those who came in contact with it. With the Moors still occupying most of Spain, by the time the Cathar heresy had reached Languedoc, on the fringes of the Pyrenees, it could hardly spread further west in Christendom.

At first the reaction of the Catholic church was to combat the heresy by reasoned argument and debate. Preachers inveighed against it. Even St Bernard himself said in the mid-twelfth century that 'errors are refuted by argument, not by force', but when the arguments failed and heresy persisted, then he concluded 'if it appears they [the heretics] would prefer to die than to believe, then let them die'. The year 1163 saw a major burning of heretics in Cologne. Elsewhere lynch mobs moved in where the church held back. The view (later to be expressed by St Thomas Aquinas) was forming that, just as counterfeiters of currency undermined the world of trade, so heresy undermined the world of the spirit: neither could be tolerated. By 1208, despite the spate of intellectual debates, theological tracts and didactic sermons, patience was running out: action had to replace discussion.

The danger of heresies such as Catharism was accentuated by the failing prestige of the established church. The conspicuous wealth and worldliness of prelates and abbots was arousing criticism even in the illiberal atmosphere of twelfth-century France; corruption and loose living within the church were breeding anti-clericalism; an ascetic movement within the church was to prove widely appealing (as St Francis was to discover at Assisi only a few years later); an ascetic movement outside the established church looked distinctly alarming.

Apart from its geographical position on the western flank of Christendom, there were special reasons why Languedoc was a natural haven for heretics. The great landowners and feudal lords of the region, like the Count of Toulouse, owed only the most tenuous fealty to the crown of France. The King of Aragon was an ever-present rival for their alliance. Acquiescence in Cathar practices and views made for an easy life for feudal overlords and a tranquil local regime in which craft guilds could flourish. Many of the aristocracy of Languedoc shared the Cathar beliefs themselves, and even those who did not tended to shelter them and afford protection against overzealous Catholic bishops: Catharism was part of the local culture.

The Pope and the King of France were both deeply unhappy about this state of affairs, and for different reasons. The aspects of Catharism that gave most offence to the Pope were twofold: first, it followed from their dualism that they stressed the humanity rather than the divinity of Jesus (he was, they argued, on earth and not in heaven); and second, they felt that the Pope and the established church were at best superfluous and at worst an obstacle to salvation. The former was evidence of heresy and provided grounds for burning at the stake; the latter provided an urgent motive for carrying out such burning before the privileges and power of the church were further brought in question. The King of France for his part wanted to absorb Languedoc securely within the bounds of his realm.

All that was needed to launch a crusade or a punitive military campaign was an immediate pretext. This was provided on 14 January 1208 by the murder of the Papal Legate, Peter of Castelnau, by an officer of the offending Count of Toulouse. The Legate had just quarrelled with the count about the latter's protection of Cathars, and after the murder the count was reported as having honoured the assassin as the man who had rid him of his enemy: echoes of the murder of Becket at the alleged instigation of King Henry II of England less than forty years before were all too resonant.

Pope Innocent III was not a man to take such an affront lying down. Within two months he had excommunicated (or to be more accurate re-excommunicated) the Count of Toulouse and despatched a letter to the barons and knights of France urging them to 'avenge the insult done to the Lord' and, incidentally, to help themselves to conquered land and properties. The papal indulgence that would provide a further inducement was less than clear on whether it absolved the crusaders from the guilt of their sins, or merely from the penance due for such sins; but with the prospect of an exciting and lucrative crusade so much nearer home than the Holy Land, few were in a mood to raise such theological niceties. The King of France was initially less than enthusiastic about releasing his knights for this semi-domestic crusade because he was currently involved in one of the many preludes to the Hundred Years War with England; but he came round when the material advantages were explained.

In the event the crusade was led by the Duke of Burgundy and a cross-section of knights and feudal lords from across France, supported by a clutch of archbishops, bishops and abbots. The most dashing of the knights was Simon de Montfort, a minor aristocrat from Île-de-France who distinguished himself by rescuing a fellow knight who lay wounded under the enemy's fire, and who was the father of the English parliamentary pioneer. The most notable, not to say notorious, of the clerical group was Abbot Arnald-Amaury of

Cîteaux, who was to prove more bloodthirsty than most of his lay companions.

The Count of Toulouse, who was the original target of the crusade, quickly managed to patch up a personal truce with the invaders of his territory and to shift the main thrust of their attack to the lands and property of his nephew the Viscount of Béziers. So it came about that the city of Béziers was the first Cathar stronghold to be attacked in July 1209. An offer of an amnesty if the garrison surrendered and gave up their known Cathar leaders was conveyed by an aged bishop sent ahead on a donkey, and was rejected out-of-hand. On the day they arrived, the crusaders were just beginning to establish their siege and their first casualty had just been inflicted on them when, to general surprise, the camp-followers, who were setting up the tents for their lords and masters, took matters into their own hands and stormed the gates of the city using their tent poles as battering rams. To the consternation of the besieged and to the amazement of the besiegers, this motley group succeeded in forcing an entry. No sooner had they done so than the onlooking knights charged through the breach and caught the defenders so much by surprise that in a matter of little more than an hour they had captured the city.

The immediate question was how could they tell the innocent citizens from the Cathar heretics who had taken shelter among them? According to legend, the knights turned for guidance to Abbot Arnald-Amaury who promptly replied: 'Kill them all: God will know His own.' Whether the abbot had in fact uttered these oft-quoted words or not, the result was the same: the crusaders set about an orgy of slaughter from which neither men, women, children nor those seeking sanctuary in the churches survived. They then set fire to the town. The massacre was to set the bloody tone of the Albigensian crusade.

The Viscount of Béziers' other stronghold was more formidable. The medieval walled town of Carcassonne stood in 1209 much as it does today: crenellated, high-walled, turreted, forbidding and dominating. The crusaders had no quick fix in this case, but they realized that the fortified districts outside the walls offered the key. These were less heavily defended than the main citadel, but once captured they offered opportunities to advance under cover and mine the walls of the citadel itself. But despite some progress, and a confusing intervention by the neighbouring King of Aragon, the city remained uncaptured. Eventually, having no desire to be left with another burnt-out shell and another pile of bodies, the crusaders offered terms: the garrison could leave with nothing but the shirts they wore 'and their sins'. Their leader, the Viscount of Béziers (and also incidentally Viscount of Carcassonne) was tricked into accepting a false safe-conduct. Simon de Montfort was granted the viscount's titles and possessions. Carcassonne survived intact as a rich piece of plunder for the crusaders.

The progress of the crusade after this was slower and more confused. The Cathars retreated to mountain redoubts built or owned by sympathetic local lords. One after another these bastions built on the pinnacles of rocky outcrops in the foothills of the Pyrenees (their ruins are still to be seen at Termes, Quéribus, Peyrepertuse, Puilaurens and other sites) fell to the crusaders. Toulouse itself changed and rechanged hands. A pattern of bonfires emerged: when bastions surrendered often the garrisons were granted immunity if they recanted, but the Cathar leaders themselves ('the Perfect ones' as they were known) seldom recanted and almost invariably ended up being burnt at the stake in large numbers – four hundred at Lavaur alone (more than 'Bloody Mary' was to burn during the whole of her reign in England four centuries later).

As the crusaders returned home (often claiming that their operational commitment did not bind them beyond forty days) Simon de Montfort fought on with a nucleus of hardened troops. In

1218 he was himself killed by a stone thrown by a catapult from one of the positions he was besieging at Toulouse. Arnald-Amaury, that other pillar of the early crusade, lost the confidence of the Pope. And still the Cathars and the local warlords continued their guerrilla resistance to the Pope and the central authority of the King of France.

Eventually, in 1224, King Louis VIII of France launched his own more secular campaign – though still dubbed a crusade – against the remaining Cathars and their protectors. Although this time the driving force was the King of France and not the Pope, the campaign train still included a full complement of bishops and abbots, as well as a vast tail of the sick and the sinning, who had (in Jonathan Sumption's words) 'been drawn by an older tradition which made the crusade a form of mass-pilgrimage' which would include indulgences and benefits even for mere camp-followers. The campaign ended in 1229 with the total absorption of Languedoc and the surrounding territory into the consolidated kingdom of France. Temporal victory was complete, but still nests of heresy persisted. A final solution was required.

St Dominic had early in his career established his reputation as a preacher when deployed to argue against the Cathar heresy at the time of the original crusade against them. After his death, the Dominican order which he had founded was to play a somewhat different role in combatting heresy in Languedoc. Dominican monks were to be the main prop of the newly instituted Inquisition which was set up in Albi and other parts of Languedoc to flush out the remaining heretics after the French king's campaign. As a new papal institution, the Inquisition had unparalleled powers: they were answerable to no one but the Pope himself; they were not only the investigators of heresy, but the prosecutors and judges of the heretics they uncovered; there was no appeal against their verdicts; they tried by every means possible – including torture – to extract confessions from the accused, because such confessions usually implicated others also; those who ran away before interrogation were excommunicated and their property seized; they meticulously recorded all their findings (and it is from such records that much of our knowledge of the Cathars derives); lawyers who attempted to defend the accused were treated as accomplices in heresy; witnesses were allowed anonymity, so the accused seldom knew the origin of the charges against them; nor were the Inquisition above using agents provocateurs when they ran out of evidence. In short, many of the methods associated in the twentieth century with the KGB or the Gestapo could be traced back to these early Inquisitors.

An element of hypocrisy also accompanied some of the Inquisition's practices. Not all those convicted were burnt or condemned to life imprisonment in fettered solitary confinement; some were prescribed punitive pilgrimages to difficult or dangerous destinations; other were stripped of their fortunes by onerous fines; some had to wear marks of their disgrace whenever they went out of doors (again, an ugly foretaste of Nazi anti-Semitism). The hypocrisy emerged from the fact that all these penalties were nominally 'voluntary penance' and not punishments. The catch-22 provision was that if the convicted did not accept his penalty (if he tried to escape from prison or ran away from his pilgrim route) this was taken as evidence that he had lapsed into his former heresy and was therefore a proper subject for excommunication and hand-over to the secular authorities for 'the usual treatment' – burning alive.

It was little wonder that such methods often provoked a hostile reaction. In Cordes-sur-ciel (one of the most charming of Cathar hill-towns, to the north of Albi) some Inquisitors were lynched; elsewhere their offices were ransacked and their records were burnt. All over Languedoc there were instances of them being in physical danger as a consequence of the fear and hatred in which they were held. The Inquisition responded by entrenching itself more firmly and conspicuously in the region. The massive red-brick walls and fortress-like appearance of the cathedral in Albi reflects the fact that it was built to provide a headquarters and shelter for the Inquisitors, as well as to intimidate the citizens of a town which had traditionally been a hotbed of Catharism and had indeed given its name to the Albigensian Crusade.

Montségur, a mountain-top fortress which had taken in Cathar refugees over many years, surrendered in 1244 with two hundred unrepentant Cathars throwing themselves on to the bonfires that had been prepared for them; and the last Cathar castle, Quéribus, fell in 1255; but the last Cathar spiritual leader, Guilhem Bélibaste, was not betrayed and burnt until 1321. Long before that date the Inquisition had effectively eradicated the Cathar heresy from Languedoc. The process had been aided by the fact that the heretics' protectors were feudal lords with much – castles and lands – to lose; they had therefore either collaborated with the Inquisition or moved to other properties elsewhere. In their absence the Cathar leaders and rank-and-file had nowhere to find permanent refuge; they were reduced to moving from one safe-house or another, or from one forest hideout to another; eventually one of their hosts would betray them or one of those they encountered in their travels would turn informer. And as surely as the heretics had disappeared from the scene, so the crusaders had returned to their native lands. Only the agents of the King of France, the newly established French nobility and the remnants of the Inquisition remained.

What had started as a fancied 'pilgrimage' by Cathar enthusiasts and by militant crusaders, both intent on an adventure, had – in the event – proved to have little in common with the mainstream of European pilgrimage. The church had seen itself as threatened and had overreacted. The events that had taken place had left behind them charred bodies, ruined castles and much bitterness, rather than that aura of sanctity that hung over the sites of true pilgrimage.

One armed uprising which was determined to establish its credentials as a pilgrimage occurred in the north of England in the 1530s,
during the reign of Henry VIII. The motivation for the uprising was,
at least in large part, religious: the peasants of Yorkshire and other
parts of the northern counties were distressed by the Dissolution of
the Monasteries, which deprived them of their most generous
patrons in an age when social security and support for the poor was
seldom seen as a responsibility of the monarch or his government,
and was far more usually left to the church. The abolition of most
saints' days, with their attendant holidays and festivals, was also
deeply resented. Many of the clergy and some of the gentry shared
these feelings with their tenants and labourers. The recently introduced new order of prayer upset conservatives across all classes of
society, and — added to their social grievances — provided a further
focus for discontent.

It was against this background that Robert Aske, a London lawyer
from a landowning Yorkshire family, raised a rebel army and captured the city of York on 16 October 1536. He immediately set
about justifying his actions in a series of public manifestos and
proclamations. These took the novel step of referring to the uprising
as 'a pilgrimage for grace' or 'a pilgrimage of grace for the commonwealth'. Like most uprisings in medieval and Tudor times (such
as the Peasants' Revolt of 1381 which had claimed Richard II as their
friend) its leaders professed their loyalty to the crown and that
their purpose was to rid the monarch of his evil or misguided
advisers. In this case the villain in their pack was Thomas Cromwell,
the king's chief minister, whose humble (or 'vulgar') origins caused

added resentment to the gentry and aristocracy who still felt that royal counsellors should be drawn from their own ranks.

The Pilgrimage of Grace – for as such it was henceforth to be known – professed therefore to be guided by religious and loyalist motives: a pilgrimage to invoke not only God's grace but the king's grace also. Henry VIII would, the rebels hoped, be retrieved from his heresies and would respect the rights of the people – or commonwealth. By dubbing the rising a pilgrimage, Aske was also being deliberately provocative, because among the royal injunctions of the previous year had been one ordering priests to denounce pilgrimages on the grounds that they encouraged parishioners to indulge in undue adoration of saints and their relics, rather than of God himself. The name was an ingenious but also disingenuous device of Robert Aske (as Professor Michael Bush, a leading historian of the event, has pointed out) to give his movement an added mantle of respectability.

Having once decided they were on a pilgrimage, the rebels tried to consolidate and embroider the idea with various practices and props. They took pilgrim oaths and vows. They adopted crosses as their emblems, and enlisted priests to carry them at the head of their columns. (The priests were often alarmed at the implications of being so publicly associated with the revolt and often slipped away in the night back to their cathedrals or parish churches.) To make the point even more strongly, the banner of St Cuthbert – a northern saint and hero – was also borrowed from Durham to be carried by the rebels. One of their supporters, Lord Lumley, who had crusader connections, supplied a banner which represented the five wounds of Christ (as on the Portuguese national coat of arms). As they marched south, the rebels chanted a song which spoke of 'Christ crucified, for Thy wounds wide, Us commons guide, which pilgrims be'. Everything was done to stress the pious and dedicated nature of the enterprise.

But in reality there was no disguising the fact that it was an armed rebellion first and foremost and the pilgrimage element was a cosmetic device. Equally, it was primarily a peasant and labourer movement. The clergy who went along with it were often coerced, and they had in any case already collectively accepted (in Convocation and in the House of Lords) the changes and reforms which they were now being pressed into opposing. The aristocracy and gentry were generally no more enthusiastic than the clergy; most of them only joined the movement as an alternative to having their castles or houses burnt down by the rebels. Many wrote to the king explaining they were only acting under duress and would revert to loyal conduct at the earliest opportunity. (Henry VIII was predictably unimpressed with such feeble protestations, though he pretended to go along with them to avoid further antagonising the landowners.) More selfishly, many of the northern grandees were not at all opposed to the Dissolution of the Monasteries as this often meant the redistribution of church lands to them. So the uprising was not all it was presented as being.

Certainly Henry VIII had no doubts from the start that he was dealing with naked treason and that the revolt deserved to be put down with all the ferocity that such treacherous actions justified. Talk of pilgrimages and seeking the king's grace fell on deaf ears in Whitehall and Hampton Court. The uprising had initially begun in Lincolnshire and had been promptly classified as 'a traitorous assembly' there; the more extensive Yorkshire movement was to be treated the same. Henry despatched an army to the north and told Cromwell that he should make 'the fat priests pay for it'. The rebels for their part were by now heavily armed and, having coerced many of the local gentry to their side, seemed less intent on seeking grace than on imposing their demands by brute force.

Whether or not the uprising could properly be described as a pilgrimage, it was undeniably the case that religious issues were at the forefront of the conflict. At Sawley Abbey, near Clitheroe, the rebels ejected the squire who had taken over the property from the church and reinstalled the abbot and his monks. When Henry heard this he ordered the Earl of Derby to go to Sawley and hang the abbot and all his monks in their habits from gibbets attached to the steeple of the abbey church, so that the whole countryside might see their fate and draw appropriate conclusions.

Lord Derby found himself with too few troops to carry out such orders, and even the Duke of Norfolk (who was sent by Henry to command the royal army) argued that it would be more expedient to grant the rebels a pardon and discuss their grievances with their leader. Very reluctantly Henry agreed, and sent a safe-conduct to Aske, saying he understood he had repented of his actions and inviting him to come to London to be his guest over Christmas at Greenwich. Aske accepted and fell under the spell of Henry's false charm and hospitality. Aske believed the king's assurances that he would make a royal progress through the north of England and hold a meeting of Parliament there to address any supposed wrongs. When Aske travelled north again himself after Christmas, it was to pass on these assurances and to try to frustrate any further spread of the revolt.

But Henry – who had wanted to hang Aske from the start – was in an unforgiving frame of mind. He decreed that his pardon had expired and all those who had come out in revolt after 7 December 1536 ('the eve of the Nativity of the Virgin') were not covered by it. The king even recruited notorious robber barons from the Scottish border region of the Cheviots to help arrest suspected rebels; these borderers behaved so badly that they provoked an armed response from formerly quiescent regions of Westmorland. The king then ordered 'dreadful execution' by hanging and quartering was to be done on those who had been provoked into further revolt; those monks who had escaped the first wave of hangings at Sawley and the monks from some half dozen other northern abbeys were also hanged without more ado. The Duke of Norfolk reported that he had hanged so many in chains that he had run out of iron to make the chains. But still Henry's desire for vengeance was not sated: he had a score to settle with Aske.

Henry wrote to Aske thanking him for his part in discouraging further revolt and again inviting him to London. This time he did not offer a specific safe-conduct, but Aske – confident of the king's gratitude – came south. No sooner had he arrived than he was clapped into the Tower. Here he was interrogated by the dreaded Thomas Cromwell who was at his most devious. Cromwell fastened on the fact that Aske had used the king's promise that he was going to come north to hold a Parliament as an argument for persuading potential rebels that they should stay at home in the confidence that their grievances would be addressed; but, Cromwell went on to argue, this implied that if the king had not given such an assurance they would have been justified in coming out in revolt; that implication amounted to high treason on Aske's part. In the face of such malign tortuosity there was no hope of a fair trial or pardon. Aske was duly hanged in chains at York, and numerous other 'fellow conspirators', including abbots and priors of disaffected religious houses, were duly beheaded, burnt alive, or hanged, drawn and quartered.

The rebellion had not spread. Only the misguided citizens of Walsingham were foolish enough to declare themselves in sympathy with the northern rebels, and a number of them were also hanged, drawn and quartered in consequence. It had been a bloody end to a supposed 'pilgrimage'.

14

Pilgrimage and the Black Death

THE BLACK DEATH struck Europe at the very height of the medieval enthusiasm for pilgrimages. By the middle of the fourteenth century, the journey to Jerusalem had been reinstated after the crusades. The journey to Rome had been given an immense fillip by the centenary Holy Year of 1300. Santiago de Compostela was enjoying the prospect of permanent liberation from the Moorish occupation. Canterbury was basking in more than a century of adulation for its martyred St Thomas. The Reformation, with all its awkward questions and criticisms, was still well into the future. The devout of Europe were taking to the sacred tracks in larger numbers than ever before.

Then, quite suddenly, in 1348 a disaster was unleashed on Europe which was not only unprecedented but which called in question the very foundation of faith and the very fabric of society. It might have been foreseen, but it was not. Even before 1346 there had been vague and possibly fanciful reports of a series of natural disasters in China – the far-away and unknown kingdom of Cathay. Floods and famines, earthquakes and swarms of locusts, plagues of serpents and scorpions, pestilence and death were reputed to be stalking that twilight land fleetingly revealed by Marco Polo but both before and since shrouded in mystery. Whatever happened in the distant Orient could hardly be considered relevant to emergent Europe. Trade routes were tenuous at best and hardly to be thought of as sources of contamination.

So it was hardly surprising that no precautions were taken. Even when the pestilence reached as far west as the Crimea, and the Tartars who inhabited the region blamed this on their Christian minority, it occurred to no one that Christian refugees from Asia Minor to the seaboard cities of Italy might be dangerous guests. In fact, the refugees in question had had contaminated bodies catapulted into their fortified trading stations by the besieging Tartars, and they brought the infection directly from Feodosia to Genoa.

When the good citizens of Genoa realized that their visitors were responsible for an outbreak of plague, they reacted with a natural selfishness that spread a local disaster into first a regional and then a continental one: they banned their port to further galleys from the East, and these dispersed to other mercantile ports. Soon Venice, Messina, Marseille and other centres of Mediterranean population were experiencing the oriental pestilence – bubonic plague.

Because trade routes, like pilgrim routes, had proliferated in previous decades, the plague spread with extraordinary rapidity. By June 1348 it had reached as far west as Andalusia, as far north as Bordeaux and Paris, and as far east again as Dubrovnik; by the end of 1348 Calais and Bristol were collecting their dead; by June 1349 London, Norwich, Strasbourg and Bavaria had succumbed; and finally by the end of 1349 nowhere was safe from Dublin and York to Denmark and Cologne.

Although rats and fleas – the main carriers – were not the prime suspects, it was early recognized that contagion could be immediate and fatal. The touch, breath and proximity of the infected – identified by their sinister boils – were abhorred. Whole families were bricked up, dead and alive together, in Milan and elsewhere. In other places, walls were constructed to incarcerate the privileged uninfected – together with their food and necessities – to try to insulate them from the infected common herd. Like most disasters, the plague brought out the best and the worst in humanity: some priests and many friars tended the dying with a selfless disregard of danger; others deserted family, friends or flock at the first whisper of fear.

But however well administered or slipshod the measures taken by the authorities to stem the plague, the bulk of the population of medieval Europe did not view this as primarily a medical or administrative problem: it was a religious and ethical one. Even the administrative measures taken to control the immigration of poss-ibly infected travellers were influenced by considerations of religion: in Venice a quarantine station was set up at the Nazarethum where new arrivals were detained for forty days and forty nights – a figure fixed not from any medical calculation but because of its significance as the period of Christ's sojourn in the wilderness. A disaster of such proportions (it was calculated that a third of the urban population of western Europe died of the plague within three years) could only be an act of God – a retribution on a guilt-ridden humanity. The fact that the clergy suffered as severely as the laity, the rich as severely (at least in some cases) as the poor, only showed that sin was not a monopoly of the uneducated and unprivileged. The plague may have fostered anti-clericalism among Lollards and thoughts of revolt among peasants, but it did not turn Christians against their God. Rather, it brought religion to the forefront of the mind in an age already obsessed with religion.

How did this affect pilgrimage? It appears to have done so in a variety of ways not always consistent with each other. Two factors conspired to make the decision to set off on any long journey less than an attractive one.

First, it had rapidly become apparent to the authorities in cities across the continent – be they Canterbury, Cologne, Santiago or

Rome – that visitors could be couriers of the plague. Their access to wells was viewed as a likely source of infection. Lopez de Meneses records that in June 1348 a group of Portuguese pilgrims were suspected of poisoning (presumably unintentionally) the wells in Aragon and had to be given a safe-conduct home. Similar charges were brought against English pilgrims at Narbonne in France.

Secondly, pilgrims – however self-sufficient they might aspire to be – were dependent on local facilities and administration. If bridges fell into disrepair, hostelries were closed, roads flooded and mountain passes left unsigned, progress was virtually impossible. And if, coupled with this, churches and monasteries were shut down because of the death or evacuation of the inmates, the prospect of hospitality – or even the objective of the pilgrimage itself – could be undermined. On the other hand, all over Europe there were Christians who had vowed that if they or their loved ones survived the plague they would demonstrate their gratitude by going on a major pilgrimage on the first possible occasion. As congregations across Europe contemplated the awesome effects of the plague, rather than a growth of scepticism or revulsion (as might be expected today) there was in fact a growth of religious fervour. God might move in a mysterious way, but his wrath and power had been alarmingly demonstrated. Death had always been an ever-present companion to medieval life, but in the years of the plague the grim reaper had focused men's minds on the after-life with a vividness never experienced before. Memento mori did not need to be inscribed on pictures and monuments: it was explicit in all around.

And so – although the health-conscious citizens of Rome were somewhat taken aback – it did not come as a total surprise when Pope Clement VI succumbed to pilgrim pressure from communities throughout Europe and declared 1350 (only a bare year after the plague had peaked) to be another Holy Year with special indulgences for pilgrims. They flocked in. In fact, the number was as great as in 1300, although the population of Europe had decreased by between a quarter and third. One local chronicler, Matteo Villani, estimated the influx at a million souls. As Philip Ziegler – the author of the still unsurpassed history of the Black Death – comments, although this figure may be exaggerated, the influx of pilgrims from all over Europe was immense.

The Pope was taking a considerable gamble by inviting so many pilgrims so soon after the worst of the plague, as one early arrival was to discover. The Lady Bridget of Sweden (later to become St Bridget) timed her pilgrimage to reach Rome in 1349, and she preached the renunciation of worldly goods – especially rich clothing – in favour of giving alms to the sick and poor. Her message was greatly boosted by her intervention in the case of a plague victim who had been despaired of by his doctors; Bridget came to his bedside and laid her hands on him undeterred by risks of infection, and the patient made an immediate and complete recovery. It was a case of a pilgrim bringing healing and redemption rather than seeking it as a reward: even the Pope was impressed.

At Canterbury, too, the flow of pilgrims was not noticeably reduced by the plague: indeed, many Englishmen thought a quick pilgrimage might be timely. The burghers of Canterbury were less enthusiastic about arrivals from other parts of the country more affected than Kent, but they took no measures to stop the flow which had by then become part of the ethos as well as part of the economy of the town. The citizens of Kent and London have never been easily deterred by blitz, unexploded bombs or other hazards from going about their normal business.

Neither the Pope, the Archbishop of Canterbury, nor anyone else had reckoned with one new sort of pilgrim who emerged from the horrors of the Black Death. The Flagellants were a German phenomenon, but not a very attractive one. They were bands of men and, surprisingly often, of women too, who were so obsessed with the need to expiate their sins, in the face of the massive divine retribution that was taking place, that they chastised themselves with whips which would now be described as cat-o'-nine-tails – leather thongs with leaded weights or implanted nails. As so often, self-inflicted violence led to more widespread violence.

The Flagellants marched from town to town and from village to village on self-dubbed 'pilgrimages' moving from one church to another and from one religious community to the next. The 'Brotherhood of the Cross', as they called themselves, had originated further east in Hungary, but as they marched and counter-marched across Bavaria, Saxony and other parts of Germany they struck fear and awe into the communities which they invaded. They had a military appearance which led many of their 'hosts' to see them more as a predatory crusading unit than as a contrite band of pilgrims. They marched in column, or crocodile, two abreast with the Master and his standard-bearers at their head. Parish priests and congregations that did not welcome them were bullied and cajoled into providing an arena and an audience for their brutal spectacle of self-flagellation. Their chants were menacing:

> Ye murderers and ye robbers all,
> The wrath of God on you shall fall.
> Had it not been for our contrition
> All Christendom had met perdition.

Usurers were singled out for special condemnation.

And usurers were of course usually Jews. Just as the Tartars of the Crimea had blamed the unpopular Christian community for the first outbreaks of the plague there, so the Flagellants blamed the Jews for poisoning wells and spreading the plague in other ways. Although usury – under its more user-friendly name of banking – was already surfacing as an acceptable activity in some of the Italian city states and elsewhere, money-lending at street level was essentially a Jewish occupation. With so many small traders and impoverished farmers in debt to a seemingly grasping and alien race, it was not surprising that the Jews became a natural target for blame and

192

hatred, and their extermination a tempting economic objective for many: debts would cease to exist if the creditor ceased to exist.

So it came about that the Black Death and the Flagellant pilgrimages resulted in one of the worst pogroms in medieval history. As Ziegler observes: 'Few doubted that the Black Death was God's will but, by a curious quirk of reasoning, medieval men also concluded that His instruments were to be found on earth and that . . . it was legitimate to destroy them.' And destroy them they did. There was a massacre of Jews in Provence in the spring of 1348. At Chillon later the same year a number of Jews under torture confessed to poisoning the wells. This became the most general charge against them and recurred in different cities and provinces all over Europe. The fact that the Jewish community were often more fastidious than their Christian neighbours and so avoided the use of wells situated close to sewage outlets – preferring to draw their water from fresh-water streams – lent credence to the concept that they were responsible for polluting the urban and village wells. Lepers (another feared and despised minority) were often accused of the same crime, and sometimes of acting as paid agents of the Jews. Among the horrific legacy of a Flagellant pilgrimage was a trail of Jews burnt at the stake or crippled by torture. In Strasbourg alone, two thousand Jews were murdered in 1349. The following year, Jewish families in various Hanseatic towns were bricked up in their houses and left to starve to death, even when they were not plague-carriers. Only in England was there no general persecution of the Jews in the wake of the plague, but this was largely because, after the expulsions of 1290 when Jewish money-lenders were largely replaced by Lombards, they were thinner on the ground and represented less of an economic threat.

Eventually, the grossness of the Flagellants' behaviour, coupled with the suspicion that – moving as they did from one centre of population to another – they were spreading the very plague they purported to be campaigning against, led the church to take a stand against them. Pope Clement VI published a bull calling for the end of practices which offended all but the most brutal and frightened of Christians.

What then was the conclusion of the whole affair? The arrival in Europe of the Black Death, at the peak of the medieval passion for pilgrimages, could well have been a permanent set-back for that activity. The criss-crossing of Europe's highways and byways by bands of travellers whose journeys had no economic necessity was a self-evident health hazard. Ignorant the authorities might have been about the causes and carriers of the plague, but its infectious nature was never in doubt. When one considers the immediate fall-off in travel in the twenty-first century following incidents of terrorism, one can only wonder at the resilience or rashness of medieval authorities who allowed the cult of pilgrimage to continue almost without faltering.

Equally, when one considers the shock that was inflicted on a religion-obsessed society by an unprecedented 'act of God' which destroyed nearly one in three of the population, one wonders that faith and devotion survived. But not only did faith survive, so did the practice of pilgrimage. The great adventure of the Middle Ages was not deterred by an extra quota of danger both to the pilgrims themselves and to their hosts. An act of God of such awesome scale only seemed to reinforce men's desire to prepare themselves for that death which so obviously and dramatically lay in ambush for them. Indeed, in the emergence of the Flagellant movement in Germany a new and perverse form of pilgrimage emerged for the first time: movement of religious activists for its own sake and unrelated to any particular shrine. Happily this consequence of the plague was a short-lived phenomenon, because its violence and its attendant anti-Semitism – always a light sleeper in medieval Europe – were seen as pernicious.

In one respect it could perhaps be argued that the Black Death had diminished the urge of the lower strata of medieval society to go on pilgrimage. After the Black Death there was some scarcity of labour and a consequent greater mobility. It was easier to slip away from a village or estate, to cross over the parish border or even into another county. A market for itinerant labour developed which had not existed before. For peasants, pilgrimage was no longer quite so uniquely the only way of leaving the feudal estate. But peasant pilgrims were so few on the ground that this factor did not represent a major change.

The overall conclusion remains: despite all the odds, the biggest natural disaster in Europe's recorded history changed little for those whose resolve was to be a pilgrim.

15

Sir John Mandeville: the Literary Pilgrim

Among all the tales of the returning crusaders and pilgrims from the Holy Land, one had an overwhelming influence – and that one was a total prefabrication, if not a fraud.

Sir John Mandeville's *Travels* which appeared, originally in French, in *c*.1357 purported to be an account of a journey first to the Holy Land and then on to the far Orient. It was soon translated into English and had an immense and enduring success, ranking alongside Marco Polo's account of his travels (both books being taken by Columbus on his original transatlantic voyage more than a century later).

The first and foremost of the book's dubious aspects is the existence of the author himself. Mandeville claims to have been an English knight, born in St Albans in 1322. He then allegedly 'had been long time over the sea, and have seen and gone through many diverse lands'. In view of the origin of the book in French, many scholars, including those responsible for earlier editions of the British Library catalogue, have attributed it to another shadowy figure, one Jean de Bourgogne. Some theories maintain that the two men were one and the same. One reason for a possible change of name was that Mandeville had killed 'a person of rank' in his youth and had thereafter been obliged to go on the run – or on 'his travels', as the case may be. Some internal evidence in the book also suggests that the author was an Englishman: there are references to 'we in England'. But from the point of view of his readers and generations of potential pilgrims, the question of authorship is less material than a number of other questions.

Chief among these is: were the travels genuine? The answer is a resounding negative. Much of the material included is palpably false: even in the fourteenth century and even in the remotest sectors of the road to Cathay, there were not to be found men with their heads growing below their shoulders. Nor were giants fifty feet high to be encountered. Neither were there 'Sciapods' – men with one foot who could sit using their outsized leg as an umbrella – to be found in Ethiopia.

Many of the most bizarre features of Mandeville's book are related to, or at least interconnected with, the whole raft of mythical tales centring on the figure of Prester John, the supposedly Christian monarch who reigned somewhere in the Orient. Some thought Prester John was descended from the Magi and had set out on an armed pilgrimage to assist the Christians in the Holy Land, devastating the Medes and Persians on the way. Pope Alexander III in the twelfth century was so convinced of the existence of this allied monarch that he addressed a letter to him. Marco Polo in the thirteenth century placed Prester John in India and thought he had been killed by Genghis Khan. Peter Covillanus in the fifteenth century placed him in Ethiopia, as did others. Medieval Christians who headed further east than Jerusalem always thought that they might encounter this legendary figure or his descendants, and turn their journey into a pilgrimage or a holy quest by so doing. Even Prince Henry the Navigator of Portugal in the fifteenth century hoped that his sea captains – financed as they were by the Order of Christ – might come across evidence of this Christian figure. Mandeville himself tended to place Prester John in some extreme quarter of the Orient beyond China, and to think that he was descended from Ogier the Dane – one of Charlemagne's paladins. No provenance was too extraordinary, no locality too remote. And so the Prester John legend made Mandeville's other bizarre tales somewhat less improbable to medieval – and even Renaissance – minds.

But despite this Mandeville uses some elaborate devices to suggest that the contents of his book are the literal facts: he refers to having broken his journey at Rome to show his account to the Pope who accepted it as true. He also interpolates remarks such as 'this I saw not' or 'I was not there', which imply that other reportage without such qualifications was first-hand experience. Many were convinced, even centuries later, of the basic veracity of his account: Samuel Purchas (writing about 'his pilgrims' in the early seventeenth century) described Mandeville as 'the greatest Asian traveller that ever the World had', and explains away the more obvious falsehoods by suggesting that there were fables added by itinerant friars with more imagination that credibility.

Other writers were less convinced. Robert Burton, the seventeenth-century author of *The Anatomy of Melancholy*, declared that Mandeville was a liar; this had also been his verdict on Marco Polo. Sir Thomas Browne, whose seventeenth-century writings also spanned the whole range between theology and science, reached much the same conclusion.

But even his most sceptical later critics could not deny that many of the strange facts related by Mandeville turned out to be based on truth, and often very surprising truth. Just as some of Marco Polo's wildest inventions were believed, and some of his more accurate observations were totally disbelieved, so Mandeville's readers often repudiated the fact and accepted the fiction.

In reality, the book is a compendium of earlier travellers' tales, some true, some false. Chief among his sources was Friar Oderic, who wrote a similar travelogue some thirty years earlier. Mandeville implies that for part of the journey he was in company with another friar, which some commentators (notably Malcolm Letts) have interpreted as an attempt by Mandeville to suggest that he was travelling with Oderic and therefore not guilty of plagiarism. He had shared the experiences, not borrowed or invented them. Just as Mandeville was in fact lifting much of his narrative from other writers, so later writers were to lift much from Mandeville: Münster's *Cosmographia*, which ran to nearly fifty editions in seven languages in the century following its publication in 1544, was just one example of 'borrowing' from Mandeville.

Mandeville's great achievement lay in inspiring his contemporaries and successors to go on travels and, more particularly, on pilgrimages. But he was also an advocate of renewing the crusading ardour of the previous centuries. The disasters of St Louis (Louis IX of France) on his crusade a century before, the fall of Acre and the subsequent set-backs for militant Christendom, made another attempt to reconquer the formerly Christian kingdom of Outremer unlikely. But at the time Mandeville was writing it was not only unlikely but virtually impossible, because Christendom was at war with itself. The Hundred Years War between France and England had broken out some twenty years before, and was at its most active stage: the battle of Poitiers was the year before the estimated date of the *Travels* appearing. Nor was it likely that the church could present a unified front any more than the lay rulers could do: the Pope had been driven from Rome in 1309 and moved to Avignon, and the luxurious lifestyle of the church establishment was attracting criticism from new and more frugal orders such as the Franciscans. There was neither the civil nor the ecclesiastical motivation for another crusade to the Holy Land.

And it was not only in the Levant that Christendom had received a set-back. Further east the Tartar hordes had swept across Asia to the point where – effectively for the first time – they were confronting the West. There was a new awareness in Europe about the far horizons. Many were in shock at the prospect of these invaders; their success was a symptom of the decadence of Christendom, and – like the concurrent Black Death – a sign that divine wrath had descended on the principalities of the West. Something had to be done if anything was to be saved.

To others in the West, the Tartar incursions presented an opportunity and a challenge. If the intruders could be converted to Christianity, or even loosely harnessed to the church's chariot, then they might prove a decisive ally in the war against the old enemy, Islam. Missionary friars and other daring and resolute Christians set out to contact and persuade the Tartar warlords of the possibility of an alliance or at least an accommodation. Perhaps the Tartars were not unmitigated bad news after all. Journeys eastward were not restricted to missionaries; traders too had begun to explore the caravan routes to the East and to exchange merchandise with those who had come from far-off Cathay. Travel and adventure were in the air in the second half of the fourteenth century and some of Mandeville's sources (if not Mandeville himself) were among the pioneers.

Jerusalem was for Mandeville not just the obvious and ultimate pilgrimage destination, it was also the centre of the world as he defined it. He was still living in the mindset of the Middle Ages: the world was round and, as the Old Testament Book of Ezekiel made plain, 'I [God] have set it [Jerusalem] in the midst of the nations.' Mandeville might or might not have been familiar with the *Mapa Mundi* (now in Hereford Cathedral) but he certainly shared its vision of a world centred on the Holy Places and peopled with weird monsters – of the sort he describes – round its periphery.

Against this background, where exactly did Mandeville's supposed travels take him? The first part of his book is devoted to the route to the Holy Land. Mandeville assumes that most of his pilgrims will go overland, passing through the lands bordering the Danube and on to Constantinople, and then down the Syrian coast to Palestine. All sorts of details intended to convey verisimilitude are included: the waters of the Danube, for instance, are said to enter the sea with such force that their 'fresschness and swetness' is carried twenty miles out from the coast; and the statue of Justinian in Constantinople has lost the golden apple from the emperor's hand which is indicative of the territories he has lost in his empire. Mandeville is greatly impressed with the opulence of the Byzantine capital and remarks that even in the emperor's stables the pillars are made of marble. There is a strong flavour of tourist guidebook about his descriptions.

Mandeville also dips into the troubled waters of the doctrinal differences between the eastern and western churches. He notes with displeasure that in Constantinople they say that the Patriarch has 'as meche power ouer the see as the Pope hath on this syde the see' and goes on to argue that the Christian faith should all be one. He disapproves of the fact that the emperor has both spiritual and temporal jurisdiction over his subjects. He also records with displeasure the fact that their priests are married and they do not consider usury a sin, and – worse – that fornication is not a deadly sin 'but a thing that is kyndely [natural]'. He is also appalled that in the Byzantine empire shaving off beards is considered to be a deadly sin because they argue that 'the berd is tokene of a man and gifte of our Lord'. This is not only a guidebook but also a moral manual.

Like all medieval pilgrims, Mandeville was obsessed with relics. When he reaches Constantinople he devotes much space to analysing the nature of the True Cross (what wood was it made of?) and the Crown of Thorns (how much of it was still there and how much had been sent by St Louis to Paris?). He is at pains to point out that this is the real True Cross and that the other claimant to the title – in Cyprus – is in fact only the cross on which the good thief was hung at Christ's side. Having traversed Asia Minor, Mandeville includes in his pilgrim route a number of the Aegean islands. Patmos is particularly recommended as the island where St John wrote the

202

Apocalypse before, Mandeville maintains, dying at the age of a hundred in nearby Ephesus. That city is also an important staging post where the ground around St John's grave, Mandeville tells his readers, is continually being stirred up and opening because the saint is not dead but resting there under the Day of Doom: 'forsooth,' he declares, 'it is a great marvel.' In fact, Mandeville never misses a chance to provide the sort of fascinating and controversial detail that would intrigue potential pilgrims and make them feel they ought to go and see these things for themselves.

His enthusiasm for another crusade, another military campaign to the Holy Land, is illustrated by the detail with which he describes the approach routes to Jerusalem; some passages are almost as if he were writing a manual for military commanders, with details of the Saracen forces and the potential of cities to resist sieges. Such a campaign was extremely unlikely to occur and, if it had, the commanders would have been very ill-advised to follow Mandeville's data. As always, this is lifted from other sources, with more imagination than accuracy. It is however an indication of his preoccupation with establishing a viable route to Jerusalem, both for pilgrims and for those (the Knights Templar had just been disbanded but the Knights Hospitaller were still active) clearing the way for pilgrims.

When he reaches the island of Longo (Kos), Mandeville embarks on one of his more fantastical tales: the daughter of Hippocrates has been transformed into a great dragon that is a hundred fathoms long. The author is careful at the outset to take no responsibility for this story, declaring that he has not personally seen the dragon in question. The tale that follows must have been a familiar one, even by the fourteenth century, but is none the worse for that. It seems that the only way for the dragon to be restored to being a maiden is for some knight to come along and kiss the dragon on the mouth; a knight of Rhodes (the Hospitallers had moved there in 1310, thus establishing for Mandeville a crusading and pilgrim link) volunteers for the job, but when confronted with the full horror of the dragon's appearance, takes fright and is duly cast into the sea by the dragon – 'and so was lost bothe hors and man'. Later we are told that another young man surprises the dragon in her maiden form and asks to become her paramour; on discovering however that he is not a knight, the maiden sends him away and tells him to return when he has won his spurs, to kiss her on the mouth – even if she happens to be in her dragon mode – and to become her lord and inherit her wealth and the whole island. The young man manages to get himself made a knight and returns, but – like his predecessor – is so alarmed by her dragon form that he runs back to his ship. On seeing this the dragon sheds a princess-like tear 'as a thing that had meche sorwe [sorrow]' and returns to her cave – disillusioned no doubt with the chivalric credentials of the Order of Hospitallers. Mandeville has managed to turn an old fable into a piece of current folklore and relate it to his preoccupation with crusades and pilgrimages.

And so the tour continues. Practical details about wines and local customs in Cyprus alternate with historical information about the sultans of Babylon. Here Mandeville says he has some special knowledge, as he claims to have dwelt with the sultan as a soldier in his wars against the Bedouin. He certainly has a distaste for everything to do with the Bedouin, describing them as 'folk fulle of euyille [evil] conditions' and scorns the idea of living in tents made out of the skin of camels 'and other beasts that they eat'. He cannot sympathize with people who do not till the land and only scrounge bread from neighbouring settlements. His account of how the Bedouin roast meat and fish on stones heated by the sun suggests that he was, as usual, basing his story on fairly sketchy sources. Altogether he concludes that the Bedouin are 'right felonouse and foule and cursed kynde', which probably reflects the fact that they tended to harass the pilgrim routes and occasionally to kidnap pilgrims for ransom.

Like so many subsequent western travellers in the Middle East, Mandeville also reveals his fascination with the sexual practices of the harem. He recounts how the sultans have their concubines paraded before them and choose whichever takes their fancy on any particular night. In thus titillating the interest of pilgrims by recounting the more exotic and erotic aspects of Arabian culture, Mandeville is an early pioneer among the many travel writers who were to do the same in succeeding centuries, including during the supposedly shockable Victorian era.

When he comes to Egypt, Mandeville is predictably interested in aspects which would appeal to pilgrims. He writes at some length about the garden outside Cairo where the Virgin Mary was said to have rested on the flight into Egypt, and a nearby field where the wells were made by 'our lord Jesus Christ with one of his feet when He wente to pleyen with other children'. Even the pyramids of Egypt are given a biblical connotation: Mandeville claims they are the granaries where Joseph stored corn during the seven 'lean years' of famine, and dismisses the more accurate findings of other travellers that they were burial monuments. Mount Sinai and St Catherine's monastery are included in the itinerary, and there are descriptions of the site of the burning bush and the various wells and springs from which Moses was able to refresh the Children of Israel during their long years in the wilderness, including the one which sprang from the stone which Moses smote with his rod. Later we are introduced to the Dry Tree, which was in the Garden of Eden and which shrivelled on the day of the Crucifixion and can be expected to sprout again only when 'a lord, a prince of the west syde of the world' shall recapture the Promised Land and sing a celebratory Mass under the tree. Later still, he tells us of a monk who climbed Mount Ararat in Turkey (seven miles high and covered in snow all the year round according to Mandeville) to bring down a plank from the Ark as a relic to reside in a local monastery. Every step of the way is enlivened with relevant stories of pilgrim attractions and hints that it is up to Christians to keep open the way to the Holy Land.

When he reaches Bethlehem he introduces a story which appears more original than most. He describes how 'a faire mayden' was falsely accused of fornication and condemned to death. When the faggots were lit, she prayed to God for proof of her innocence and immediately red roses sprouted where the flames had been and white roses where the faggots had not yet been kindled. This, Mandeville confidently asserts, is the origin of the rose – a highly symbolic flower in the age of chivalry.

Now, by Chapter 10 of his book, he is approaching Jerusalem itself, where he lays out the whole range of attractions for pilgrims who may follow in his supposed footsteps. One such is the wall built round the Holy Sepulchre to protect it from the overenthusiastic attentions of devotees who 'breke the stone in peses or in poudre'. Another is the pillar to which Christ was bound before he was scourged, and which is surrounded by other pillars of stone which are always dripping water, indicating that they are 'weeping for our lordes deth'. A further highlight is the circle on the church floor in which Joseph of Arimathaea laid Christ's body after the deposition from the cross: this spot is designated the centre of the earth. There is, Mandeville insists, so much for the Christian pilgrim to see.

Although Jerusalem is the culmination of the early part of Mandeville's *Travels*, he goes on to describe in the second and longest part of his book the regions further east. Now he is leaving the pilgrim routes behind him and is away in the world of Marco Polo with ever less credible accounts of events and natural features in pre-Mogul India and the Cathay of the Great Khan. It is here that the headless men with faces below their shoulders and the other weird and wonderful flights of imagination really take off. He is no longer bound by the conventions of Christian mythology, legend and tradition.

Mandeville's *Travels* were an instant success across Europe. Of the 250 surviving manuscript copies, only some forty are in English, but there are about fifty in Latin, about forty in French, about seventy in German or Dutch, and the remainder in a variety of European languages. It appealed to laymen who preferred French or English to Latin, because it was essentially a 'popular' rather than a theological work. Jean sans Peur, the leader of the disastrous crusade in 1396 that ended in the defeat at Nicopolis, possessed his own copy (a fact that would doubtless have gratified Mandeville). Some abbeys and launching points for pilgrimages – notably St Albans in England – disseminated the book widely. With the introduction of printing a whole new popularity was given to the work, doubtless in part because this coincided with a new age of discovery and exploration.

Where Mandeville breaks new ground is the implicit link he establishes between pilgrimage and adventure, between going on a journey for the sake of redemption and going on a journey for the sake of sightseeing and curiosity about the world beyond the accepted horizons. His book was the spur to generations of travellers setting out from western Europe to the Middle and Far East. Just as the exploits of Patrick Leigh Fermor or Fitzroy Maclean might have inspired a generation of young British men in the second half of the twentieth century to take the road to Constantinople or the Golden Road to Samarkand in search of self-enlightenment and random encounters, so Mandeville inspired multiple generations across a whole continent to take to the road on a quest into the unknown. However flawed his provenance and veracity, Mandeville was the best advocate ever of the daring pilgrimage.

16

John Bunyan: the Allegorical Pilgrim

WITH THE DISSOLUTION of the Monasteries in England, and the Reformation and Counter-Reformation on the continent, the late sixteenth century seemed to mark the end of the age of pilgrimage in Europe. The adoration and veneration of saints, the sanctity of their shrines, and the efficacy of their relics were all being denied, called in question or – at least – discounted.

John Foxe in his *Book of Martyrs*, published in England in 1563, had inveighed against pilgrimages: his heroes were quoted as denouncing a practice that smacked of idolatry by suggesting that miracles could be worked by 'dead images' rather than by God alone; money was better given to the poor than spent on self-indulgent pilgrimages; women in particular should stay at home and look after their husbands rather than go cavorting around the countryside. A number of popular pilgrim attractions – notably the Rood of Grace at Boxley Abbey in Kent – had been exposed as total frauds: figures were manipulated 'to goggle and nod' by monks working wires and levers for the purpose of encouraging donations, which often ended up by swelling the coffers of the Pope in Rome. Among the homilies to be read in Elizabethan churches were ones which decried the 'madness of men' who wasted their time and substance journeying by land and sea to 'Compostela, Rome, Jerusalem and other far countries'.

All this caused a dramatic fall-off in the numbers taking to the pilgrim roads in England, and a serious reduction of those on the continental routes also. Not only had Protestant countries firmly set their faces against the practice, but Roman Catholics too – in the aftermath of the Counter-Reformation – were being discouraged from practices long associated with abuse, such as excessive attention to shrines and relics, and the earning or purchase of indulgences which often went hand in glove with pilgrim visits to designated Holy Places. It might have been predicted that preoccupation with pilgrimages would go the same way as the pilgrimages themselves – into obscurity if not into terminal decline.

In fact, nothing could have been further from the case: the closing years of the sixteenth century and the opening years of the seventeenth century saw something akin to an obsession with pilgrimages. As Professor N.H. Keeble has pointed out,* Protestant preachers were forever comparing the Christian life to a journey. Ever since the days of the Lollards in the fifteenth century, even those who disapproved of going on a pilgrimage to a shrine were perfectly happy to use the *language* of pilgrimage as a metaphor for the Christian life. Now these Lollard views (which would have been heresies earlier) were gaining a new and wider currency. In the 1540s, a record was published of the trial of Sir John Oldcastle, who – more than a century earlier – had made the distinction between the physical and the moral pilgrimage: 'every man dwelling on this earth is a pilgrim,' he says, but goes on to point out that this is equally so even if, 'he never in his life go on pilgrimage . . . to Canterbury, Walsingham, Compostela, and Rome, or any other

* In his essay in *Pilgrimage*, edited by Morris and Roberts (see bibliography).

such place else'. In fact, he argues, pilgrimage is a frame of mind rather than a literal achievement.

Another Lollard whose views were published in the mid-sixteenth century (when those views were becoming fashionable for the first time) was William Thorpe. He identified elements in the appeal of pilgrimages which had always existed, but which had not usually been so explicitly recognized, when he said that many undertook pilgrimages 'more for the health of their bodies than of their souls . . . more to have here worldly and fleshly friendship, than for the friendship of God'. In fact, as in the case of the Wife of Bath and so many others, a springtime pilgrimage was more a recreational activity than a spiritual one. Now this was being condemned as evidence that physical pilgrimages were not true pilgrimages.

The issue was further complicated by the fact that by the early seventeenth century the words pilgrim and pilgrimage were beginning to be given an extended non-religious meaning which enveloped other sorts of travel. The record of English exploration entitled *Purchas his Pilgrims*, published in 1625, was in practice a continuation of Hakluyt's *Principal Navigations, Voyages and Discoveries of the English Nation* and had nothing at all to do with religion. With this wider meaning, journeys that had other motives altogether – such as art-purchasing jaunts to Italy (the precursors of the Grand Tour) – might be described as pilgrimages. The blurred terminology could be useful in practical ways too: Professor Colin Morris has pointed out that when Nicholas Lanier went to Italy in 1625 to buy pictures for Charles I's royal collection, it was convenient to describe the trip as part of a pilgrimage to the Holy Land so as to disguise its commercial nature and avoid raising expectations of paying high prices.

But at the more thoughtful and reflective level, for the Protestant, and even more for the Puritan, the true pilgrimage was not a progression from one place to another but a steady spiritual development. Bishop Hugh Latimer, preaching in 1552 just three years before he was burnt at the stake for his Protestant views, made the explicit distinction between a spiritual experience which he described as 'a certain pilgrimage which may be called the Christian man's pilgrimage' and 'the Popish pilgrimage, which we were wont to use in past times, running hither and thither'. By extension, Jerusalem becomes for the first time a concept rather than a place (even if Blake's vision of having 'built Jerusalem in England's green and pleasant land' was not to emerge for another two centuries). George Herbert and Henry Vaughan, those leading lights among the Metaphysical poets of the seventeenth century, both wrote poems about spiritual pilgrimages. Sir Walter Raleigh, never a great one for political correctness, went even further in his 'Passionate Man's Pilgrimage' (supposedly written when he was awaiting execution) and rehearsed all the details of a pilgrim's kit – his scallop-shell of quiet, his staff of faith, his scrip of joy – all having an allegorical significance.

Despite the theological emphasis on spiritual rather than physical progress, there was still a great preoccupation with movement as a Christian activity. John Milton (a much more puritanical figure than Raleigh) found that the true Christian was a 'wayfaring Christian'. Reformation divines extolled biblical figures such as Abraham and Moses as nomads and travellers; they were much given to quoting the passage from St Paul's Letter to the Hebrews in which he praises the ancient Fathers who 'confessed that they were strangers and pilgrims on the earth' and who thereby demonstrated that they 'seek a country'; evangelists and nonconformist ministers travelled widely propagating their faith; and it was significant that when a group of Puritans set out from Plymouth in 1620 to seek greater religious freedom in the New World, they were dubbed 'the Pilgrim Fathers'. Travel and pilgrimage remained valid Christian concepts, however discredited the old pilgrim routes and pilgrim destinations of Europe might have become. Adventure might no longer be looked for on the highways and byways of Kent or northern Spain, on the plains of Lombardy or in the deserts of Syria, but it was to be found in the struggle for salvation: the country they sought was no longer Jerusalem but the New Jerusalem.

But by far the most influential of all the puritanical thinkers and writers about this new style of pilgrimage was of course John Bunyan. And Bunyan's story follows in great detail the form of a real-life pilgrimage, basing its spiritual adventures on the actual hazards which had for so long beset those who walked the great pilgrim routes of Europe. It is in many ways ironic that the greatest literary homage to pilgrimage should have been written at a moment when the actual practice of pilgrimage was in sharp disfavour and decline.

If Chaucer's *Canterbury Tales* is the most obvious pilgrimage in English literature, John Bunyan's *The Pilgrim's Progress* must be the most celebrated allegorical pilgrimage not only in English literature but in any literature. It has been translated into 108 different languages and is believed never to have been out of print since it first appeared in 1678. As a work of fiction it pre-dates Defoe's *Robinson Crusoe* by more than forty years; and as a religious and spiritual guide it has outstripped every work in English except the Bible itself.

There is no record of Bunyan himself ever having been on a pilgrimage, but he had seen a lot of the highways and byways of life before he wrote his great work. Born in 1628, the son of a tinker in Bedfordshire (and in consequence taunted throughout his life with being a vagabond), he had fought as a soldier on the Parliamentarian side in the English Civil War, and narrowly escaped being killed when another soldier who had taken over his watch was shot through the head. Returning to civilian life, and possibly having been influenced by the Puritan preachers in the army, he turned to religion – giving up such dangerous vices as reading ballads and bell-ringing. Soon he was notorious as a controversial preacher, but the regular clergy resented such uneducated and unordained 'mechanick preachers' and – on the restoration of Charles II in 1660 – he was imprisoned for unlicensed activities. He was to remain in Bedford prison (though sometimes apparently allowed out on parole) for the next twelve years, largely because he refused to give an undertaking not to revert to preaching. Even after he was released – following a generalized royal pardon – in 1672, the fear of rearrest hung over him, and he spent one further short spell in gaol. He had been a prolific writer as well as preacher for most of his life, and by the time of his death in 1688 he was famous not only in his own country but across the Atlantic in New England also.

And this fame was essentially based on the masterpiece he had worked on throughout most of his time in prison and which he entitled *The Pilgrim's Progress from this world to that which is to come, delivered under the similitude of a Dream, wherein is discovered the manner of his setting out, his dangerous journey, and safe arrival at the desired country*. It might not instantly have been a bestseller under the same title today, but the seventeenth-century enthusiasm for religious controversy was unbounded.

Although the popularity of *The Pilgrim's Progress* has never been in doubt, its originality has sometimes been disputed. There had been other allegories of a Christian's progress through this world's temptations and dangers, mostly published in France or Holland, before Bunyan's time, just as there were to be many afterwards – notably C.S. Lewis's *The Pilgrim's Regress*; but Bunyan certainly would not or could not have come across them. A more likely source of allegorical method and ideas was Spenser's *The Faerie Queene* written nearly a century earlier, in which an individual Christian (in Book I) is seduced by false religion and finally triumphs with the help of Truth. But again it is unlikely that Bunyan would have studied Spenser's poem, and in any case the differences are far greater than any similarities. His flashes of humour, his pungent use of quotations from the King James version of the English Bible, and his feeling for the Bedfordshire countryside (much augmented by a wild *Lord of the*

Rings-type dramatic scenery) are all his own. Above all, the idea of setting his parable as a pilgrimage was Bunyan's own.

Of course the main allegory is a representation of the trials and tribulations of Christian life in general, transposed into the dangers and hazards of a pilgrim's journey; but there is also the allegory of the specific real-life dangers of a pilgrim's journey, transposed into the imagined and fanciful dangers of his mythical hero's adventures. It is worth looking at just some of those dangers and hazards facing a seventeenth-century pilgrim, and how Bunyan portrayed them.

Losing the way was the most frequent hazard. Even on the well-marked routes to Canterbury or Santiago de Compostela, directions were often not identifiable and pilgrims strayed off the route: easier terrain lured them off the straight and narrow. Bunyan's hero – the aptly named Christian – and his companion Hopeful find that the way along the river they are following is rough and 'their feet tender by reason of their travels'. When therefore Christian spies 'a meadow and a stile to go over into it', he sets about persuading Hopeful that 'here is the easiest going . . . let us go over'. Hopeful, a maddeningly smug and cautious character, replies: 'But how if this path should lead us out of the way?'

Once they have left their proper path they fall in with a certain Mr Vain-Confidence who encourages them further out of the way. Things start to go wrong. First Mr Vain-Confidence falls down a deep pit and is heard groaning at the bottom. Then the weather breaks and it begins to 'rain and thunder, and lighten in a very dreadful manner'. Hopeful immediately begins to moan: 'Oh that I had kept my way! . . . I was afraid on't at very first, and therefore gave you that gentle caution. I would have spoke plainer, but that you are older than I.' (It could be a conversation about where to picnic from any century.) There then follows an argument as to who shall lead them back to the correct route, with the insufferable Hopeful saying: 'You shall not go first, for your mind being troubled, may lead you out of the way again.' Eventually, with rising waters from the river cutting off their retreat, they lie down where they are and fall asleep. Worse troubles await them.

As well as the fear of losing the way, seventeenth-century pilgrims had the much worse fear of falling into the hands of local robber barons – often on the pretext that they had been trespassing on the baron's lands and estates and were therefore fair game to be robbed or held to ransom. This is exactly what now happens to Bunyan's hapless hero.

Christian and Hopeful wake in the morning to find none other than Giant Despair looming over them and asking 'with a grim and surly voice' what they are doing trespassing on his property and 'trampling in and lying on my grounds'. He drags them off to Doubting Castle and throws them into a dungeon without food, water or light, where he beats them up with his 'grievous crab-wood cudgel' before advising them to 'make away with themselves either with knife, halter or poison'. Hopeful argues against suicide and eventually, just when they are about to die of hunger and thirst, Christian remembers that he has 'a key in his bosom called Promise' which miraculously opens the inner and outer gates of the dungeon and castle and they both escape back over the stile and out of the giant's jurisdiction. Not many of Bunyan's contemporaries who fell foul of the authorities – whether on pilgrimage, in the Civil War or as a result of unlicensed preaching – would have been so fortunate. The message is clear: do not give in to Despair, however dire the circumstances.

Just as real a danger to seventeenth-century pilgrims as losing the way or being captured would have been falling into vice and corruption. Wealthy pilgrims were inclined to treat their pilgrimage as a Grand Tour, stopping to make luxury purchases or follow up introductions to affluent gentry along the way, thus undermining the penitential purpose of the journey. Poorer pilgrims were more likely to fall prey to bouts of drunkenness or even to the charms of loose women who frequented the inns and hostelries. Bunyan's hero had his share of these temptations too.

Early in his pilgrimage Christian finds his route takes him through the town of Vanity, renowned for its year-long Vanity Fair. The merchandise at the fair includes 'places, honours, preferments, titles, lusts, pleasures and delights of all sorts, as whores, bawds . . . silver, gold, precious stones, and what not'. At all times the fair is frequented by jugglers, cheats, fools, knaves and rogues and 'here are to be seen too, and that for nothing, thefts, murders, adulteries, false-swearers' and other distractions. Bunyan — like the good puritan he is — is at pains to point out that 'the ware of Rome and her merchandise is greatly promoted in this fair . . . only our English nation, with some others, have taken a dislike thereat'.

When Christian and his then companion Faithful arrive at the fair they cause consternation on three counts: their plain clothes, their biblical speech and their lack of interest in the goods offered. This last causes particular offence and the pilgrims are duly arrested and put into a cage where they can better be mocked and reviled by the inhabitants. Predictably, their behaviour is so impeccable that some of the citizens start taking their side and a brawl ensues for which Christian and Faithful are blamed as provocateurs. They are brought to trial and accused by witnesses with names such as Envy and Superstition of speaking ill of such prominent citizens of the town as Lord Carnal-Delight and Sir Having Greedy. Finally they are condemned to death and the unfortunate Faithful is burnt at the stake. Christian inexplicably escapes again, having resisted all the temptations of the fair. Once more they prove to be models of how a puritanical pilgrim should conduct himself on pilgrimage and resist the lures of greed and the temptations of the flesh.

The most obvious problem for any long-distance walker, be he a pilgrim or a hiker, is having to carry the weight of all his clothes and essential gear. Bunyan makes his pilgrim's backpack into a deeply allegorical burden: when Christian scrambles up hills he does so 'not without great difficulty, because of the load on his back' which represents the weight of troubles and commitments he has brought with him from his former life. But when he is startled by a vision of the cross, his burden falls from his shoulders and is a problem no longer. The moral is surely not just that the burden of sin is relieved by forgiveness, but also that true pilgrims should not bring too many unnecessary goods with them, and that they should leave behind them the anxieties and ambitions of their previous worldly lives.

Another concern of all who went on pilgrimage in the seventeenth century or at any other period was the company and companionship they would have on their journey. Chaucer's Canterbury pilgrims had been a diverse group, but had gone to great lengths to entertain each other en route. Bunyan's pilgrims soon fall in with a certain Mr Talkative who overtakes them and engages them in conversation, claiming to be going to the same destination and suggesting they travel together. Faithful is at first taken in by him and suggests (for he too can be somewhat smug) that they should 'spend our time discoursing of things that are profitable'. Mr Talkative displays a marked capacity to witter on in a platitudinous way on any subject: 'I will talk of things heavenly, or things earthly; things sacred, or things profane; things past, or things to come; things foreign, or things at home . . .' There is no end to his well-meant offers of conversational topics. But Christian has previously met Mr Talkative in his home town, where he came from the Saywell family and lived predictably in Prating-row, and has the measure of him. He is, it seems, all talk and no action. So after an excruciatingly boring few pages of dialogue with Faithful, Mr Talkative is dismissed as a good riddance. Once again, Bunyan has put his finger on one of the recurring hazards of the pilgrimage: the sort of companion whose over-friendly first advances seem initially to be welcome, but who soon becomes a tedious and unwanted hanger-on. The road to

Glastonbury or Canterbury must have been crowded with such over-gregarious characters.

Worse than the unwanted companion was, of course, the companion who deserts in time of need. Christian's original companion is one such – Mr Pliable. When they both fall into the mire known as the Slough of Despond, Pliable manages to scramble out on the near side and – after a few accusatory remarks – abandons Christian to struggle alone in the bog while he sets off back home. When Pliable gets back he sits with his neighbours 'sneaking among them' and deriding Christian for the folly of having set out on such a perilous enterprise. Christian meanwhile wallows on across the Slough of Despond, much weighed down by his backpack of which he has not yet been relieved, until helped out on the far side by a friendly hand. The need to choose staunch companions from the start is clearly the moral of this incident.

The Slough of Despond is representative of the natural hazards that lay across most pilgrim routes in the seventeenth century. We have seen how forests that lay across the Pilgrims' Way between Winchester and Canterbury had necessitated halts to collect up a sufficiently strong party to risk venturing into terrain that was vulnerable to ambush. Pilgrims to Glastonbury in the west country risked stumbling into the sort of moorland bogs that were to swallow up the villains in *Lorna Doone*. On the road to Santiago there were ravines into which the unwary or overtired could fall. And deserts had always taken their toll of those venturing as far afield as the Holy Land. Bunyan's tale would not have been complete as an allegory of pilgrimage without some such natural obstacles.

A more minor set-back, but a very real and recurring one to most pilgrims, was due to absent-mindedness or tiredness leaving behind or forgetting vital items of equipment. Bunyan makes both Christian and his wife Christina (the heroine of the second part of his book) lose through carelessness items they can ill afford to be without. In Christian's case it is his roll (a sort of passport that will ensure his entry to the Celestial City) which he drops while taking an afternoon nap in a pleasant arbour when he should have been pressing on with this day's journey. When he discovers his loss he is disconsolate and retraces his steps, happily finding the roll (or scroll) where he had dropped it. Christina, following in his footsteps on her later journey, loses her Bottle of Spirits (which must presumably have been purely medicinal) at almost the same spot and sends a boy back to fetch it. Her companion reads her a pious lecture about staying alert at all times. Certainly for Bunyan's contemporaries losing documents on a pilgrimage could be as serious as losing a passport today, since on many routes – notably that to Compostela – it was often necessary to have a licence from the pilgrim's home bishop (in England or in France) to ensure a proper reception as a genuine pilgrim on arrival at the destination, where many bogus pilgrims – vagabonds or traders – tried to cash in on the hospitality offered. Once again Bunyan was making a valid point.

In Bunyan's book it falls to the arch-villain Apollyon to enunciate one of the most insidious dangers that can befall the pilgrim on any route and at any time: 'to be inwardly desirous of vain-glory in all that thou doest', in other words, to go on pilgrimage with the motive of gaining admiration and worldly credit for so doing, rather than with the proper motive of seeking spiritual benefit. Christian does not deny this charge, but tells Apollyon he is confident that 'the Prince whom I serve is ready to forgive'. Bunyan, with his ever-sensitive puritan preoccupation as to whether he himself was in truth one of the Lord's Elect and therefore destined for heaven, must have seen wrongly motivated pilgrims as one of the many categories of persons he despised and against whom he wished to warn his readers.

Another category towards whom Bunyan was explicitly opposed was of course the Roman Catholics. We have already seen that the wares of Rome were looked upon as among the most pernicious in Vanity Fair. Even before Christian reaches the town of Vanity he has been exposed to Giant Pope sitting at the mouth of a cave in front of which Christian has to pass by on foot. But although the Pope is surrounded by the bones of earlier pilgrims whom he has 'cruelly put to death', Bunyan tells his readers that 'by this place Christian went without much danger' because Giant Pope 'though he be yet alive, he is by reason of age, and also of the many shrewd brushes that he met with in his younger days, grown so crazy, and stiff in his joints, that he can now do little more than sit in his cave's mouth, grinning at pilgrims as they go by, and biting his nails, because he cannot come at them'. In other words, Bunyan is saying that Rome and Catholicism are a spent force. But the words which Giant Pope is reported as muttering as Christian goes by still have a sinister ring: 'You will never mend, till more of you be burned.' The Marian persecutions of a century earlier in England had clearly not been forgotten.

This anti-papist prejudice makes it all the more extraordinary that in the Palace Beautiful, which Christian is shown round by such delectable damsels as Discretion, Prudence and Piety, he is taken to view a collection of sacred souvenirs: such objects as Moses' Rod, the Trumpets with which Joseph put to flight the armies of Midian, the Jaw bone with which Samson slew so many, and even the Sling and Stone with which David killed Goliath. It might have been thought that for a Puritan, who tended to discount the cult of relics – such as the ubiquitous pieces of the True Cross – such objects would have aroused scepticism rather than uncritical admiration.

But Bunyan must have known that viewing relics of this kind was an important part of most pilgrimages, so they too found their place in his allegory of the Christian life, which he tied so closely to the real, everyday hazards of those who set out with staff and scrip to tread the rough routes across Britain and Europe.

17

A Personal Epilogue

Not only when writing this book, but for many years before, I have indulged my fascination with pilgrimages. I have made them the theme and objective of holidays. I have gone out of my way to seek out significant features of pilgrim routes: a castle here, a monastery there. I have wanted to see the sights that the medieval characters in this book had seen. I have wanted to stand where they had stood, to be awed and exhilarated by the experiences they had had.

This has made me not so much a pilgrim myself as a traveller with a pilgrim fixation: it was not the destination, still less the relics that were believed to make the destination holy, that attracted me. It was the path. For me to travel was always better than to arrive: to glimpse the distant view of Santiago or Canterbury, of the mountain of Sinai or the island of Iona, of the cupolas and vineyards of Mount Athos . . . this was what I sought rather than to receive absolution in that Catholic, Orthodox, Presbyterian or Anglican basilica towards which I had directed my steps.

But this is not to imply that I was in any way cynical in my approach to pilgrimage, or even to the pilgrims whom I have selected to describe in earlier chapters. Some of the latter may have been snobs, bullies or bigots, tiresomely mystical or dubiously pious, but I respect them all for what they did. Their journeys were dangerous; and a journey should have an objective and what better than a spiritual one?

Nor do I wish to imply that I was unmoved by the atmosphere of the pilgrim destinations. To me, the sacred qualities of the places which my chosen characters have visited half a millennium ago, and which I have visited in recent years, were derived not so much from the bulging reliquaries and the assorted bones of saints as from the atmosphere of sanctity that comes from prayer, and the atmosphere of peace that comes from fulfilment. So it is in that spirit that I shall end my book with some brief recollections and reflections on my own pilgrim travels.

The Sinai desert is one of the world's bleakest quarters: Moses and the Children of Israel found that their forty years there often seemed more dire than their slavery in Egypt. The desert itself is harsh; the mountains are high, rocky and bare; everything is dusty; and on the rare occasions when it rains, flash floods make the gullies into death traps. I found myself there after I had read Brother Felix Fabri's description of his pilgrimage to Mount Sinai and St Catherine's Monastery, so I knew what to expect, and was careful not to wander off and lose my bearings and my companions as he had done.

The climb to the top of Mount Sinai (or Mount Moses, Mount Musa or Mount Horeb as it is variously known) is still a steep one, though the cutting of 3,750 steps by pious monks has made it easier than it was when Brother Felix was needing to pull and push one of his fatter companions up the vertiginous slope. (Some of the steps – one wonders which? – had already been cut before Brother Felix's ascent in 1483.) On the top there is a chapel dedicated to the Holy Trinity and built in 1934 on the site of an earlier one that was already there in Brother Felix's time. The view is as inspirational as he said: 'a mount inhabited by God and frequented by angels; a mount of light, fire and burning; a mount of trumpets and noise, and a mount of visions and contemplation'.

If architecture should be a reflection of the purpose of a building, then there is no doubt that St Catherine's Monastery is primarily a fortress. Four-square, with walls nearly fifteen metres high and several metres thick, with its towers, and with a conglomeration of disparate buildings – churches, belfries, even a mosque – within its walls, it resembles a small medieval village. There was good reason for the fortification: Bedouin tribes have always roamed this region and their inclination to loot any settlement would have been enhanced by the fact that this settlement was so conspicuously an infidel one. After the sack of Constantinople by the western crusaders in 1204, the monks must have feared Christian as well as Moslem incursions. But the Orthodox monks did not only build high walls to protect them from the Bedouin and others; they also tried to fend them off by kindness and to placate their Moslem neighbours. The original gateway to the monastery had not been at ground level, but – for security reasons – nine metres up the wall; it had not only been used to hoist up visitors and provisions, but also to lower provisions to the Bedouin without the walls in time of famine or hardship. The tiny mosque within the walls was not only an insurance against attack by belligerent Moslems, but an active centre of worship for the casual Bedouin workers who were intermittently required to help the monks with their construction projects. The monks may have been unfriendly to Catholic pilgrims at the end of the fifteenth century, but they knew they could not afford to be consistently hostile to the followers of Islam who dominated the surrounding desert.

Within the walls there is a chapel dedicated to St George and another dedicated to the Burning Bush – the latter is thought to be on the exact spot where Moses first saw this remarkable phenomenon. Since God had instructed Moses to remove his footwear on approaching, it was hardly surprising that we were enjoined to do the same. The relics of St Catherine – guarded by attendant angels on the summit of her mount until carried down by the monks – are predictably preserved in a magnificent reliquary beside the altar in the basilica. There is a gallery devoted to the monastery's collection of icons: some are as early as the sixth century and most of the rest date from around the time of Brother Felix's visit in the fifteenth century. A few more recent items rigorously maintain the spirit and tradition of this medium. One is awed by the consistency of an Orthodox art form that can preserve its austere vision of Christ and his saints from the early Middle Ages until the present, while the artists of the western church stagger through fashions of mysticism, formalism, romanticism and sentimentality. The stern Pantocrator of the Greek and Russian church was at no risk of being portrayed as a benevolent Scoutmaster.

But the greatest treasure of the monastery is arguably neither the relics in the basilica, nor the icons in the gallery, nor the bushes growing behind glass cases, but the library. There are some four thousand manuscripts – many in scroll form – ranging from texts in Greek and Hebrew to others in Arabic, Coptic and Slavonic languages. They lie (or did when I was there) on dusty shelves, some with wire netting in front to repel curious or light fingers, and others alarmingly open to book-lifters. There is, alas, a long tradition of purloining treasures from this library. The German bibliophile Constantin Tischendorf made a predatory visit in the mid-nineteenth century and carried off the Codex Sinaiaticus (the earliest existing copy of the New Testament) which he stuffed

226

into the saddlebag of his camel and which was the glory of his private collection until it eventually ended up in the British Library in London. Tischendorf maintained that he found the manuscript in a log basket and about to be used to light a fire in the monks' refectory, from which he saved it for posterity; the monks claim that he got the librarian drunk and swapped the priceless treasure for a bottle of schnapps.

My own guide to the library was a young monk of Serb extraction called Brother Vladimir who was good-looking and charming, despite his somewhat tattered habit and – when in proximity to him – an aura that suggested that not only shaving but also showering was not on his daily agenda. I was the only visitor who had expressed an interest in the library and – with a welcoming courtesy in marked contrast to the cold reception Brother Felix had received – he took me off to a quiet corner of the library for a conspiratorial chat. I imagined I was going to be told some lurid story of western larceny, but he had another story in mind, a surprisingly – almost shockingly – unecclesiastical one, which I have heard since in after-dinner speeches but had not heard before.

Did I realize, he asked, that the monastery stood on the spot where Moses, after descending from the mountain with the tablets bearing the Commandments, had discovered the Children of Israel worshipping the golden calf? Yes, I assured him, I did. Did I know what Moses had said when he called the Children of Israel together after his second visit up the mountain to receive the revised Commandments, after he had smashed the first? No, I didn't, I confessed. A wicked smile spread over Brother Vladimir's face: 'Moses gathered them round him and asked them which they wanted to hear first – the good news or the bad news. The good news, they said. The good news, Moses told them, was that he had persuaded God to limit his Commandments to ten only; the bad news was the adultery was still included!' As we chuckled over his risqué story, I felt the dust off the library shelves wafting up to

227

rebuke and choke us. I murmured my thanks and emerged from the sombre gloom of the library into the harsh sunlight of the desert, and turned our Land Rover towards the coast and the Gulf of Aqaba.

Mount Sinai and St Catherine's Monastery had never been one of the major pilgrimage destinations of the Middle Ages or of any subsequent time; but to those who have been there it will always – as Brother Felix declared – be an esoteric and engagingly remote objective. And, despite an irreverent monk, a very moving one.

As we have seen, those on the pilgrim route to Santiago de Compostela in the Middle Ages varied greatly in status, style, origin and motivation: the same is true today.

Those who wish to qualify as a genuine and full pilgrim obtain a pilgrim 'passport' and have it stamped at all the main staging posts – basilicas and chapels – along the way; they then have their credentials verified in Santiago and attend the pilgrim service in the cathedral, when the mighty *botafumeiro* swings low, carrying its clouds of incense over the heads of the weary, grubby, often unshaven, but physically and spiritually fulfilled pilgrims packed into the pews. It is the culmination of many weeks of foot-slogging or – in the case of a significant minority – horse-riding.

We did not attempt the full qualification for pilgrim status, but we followed the route religiously – in every sense of the word – from Vézelay in Burgundy, over the Pyrenees and along the 'royal French path' through the Basque country, Navarre, Asturias and Galicia, until we eventually arrived at the majestic *parador* Dos Reis Catolicos facing the cathedral of Santiago de Compostela across its crowded plaza. We walked long stretches of the way, choosing those sections which ran through unspoilt countryside, snaking over hills and through forests, beside streams, and skirting fortified hill villages and ancient shrines. In this way we deliberately sought out the unchanged – indeed eternal – aspects of the route; we shunned stretches that bordered main roads or that struggled through towns and suburbs. But we did not fail to include in our halts the main features of the Camino de Santiago which had changed little from medieval times: the great basilicas of Pamplona and Burgos, of Fromista and León. In this way, although we may not have gained points in heaven, we were able to enrich our experience with constant echoes of the past, going back to the times of St Francis, John of Gaunt or Sir James Douglas, with his precious hand-luggage containing the heart of Robert the Bruce.

Vézelay is a good starting point for any religious enterprise. The lofty Dominican abbey towers over the pretty French village illustrating the dominance of the spiritual over the secular. Itself a pilgrim destination, having early acquired relics of St Mary Magdalene, it was the rallying point for the Second Crusade in 1146 and the scene of St Bernard's rousing sermon on that occasion; it was also the rendezvous for Richard Coeur de Lion of England and Philip II of France in 1189 before they set out on the Third Crusade. It was always a favourite assembly point for French pilgrims – and others from further afield in Germany or Scandinavia – who wished to make the journey across Europe to Santiago. Today, those with a head for heights can climb the wooden flights of steps to the top of the tower. (Descending is more alarming, as the wooden barriers at the corners of the flights did not appear, when I was there, to be built to stem the fall of a pilgrim who had missed his footing.) From the top one can look down on the field where St Bernard – on an equally rickety wooden platform – delivered his great clarion cry for the crusade. We felt we should have set out from Vézelay on a richly accoutred stallion rather than on the Velcro-coated seats of a modest hired car.

There is little obvious trace of the pilgrim route until one reaches the Pyrenees. The signs begin at St Jean Pied de Port and direct one into the clouds and over the passes to Roncevalles, where Count Roland – commanding Charlemagne's rearguard after a raid into Spain in the eighth century – was alleged to have been killed by the Moors (though in reality more likely by the Basques). The link between the pilgrimage and the Reconquest of Spain from the Moors by the Christian kingdoms of Castille and Aragon is a leitmotif that runs through much of the history and many of the landmarks on the Camino de Santiago. St James was, after all, the Matamoros, the Moor-slayer. Spaniards and other Christians from all over Europe flocked to his tomb in the Middle Ages not only to pay their respects to one of the greatest of the Apostles, but also to show solidarity with a Christian regime which had, exceptionally, reversed the incursions of Islam, at a time when the Holy Land had already been recaptured from the crusaders by the Saracens and had consequently become a difficult and dangerous destination.

Internationalism has also always been a feature of the Camino de Santiago. English and French, Germans and Swedes had always rubbed shoulders at the pilgrim hostelries, and still do. Today, as one stands awestruck outside the glorious façades of Burgos or León cathedrals, or shares tables at the curbside coffee shops, or joins – however fleetingly – fellow pilgrims on the path, this inter-nationalism is as apparent as in the days of Chaucer's Knight. The cockle-shell of St James is as potent a symbol of this as the stars of the European Union on the number plates of foreign cars.

As well as a mixture of nationalities, there is a total mixture of ages among the pilgrims. Healthy young Danes, sucking water from their bottles, stride along past ageing Irishmen pulling at hip flasks. Groups of young equestrians from English riding schools pass solitary French horsemen of indeterminate age. Teenagers in baseball caps from Belgian fitness clubs pass Poles or Hungarians who look as if they might have suffered in body and soul for their beliefs under half a century of Communism. We saw pilgrims as young as fifteen and as old as eighty, but if one age group tends to predominate it is the newly retired – the sixty to sixty-five-year-olds. We repeatedly met people who told us that they had wanted to make the pilgrimage for years and now that they had the time, and were not yet too decrepit to face the exertion, they had left their families and friends for many weeks to grasp the opportunity.

Just as pilgrims have always come from different countries and different generations, so also they have always come for different motives. The pious friar of the Middle Ages finds his counterpart in the theological student on a university vacation; the medieval grandee seeking absolution for war crimes or exploitation of his peasants finds his counterpart in the Austrian professor collecting material for his thesis on baroque architecture; the medieval craftsman seeking an escape from the claustrophobia of his guild or estate workshop finds his counterpart in the gap-year traveller seeking experience, adventure and fresh air.

All converge on the plaza in front of the cathedral at Santiago. When Robin Hanbury-Tenison arrived there in the late 1980s, having ridden from the Pyrenees with his wife and proudly bearing his fully stamped-up pilgrim passport, he presented himself at the palatial five-star *parador* and – mindful of the palace's original purpose as a hostelry for pilgrims – asked to be given the complimentary dinner to which all pilgrims had traditionally been entitled. We knew we had not earned any such pilgrim rights. But we had walked long and far, had wondered at the beauty of the route and of the monuments, had made friends with companions on the road, and prayed at the chapels along our way. Neither God nor the *parador* owed us anything, but we felt we owed ourselves something. We booked into the luxurious dining room and ordered an expensive dinner. Not many of the medieval pilgrims – the bishops and friars, the rogues and penitents – would have appreciated our self-indulgence. But one who we felt might have done so was John of Gaunt: he too had taken the pilgrimage on his own terms, just as we had done. And if he had earned some merit, surely we must have too, if only because – unlike him – we had accepted Santiago as we found it and not tried to remould it to our own preconceptions.

When one thinks of Spain and pilgrimages one's mind naturally turns to Santiago de Compostela but there has always been a network of local pilgrimages in Spain – the *romerias*. The fact that the word *romeria* also means picnic or excursion says something about the spirit of these pilgrimages.

When living in Spain in the early 1990s I managed to join one such *romeria* to El Rocio. It was a Chaucerian event. We assembled outside Seville and most of the men rode, dressed in traditional Andalusian garb, while families followed by car or wagon, with wives and daughters also decked out in finery that looked like a stage set from *Carmen*. There were stops for conviviality and drinking sherry; tents were set up; local grandees held court. The clouds of dust and smell of horses lent the whole occasion a timeless Iberian quality with a flavour of El Cid, Don Quixote and the bullring.

The monasteries of Montserrat, Poblet and Santes Creus are the centre of particularly active *romerias* in Catalonia, all notable architectural monuments and between them rating no less than eight stars in the Michelin guide. Montserrat stands amid the most spectacular of sierras: a mountain massif so dramatic that Wagner made it the setting for *Parsifal*. The monastery itself is more like a small market town than a single building: offices, shops, a museum

232

and a huge church clustered around a square heaving with people all of whom have come on *romerias*, usually wearing the T-shirts of their local fraternities. Some had brought bands with them, and looked more like football supporters than pilgrims. But pilgrims they were, and many queued for hours to pay their respects to the Black Madonna, an exquisitely beautiful figure said to have been carved by St Luke and brought here by St Peter in AD 50.

I was received by Father Ignasi, representing the abbot. A quiet, scholarly Benedictine, he talked to me about the troubles the monastery had survived. Napoleon's army had burnt some of the buildings and chased out the monks. But worse had happened in the Civil War of the 1930s. While the church had been saved from destruction by its usefulness as a hospital for the Republican forces, twenty-three of the monks had been taken off to Barcelona and shot. Father Ignasi told me proudly that twenty-one of them had subsequently been beatified as martyrs. I longed to ask what the other two had done to disqualify themselves, but the question seemed faintly irreverent, and good taste – or lack of courage – prevailed.

Although in a less spectacular setting, Poblet was a more heavily fortified monastery, standing within its own crenellated outer walls. The calm serenity of the cloisters and the abbey church pervaded even the draughty monks' dormitories – reminiscent of the worst of English boarding schools. Here I was received by a sombre-faced Cistercian monk who appeared to have wandered out of an El Greco painting. He explained that Poblet too had had difficult times and there were now only thirty-two monks in the whole complex – not even one dormitory full. He spoke with admiration and perhaps a touch of envy of the Catholic church in Poland, where – in part due to Pope John Paul II – the church was firmly associated in the public mind with liberalism and resistance to Communism; whereas in Spain the long association with General Franco had left a less liberal image to be inherited by the church in the new democratic kingdom of Spain. Perhaps fortunately, he was summoned by bells before he could say more.

Perhaps because the Spanish Civil War – with its fierce anti-clericalism – is still a living memory for the elderly, and a vivid if vicarious experience for many of the younger generation, there is frisson of declared commitment about regional pilgrimages in Spain which is rare in the twenty-first century. It is the same overt statement of faith which characterizes Orthodox pilgrim activity in the Islamic Near East, and which used to characterize churchgoing in Russia and Eastern Europe during the Communist era. A *romeria* may often be a picnic, but it has the poignance of a picnic on the road to Emmaus or Damascus.

St Columba's Abbey on the island of Iona off the western Highlands of Scotland has been a sacred site since the Bronze Age and, since St Columba introduced Christianity to the region in the sixth century and converted the Picts, there have been a succession of Christian churches, monasteries and convents constructed by successive Scottish patrons: Queen Margaret rebuilt the monastery and St Oran's chapel in the eleventh century; Reginald, laird of Clan Donald, built a splendid Benedictine abbey in the twelfth century; the Augustinian monastery dates from the thirteenth century, and there was further restoration and rebuilding in the fifteenth century. Just as English monasteries fell into disrepair after the Dissolution in the sixteenth century, so Iona also was allowed to crumble, until in the twentieth century the Iona Community restored it with care and skill to the reconstituted medieval splendour in which it now stands.

There have always been pilgrims to Iona, but they were unlike the pilgrims to other European destinations: most of them were already dead. Iona was for centuries a chosen resting place for Christian kings, princes, dukes and bishops. Among others, here lie Kings of Norway, Scotland and Ireland, Lords of the Isles and chieftains of Highland clans. The tradition persists: John Smith, the Labour Party leader, and the last Duke of Argyll have been laid to rest there in recent years.

Today the main pilgrim route differs slightly from the line taken by medieval mourners: a boat from Oban (rather than Loch Feochan a few miles to the south) carries pilgrims over the water to the south-east of the Isle of Mull where they land at Craignure (rather than at Port Nam Marbh – 'the harbour of the Dead'). From either landing place a track – now paralleled or in some parts replaced by a road – runs the length of the southern peninsula of Mull till it terminates at Fionnphort where a smaller ferry boat conveys passengers across the straits to Iona.

The island conveys an image of pilgrimage quite different from that of the traditional mainland or European conception. There is none of the fustiness of so many ancient shrines, none of the elaborate protocol of a grand continental cathedral, none of the strange and shabby mysticism of Mount Athos, and none of the dusty weariness of the long, hot roads to Jerusalem or Santiago. There is a timeless freshness about Iona which makes one understand its two-way traffic over the centuries; it was not only to this remote island that the great and holy of the world chose to be brought in death, but it was from this island outpost on the edge of the known world that missionaries set out to bring the Gospels to communities as far afield as the Alps and the Apennines. Few trod more perilous paths than these Celtic monks. Few tread more happy and wholesome paths today than those who in life take the Road to the Isles.

My own pilgrimage to Mount Athos some years ago involved the traditional complicated procedure of securing an invitation to the Holy Mountain via the good offices of the British embassy in Athens. Armed with a letter, from the Greek Foreign Ministry, we had taken a bus from Athens to Thessaloniki and then a local bus to Ierissos. From there we took a fishing boat to the little port of Daphni on the Athos peninsula and climbed the steep track – still clutching our wilting credentials – to Karyes. Here the representatives of the abbots of the monasteries provided us with a splendid document, signed and sealed with saintly images, which invoked the hospitality of the monks to such scholarly brethren (we were both under-graduates) as ourselves. Armed with this formidable recommenda-tion we set out with scrip and staff and canvas backpack.

The next two weeks were spent walking between one monastery and another. These are scattered along the coastlines and the interior of the peninsula, which is some thirty miles long and five miles wide. There are now twenty Orthodox monasteries and innumerable smaller *sketes*, hermitages and caves. Not all are Greek: one of the largest is Russian, and there are also Bulgarian and Serbian monasteries. At its zenith in the last century, the population of Athos numbered nearly forty thousand monks; by the 1970s that number had dwindled to 1,100, and it has now – since the fall of Communism – risen slightly to more than two thousand.

The walking was not made easier for us by the heat and the hunger. Monastery hospitality tended to consist of a greasy thin soup, a slice of black bread and a small glass of ouzo. It was hardly a satisfying dinner for two footsore travellers and much of the days would be spent picking figs or other path-side fruit or berries to eke out our slender meals. I particularly remember one evening after an unusually frugal repast at Karakallou monastery. We had repaired to the vineyard where an aged monk called Father Gregory took pity on us and fed us some spare grapes. We got into conversation and heard about his early life as a Greek immigrant to Chicago, where he had worked as a meat packer before returning home to become a reclusive monk. On account possibly of his lack of any formal education, he had tended to be given the humbler jobs such as tending the vineyard. 'It used to worry me,' he said, 'that while the other monks were chanting in the chapel I had to be here growing grapes and making wine. I sometimes thought I might as well not be on the Holy Mountain at all, but earning a fat wage in Salonika [Thessaloniki]. But then I remembered that He too made wine – at the marriage feast at Cana of Galilee – so now I feel better about it.'

As we trekked around the monasteries we discovered that there were two distinct types of monastic house on Athos: those under cenobitic rule, requiring poverty in addition to celibacy and unquestioning obedience to the abbot; and those under idio-rhythmic rule, being more indulgent, allowing the monks to bring their own funds, comforts and even acolytes to cook for them. It usually seemed our misfortune to arrive at the latter on fast days. Nights at the monasteries would be disturbed well before dawn by a monk striking a *simandro*, a wooden beam, to call the inmates to prayer in the chapel. We always felt, having accepted the hospitality of the house, we should join the vigil. What we intended as a courtesy often turned into a strangely moving experience.

When on one occasion we did arrive at an idiorhythmic monastery not on a fast day but on a feast day, it turned out to be one of the most embarrassing evenings of my life. Earlier in the day my companion and I had been walking over the steep lower slopes of the 6,600-foot mountain at the eastern end of the peninsula and had dropped down to the sea for a swim to cool off. Being far from the view of the Grand Lavra Monastery, for which we were heading, we swam naked. Having completed our swim, we strode for a few yards up a fresh-water stream to splash the salt water off each other before we put on our clothes. While we were engaged in this innocent pursuit, a hermit emerged from a cave above us, screamed and ran off, covering his eyes with his hands. We were sorry we had startled the old man as we knew how much the monks deplored nakedness (John Julius Norwich had been berated for taking a shower under a monastery pump) but we thought little more of it until the evening.

Having arrived at the Grand Lavra, we were warmly welcomed and generously invited to join the monks at their feast in the refectory. Normally such meals were taken in silence, while one of the Fathers intoned a lesson from the pulpit. But on this particular evening the monks were beside themselves with excitement: everyone was chattering to his neighbour and the lesson reading went unheeded.

With some trepidation, we enquired the reason for this unusual animation. Slowly the story emerged. There was a particularly holy hermit who lived in a cave near the sea not far from the Grand Lavra. On this very evening he had broken his vows of solitude and silence and had come to the monastery to tell them of an extraordinary occurrence. He had seen a vision: John the Baptist baptizing in his local stream. When asked by the monks how he knew it was a vision, he had replied that both the Baptist and the baptized 'had bodies of a shining whiteness unlike any normal mortal'. The monks held the hermit in the highest esteem; he would not have invented or imagined such a vision. They were already contemplating a stained-glass window in the refectory to com-memorate the event.

What could we say? We were too embarrassed or too pusillanimous to explain our encounter with the hermit. While the thought of disillusioning or humiliating the old man appalled us, so too did the thought of conniving in the inception of a spurious – and sacrilegious? – stained-glass window. In the end we left a carefully worded written confession for the abbot on our departure the following morning.

The abbot of the Grand Lavra was a man not only of great spirituality but also of considerable worldly wisdom. I am sure he knew what to do. It cannot have been the first mistaken vision to have been recorded on the Holy Mountain. But I still feel uncomfortable when viewing the massive walls and windows of the Grand Lavra, and I am relieved that since that visit I have only done so from the sea where the windows do not have the light behind them.

The right place to start any retracing of the Albigensian Crusade, that most bizarre and vicious of armed pilgrimages, is undoubtedly Carcassonne. Although there has been much restoration, Carcassonne remains probably the most complete medieval city in Europe, standing entirely within its crenellated ramparts and commanding the surrounding countryside. Its fortress and basilica still dominate the narrow cobbled streets, crowded today with boutiques, tapestry galleries, restaurants and pavement cafes. The Cathar occupants may have caused the downfall and looting of the town in the thirteenth century, but they are responsible for its distinctive historical flavour and self-evident prosperity today. Carcassonne cries out to be the backdrop of every film that is set in the Middle Ages, as it was for Ken Russell's disturbing *The Devils*.

This is the land of troubadours and music as well as knights and dungeons. We were lucky enough to be admitted on our first night to an organ concert in the Basilica of St Nazaire. Sitting in the Romanesque nave looking up at some of the finest stained-glass windows in France, dating from the period of the Albigensian

Crusade, it was easy to ponder on the nature of the heresy that had provoked so much violence and such a protracted war.

Moving on from Carcassonne, as the Cathars had done after their expulsion from the town 'carrying with them nothing but their shirts and their sins', we moved south to the hilltop fortresses. The first Cathar site we came to was far from typical. The chateau of Villerouge-Termenes stands in the centre of the village, in good repair, four-square and turreted. Inside, one steps into the world of Warwick Castle or Madame Tussaud's: an audio-visual presentation in every room tells the tale of the last Cathar martyr – Guilhem Bélibaste, who was burnt alive there in 1321. A waxwork figure of a cowled monk leaning over the balcony manages to give one an uncomfortable feeling about being a Protestant in this haunt of the Inquisition.

From now on our Cathar castles were to get more demanding. Termes, a few miles down a winding road, is a relatively easy walk up a steep path to ruined towers; none-the-less, it held out against a four-month siege by the crusaders.

Quéribus, some twenty miles further south, is an altogether different proposition. Here the castle is a tower on the very peak of an outcrop of rock, and the climbing involves scrambling up rough and sometimes disintegrating steps, beset with sharp corners and sudden gusts of wind. But the rewards of the climb are great: a vaulted Gothic hall and a labyrinth of winding passages and stairs punctuated with arrow slits commanding the approaches. One would have felt very safe here from attack, and indeed it was the last Cathar fortress to hold out – until 1255. From then on, it became a French royal lookout post towards the Spanish frontier.

By the time we reached the castle of Peyrepertuse, a mere five miles to the west, the weather had closed in. Rifts in the cloud revealed its jagged profile; a rainbow – like the rays implanting stigmata in a medieval painting – gave an eerie illumination to the scene. This is not an ascent for the vertiginously challenged: drops

240

are sheer in places beside the stone steps and rough paths, and hand-ropes and balustrades only intermittent (though generally where most needed). The keeper at the bottom told us that in high winds it was dangerous and in storms it was forbidden to attempt the ascent. Bearing in mind the three stars granted to it in the Michelin *Green Guide*, we were surprised to be alone at the top; the reason became clear when we found – on descent – that the keeper had decreed it stormy and disallowed others from following us.

The chateau of Puilaurens was the third and final destination of our stormy day. More intact than Quéribus or Peyrepertuse, it was less of a challenge to climb, which was just as well as three Cathar castles in a day – even without the necessity to storm them in crusader style – had amounted to quite an exhausting assignment. The following day we arrived at the charming provincial town of Foix. The castle, now a museum, fills the skyline from whatever angle you approach the bustling town centre. Beyond this, the Montagnes du Plantaurel provide a suitably dramatic backdrop. Even Simon de Montfort, the boldest of the Albigensian crusaders, declined to attack the chateau of Foix: perhaps he had had enough of human bonfires.

If it is right to start a journey retracing the Albigensian Crusade at Carcassonne, it is equally right to end it at Albi. If ever a town is dominated by one building it is Albi: its cathedral is to the city of sixty-six thousand inhabitants what Windsor Castle is to the town of Windsor. And the domination is entirely intended. The Cathédrale Sainte-Cecile was built to house the Inquisition (some of whose officers had been lynched nearby) and to demonstrate once and for all to the heresy-infested inhabitants of Albi and its surroundings that by 1282 the church was back in full control and intended to stay so. The sheer, high, red-brick walls look more like a power station than a church. This was for Roman Catholicism what the Lubianka was for the KGB: a visible warning to dissidents.

241

What resonance have these sites to modern pilgrims, armed or otherwise? I think that more than anywhere – more even than the divided Holy Land – they remind the visitors of the intolerant aspects of the Middle Ages. Cathars had flocked to this corner of France to support each other in a deviant – but peaceable – interpretation of Christian dogma; and they were hunted down with a savagery that has seldom if ever been surpassed. The remoteness of their castles and the bleakness of their crag-top fortifications serve as an ever-present witness to the desperation of their plight. To go there now is to be reminded of an aspect of medieval religion which is in stark contrast to the easygoing sociability of a Chaucerian pilgrimage or the cosy comradeship-in-adversity of the road to Rome or Santiago. But perhaps for this very reason it has relevance to an age when religious wars are a feature of contemporary life and when faith is once more a burning issue.

My own pilgrimage to pay homage to St Cuthbert was not in the first place directed to Durham, but to the scene of his earlier activities – Lindisfarne, or Holy Island as it is more popularly known. I chose the route that the saint had taken on numerous occasions from Melrose Abbey on the Scottish side of the borders (where he was a young monk), first over the Eildon Hills and following the River Tweed, then along an old Roman road known as Dere Street which is now an unpaved drove-road running straight as a die through wooded pastures, then across the Cheviot Hills, and so on to Lindisfarne (where Cuthbert was to become a bishop) off the Northumbrian coast of England. St Cuthbert not only knew this stretch of country well, he also knew the wildlife and flocks that grazed there – then as now. He had started life as a shepherd of sheep, but had quickly moved on to shepherding souls, while retaining his affinity for all living creatures.

The route of my chosen pilgrimage – St Cuthbert's Way – is a strikingly beautiful and varied stretch of country, which falls naturally into four or five days' walks of around twelve miles a day, mostly gentle enough but with some steep gradients in the Cheviots. The route is well signed (with St Cuthbert's cross) and, apart from a few brief link passages along minor roads, is on footpaths or open hillside all the way. There is bed-and-breakfast accommodation at most of the villages along the route.

This Scottish Border country has always been a troubled land, as the frequent castles and peel towers which one passes along the route remind one. The constant robbing and raiding of neighbours' cattle, the carrying off of daughters and the burning of homesteads (all too often with the inmates still inside) gave the region a reputation from the fourteenth to the seventeenth centuries of being the Balkans of Britain. Border reivers (or raiders) were much romanticized and are the subject of many a Border ballad, but the less glamorous side of their activities is reflected in the one word which they have bequeathed to the English language – 'bereaved'. Here Douglas-Homes and Percies pursued their vendettas with the fury of Montagues and Capulets – all of them inclined to spring into the saddle and don their steel bonnets at the drop of a lighted torch.

Having crossed the border (running perversely north–south rather than east–west at this point) we found the marker posts sparser and less clear on the English side, and on at least one occasion had to retrace our steps after the path we were following petered out in bog and heather. But the views made up for everything: the rolling Cheviots, topped with moorland and dissected with drystone walls, revealed at every ridge fresh vistas of distant valleys and stone farmsteads nestling in the folds of the hills. Among the ubiquitous sheep were little clusters of feral goats, their long, sharp horns deterring close inspection.

It was not until the fourth day that we arrived at St Cuthbert's cave in wooded country well beyond the Cheviots. Here the saint's coffin was allowed to rest on the first night of its escorted flight from Lindisfarne, when Viking raids from across the North Sea were becoming uncomfortably frequent. The cave itself is a series of huge shelving rocks that look like the background to an Italian fifteenth-century painting depicting the den of a dragon awaiting the arrival of St George. Some of the carved inscriptions look gratifyingly like medieval pilgrims' graffiti, though others all too clearly are the work of latter-day visitors who – judging by their sentiments – may have had more secular emotions in mind.

The final and fifth day of our walk was devoted to Lindisfarne itself. This offshore island can only be reached on foot at low tide, and the three miles across the sands are sloshing with water even then. A causeway road enables cars to make the crossing, though this too is under water and impassable at high tide. Both pilgrim route and causeway are punctuated part-way by wooden refuges, which resemble Boy Scout semaphore towers and are designed to enable the foolhardy or caught-short to scramble to safety. The castle, on its rocky outcrop at the furthest point of the tiny island, beckons as a final objective across the sands. It was extensively restored by Sir Edwin Lutyens and is now preserved by the National Trust: it is an evocative reconstruction romanticizing an era that never quite existed.

For followers of St Cuthbert, the ruins of the priory built to commemorate him at the beginning of the twelfth century are a more appropriate destination. Alongside the ruins is a well-preserved church and we sought shelter there from the driving rain. Throughout our walk – in early May and mostly sunny – we had met very few fellow pilgrims; not like Cuthbert's own day when so intense had been the pilgrim traffic at times that Cuthbert had withdrawn to one of the remote Farne islands. He was a natural recluse who had only taken on the duties and the social obligations of a bishop after much persuasion. Here on Lindisfarne his spirit pervaded the islands, both in life and for the century after his death, until the frequency of Viking raids persuaded the monks that they must take his body to the mainland for safe keeping.

The final resting place for St Cuthbert was to be the bluff above the River Wear at Durham where the mighty cathedral – 'the greatest Romanesque church in Christendom' – now stands to commemorate the saint. Beside his shrine behind the high altar is inscribed a prayer:

> Almighty God, who didst call Thy servant Cuthbert from keeping sheep to follow Thy Son and be a shepherd of Thy people, mercifully grant that we following his example and caring for those who are lost, may bring them home to Thy fold.

A little further off in the cloisters is a collection of the saint's relics, notably his pastoral cross. During the Middle Ages it was to this shrine with its treasures – rather than to Lindisfarne – that the pilgrims came in a steady flow. Here was a great basilica which could hold its own with Santiago de Compostela or Canterbury. But for me – and I suspect for Cuthbert – the wild rocks off Lindisfarne, echoing to the calls of the eider duck, were the true resting place of his roving spirit.

Of all the landmarks on the way to the Holy Land, the great castle of Krac des Chevaliers is surely the most striking. It stands high above the plains of Syria – daunting, massive, unscaleable, impenetrable, arguably the most formidable fortress in the world. This was the staging post and rallying point which the Knights Hospitaller built (on earlier ruins) in the twelfth century, not only to shelter those pilgrims who had come on the overland route through Asia Minor and the Levant on their way to Palestine, but also as a secure base from which the knights could sally forth across the plains to rescue beleaguered pilgrims or to avenge Saracen raids on the pilgrim caravans.

Today (or at least in April 2004) Krac des Chevaliers can be reached in a two-hour drive from the port of Tartous on the Syrian coast. The road passes through hills which are described as being the northern end of the Mount Lebanon range, and within sight of rocky peaks which have for centuries been snow-covered throughout the year, despite the surrounding shimmering heat-haze. (Only in the past two years has global warming been blamed for an unaccustomed absence of snow.)

The castle itself has all the features which suggest it could resist the sort of long siege which all crusader castles had to endure from time to time. There is a defended aqueduct to bring in drinking water, and there are outer and inner crenellated walls of immense thickness, each punctuated with a series of round towers. Within the walls there are stables, refectories, a banqueting hall, a reservoir, warehouses, kitchens and a sizeable chapel. Between the massive stone blocks (quarried locally and carried up to the hilltop by local labour conscripted by the crusaders) grow abundant wild flowers, mellowing the impression of walls that would have defied even the tallest scaling ladders.

The effect of Krac des Chevaliers on the visitor is to make him realize what a far cry the armed pilgrimages (which the crusades claimed to be) were from the gentle perambulations across the plains of northern Spain to Santiago, or across the North Downs of southern England to Canterbury, that constituted more normal

246

medieval pilgrimages. But below in the valley, some five miles away, stands another building of equal antiquity which bridges the gap and humanizes the pilgrim route.

The Monastery of St George is not literally in the shade of the castle, but one feels instinctively that it is under the latter's protection. This is a Syrian Orthodox monastery, in the direct line of descent from the ancient church of Antioch with which St Paul was familiar. One is quickly reminded that St George became a patron saint in the land which is now Syria several centuries before he was adopted (at the expense of St Edward the Confessor) as the patron saint of England. Indeed his valiant encounters with the dragon outside a cave harbouring an edible maiden seem to fit the barren landscape of the Levant much better than the verdant pastures of England's green and pleasant land.

Inside the monastery and down a steep flight of steps lies the chapel with a notable collection of icons, many of them depicting St John the Baptist as an alternative to St George. We were told that one of them had recently been stolen from the chapel and later put for sale at Sotheby's in London, where its illegal provenance had apparently been spotted by the vigilant auctioneers, resulting in its happy return to its desert home.

We arrived just as the preparations were getting under way for an Orthodox christening in the chapel. Monks in stovepipe hats tripped over the wings of small children dressed as fairies (or were they angels?); formally dressed relations (who looked as if their dark suits were enjoying their annual outing) stood aside to make way for a madonna-like mother bearing a diminutive baby, gift-wrapped like a present from heaven – which the young mother doubtless felt it was. We flattened ourselves against the cold stone wall and planned a rapid retreat before we might appear to be intruders on this scene of family celebration.

To our embarrassment a handsome young man – clearly the baby's father – accosted us before we could withdraw. Would we like to stay for the service? We were more than welcome. Being a Christian family in twenty-first-century Syria could be a lonely experience, he said. He would welcome our support and prayers for the child. His ready assumption that we were Christian pilgrims rather than mere western sightseers was humbling and we accepted his invitation.

Syrian Orthodox clerics take christenings very seriously. The baby was unwrapped by a rather shaky monk (could he be trusted not to drop it on the flagstoned floor?) and subjected to total immersion (could he be trusted to remember to bring it safely to the surface?). Small and vulnerable though the baby was – it transpired on unwrapping to be male – he did not appear to be in any way fazed by the experience: he emerged from the less-than-clear waters of the font gurgling but not crying. Much genuflecting took place; incantations and chants reverberated round the barrel-vaulted roof; the father turned to me: 'You are a pilgrim. My son here,' he pointed to the damp pink parcel, 'will be a pilgrim too . . . perhaps not to Jerusalem . . . but I hope to a world where Christians and Moslems can live together in peace.' The hopes of a thousand years echoed over the dusty desert font.

Select Bibliography

ARMITAGE-SMITH, Sidney, *John of Gaunt* (London, 1920)

BALDWIN, David, *Santiago de Compostela: the Way of St James* (London, 2001)

BELLOC, Hilaire, *The Path to Rome* (London, 1902)

BENNETT, Josephine, *The Rediscovery of Sir John Mandeville* (New York, 1954)

BOORDE, Andrew, *First Book of the Introduction of Knowledge: 1548*, edited by F.J. Furnivall (London, 1870)

BUNYAN, John, *The Pilgrim's Progress* (London, 1678)

BYRON, Robert, *The Station* (London, 1931)

CHAUCER, Geoffrey, *Canterbury Tales*, translated by Nevill Coghill (London, 1956)

CHOLMELEY, Katharine, *Margery Kempe: Genius and Mystic* (London, 1947)

CLANCHY, M.T., *Early Medieval England* (London, 1997)

DALRYMPLE, William, *From the Holy Mountain* (London, 1997)

DE SILVA-VIGIER, Anil, *John of Gaunt* (London, 1992)

ELIOT, T.S., *Murder in the Cathedral* (London, 1935)

ERASMUS, Desiderius, *Pilgrimages to Saint Mary of Walsingham and Saint Thomas of Canterbury*, translated by J.G. Nichols (London, 1875)

FABRI, Brother Felix, *The Book of the Wanderings of Brother Felix Fabri 1480–1483*, translated by Aubrey Stewart (London, 1893)

FALUDY, George, *Erasmus of Rotterdam* (London, 1970)

HALL, D.J., *English Medieval Pilgrimage* (London, 1966)

HARPUR, James, *Sacred Tracks: 2000 Years of Christian Pilgrimage* (London, 2002)

HELL, V. & H., *The Great Pilgrimage of the Middle Ages* (London, 1966)

HUIZINGA, J., *The Waning of the Middle Ages* (London, 1924)

JUSSERAND, J.J., *English Wayfaring Life in the Middle Ages* (London, 1891)

KEEN, M.H., *England in the Later Middle Ages* (London, 1973)

KEMPE, Margery, *The Book of Margery Kempe*, edited by Barry Windeatt (London, 2000)

KEMPE, Margery, *The Book of Margery Kempe, 1436*, a modern version edited by W. Butler-Bowden (London, 1936)

LETTS, Malcolm, *Sir John Mandeville: the man and his book* (London, 1949)

MANCHESTER, William, *A World Lit only by Fire* (Boston, USA, 1992)

MARTIN, C., *Roma Sancta (1581)*, edited by George B. Parks (Rome, 1969)

MORRIS, Colin and ROBERTS, Peter (editors), *Pilgrimage: the English Experience from Becket to Bunyan* (Cambridge, 2002)

NEWETT, M. Margaret, *Canon Pietro Casola's Pilgrimage to Jerusalem in the year 1494* (Manchester, 1907)

NORWICH, John Julius and SITWELL, Reresby, *Mount Athos* (London, 1966)

O'SHEA, Stephen, *The Perfect Heresy* (London, 2000)

PARKS, George B., *The English Traveller to Italy: Vol I – The Middle Ages (to 1525)* (Rome, 1954)

PRESCOTT, H.F.M., *Jerusalem Journey* (London, 1954)

PRESCOTT, H.F.M., *Once to Sinai* (London, 1957)

RAYNALD, O., *Annales Ecclesiastici*, edited by J.D. Mansi (Lucca, 1747–56)

REGINALD OF DURHAM, *De admirandis B. Cuthberti virtutibus* (edited for Surtees Society, 1835)

RIANT, P.E.D., *Expeditions des Scandinaves en Terre Sainte* (Paris, 1865)

RIDLEY, Jasper, *Henry VIII* (London, 1984)

RUNCIMAN, Steven, *A History of the Crusades: Vol I* (Cambridge, 1951)

SEWARD, Desmond, *The Monks of War: the military religious orders* (London, 1972)

SEYMOUR, M.C. (editor), *Mandeville's Travels* (Oxford, 1967)

STARKIE, Walter, *The Road to Santiago* (London, 1957)

STRAYER, Joseph R., *The Albigensian Crusades* (University of Michigan Press, USA, 1992)

SUGDEN, Keith, *Walking The Pilgrim Ways* (London, 1991)

SUMPTION, Jonathan, *Pilgrimage: An Image of Medieval Religion* (London, 1975)

SUMPTION, Jonathan, *The Albigensian Crusade* (London, 1978)

WARD, H. Snowden, *The Canterbury Pilgrims* ((London, 1904)

WATT, Francis, *Canterbury Pilgrims and their Ways* (London, 1917)

WETHERED, H. Newton, *The Four Paths to Pilgrimage* (London, 1947)

ZIEGLER, Philip, *The Black Death* (London, 1969)

Index